M000096929

Caissons Across Europe

An Artillery Captain's Personal War

CAISSONS ACROSS EUROPE

By Richard M. Hardison

EAKIN PRESS ★ Austin, Texas

FIRST EDITION

Published in the United States of America
By Eakin Press
An Imprint of Eakin Publications, Inc.
P.O. Drawer 90159 ★ Austin, TX 78709-0159

ISBN 0-89015-758-8

Library of Congress Cataloging-in-Publication Data

Hardison, Richard M.
Caissons across Europe / by Richard M. Hardison.
p. cm.
ISBN 0-89015-758-8 : $18.95
1. Hardison, Richard M. 2. World War, 1939–1945 — Campaigns — Europe. 3. World War, 1939–1945 — Personal narratives, American. 4. Soldiers — United States — Biography. 5. United States. Army — Biography. I. Title.
D756.H27 1990
940.54'21--dc20 89-25681
CIP

To

Henry E. Brooks

and the memory of

William F. Hughes, Jr.

Contents

Foreword

The story you are about to read may lead you to believe it is about the great war of 1941–45. You may also think it will depict the glory of war, or, to an opposite point of view, the futility of armed combat. It is none of the above.

Although the stage for this story is set for war and concerns itself with the trappings of war, it is really about Richard M. Hardison and his partial transformation from a normal, somewhat naive boy of West Texas into manhood. As he loses much of his innocence, he acquires the essences of cynicism, worldly knowledge, some despair, and eventually the resurgence of spiritual courage to see his new world not only as livable, but as filled with promise of fulfillment and contentment.

Tex — as his comrades in arms would call him for all the time between Camp Campbell, Kentucky, through a long training mission in the States, to, and through, most of Western Europe — tells his story from the day of his graduation from Texas A&M in June of 1941 until he returns to the same school fifty-seven months later. Most of this time, he was an officer of the 399th Armored Field Artillery Battalion of the 8th Armored Division. This is the battalion of which *Army Times* wrote in the summer of 1943 that the "Average age of the officers of this battalion is thought to be the youngest of any line battalion in the U.S. Army." At that time, Tex was an old captain of twenty-three while his battalion commander was a lieutenant colonel at the age of twenty-four.

You will find that Tex deals frankly with the performances of his fellow officers and men of the 399th during the frenzied months they were sharing their fates. Never one to equivocate, always honest and forthright, he has set out the fruit of his extraordinary memory of those times almost as if he had kept a diary. As I read the manuscript, I was amazed at the detail and the emotional and physical content of the incidents he describes, time after time. For him those months and years of his life were intensely compressive. The memories of those times represent significant high points in the whole of his life and suggest, at least for a while, that he had found his place in the scheme of things. Here was a man who, without ever shirking his duty or passing a burden to another, found the time to use the battlefields of World War II as the locale of his own personal explorations, sometimes just for his own diversion, sometimes in the company of others, always meticulously recalled and recorded. Whether he was overtaking an enemy police station or rescuing the politically harassed people of that era, Tex describes all without varnish — as it was and as he experienced it.

The closing chapters are especially important to the author for many and varied reasons. When the 8th Armored Division was disbanded in Czechoslovakia after the fighting was over, Tex and many others of his battalion were reassigned to the 94th Infantry Division. He and some of his close friends became a part of the 301st Field Artillery Battalion of that division. At that point, he was to live a very emotional experience filled with conflict. The manner in which he handles these troubled times remains an indicator of his strength of character and respect for human dignity.

Only one of his fellow officers was a West Point graduate: the battalion commander, who was good at his job, well respected, and destined to become a highly successful and now retired major general. All the others were products of other military schools, or of university ROTC programs or successful candidates of the Army Officer Candidate Schools at Fort Sill, Oklahoma. They came from all walks of life and practically from all points of the compass in the United States. Tex, a battery commander and later a battalion staff officer, G2, knew them all. He speaks in his story of almost all of them with respect, warmth, and humor. I am sure that each clearly remembers Tex and that they could have assembled enough stories about him to have doubled the pages of this book.

I have known Richard Hardison for almost fifty years and have enormous respect and admiration for him. For the past two years I have renewed acquaintances with Tex and his wife, Don, who is also very special, and with most of the officers and men of the 399th Armored Field Artillery Battalion. Our reunions were times to remember the good times and to shamelessly grow teary-eyed when recalling the less than good times. For all of us of the 399th, whether mentioned or not, time is running out. For all too many of us, time has already run out. I am glad Tex decided to tell his story; it was a labor of love which you will recognize as you read it. For me, it awakened many memories.

But more importantly, it made me reevaluate my particular commitment to my country and its people.

While I feel and think not much differently today from the way I did in the early forties, I feel renewed. I am glad to have served with Tex in those days. I pray that we will have each other for more than a few years and that you, the reader, will find enjoyment and counsel in this book.

John J. Collins
Westport, Connecticut

August 1990

Preface

In 1970, at a reunion of the former officers of the 399th Armored Field Artillery Battalion, I was asked if I would compile a history of our unit during World War II. Those present said they would furnish information regarding actions, training, etc., and since they said that I remembered more than they did I would be responsible for seeing that the events were recorded at the correct time and place. My time was then committed to business interests, so I declined.

In 1974, at a later reunion, I was again asked by this group to write a history of the unit and I was somewhat more receptive to the idea. I began to think about it and after a time found that I was much more interested. I prepared an outline and began preliminary work. Later that year, George and Laura Salisbury flew with Don and me to Paris, picked up a rented car, and began to drive east. We visited every place we had served in France, Holland, and Germany to the East German border. In Rhineberg I found the place where the medics cut off George's tank suit when he was wounded there. It brought back many memories and Laura began to cry. The trip was cleansing for me; I felt good and was enthusiastic about writing the history.

After returning in October, I wrote all of the former officers of the 399th a letter telling them of our trip back. I asked them to send me material so I could begin the project. Replies came from all of them, and almost without exception they stated that they really could remember very little or nothing. However, they were sure that others could remember, and I would have little problem compiling the needed information. One said that the only way he was sure that he was in the war was to look at a picture of himself in uniform. Another said that he was sure that we were in England because it was cold there. By this time I was quite interested and decided to proceed with the work as seen through my eyes. This is how the book came into being.

By 1981 I realized that I could not finish the history without some help. There were gaps and voids of several days in my memory. I did receive some help from a few of the fellows by telephone, but not nearly enough. By accident I found that I could hypnotize myself on occasion and under certain conditions. I developed this technique and after a time was able to "go under" when I needed details about some incident or other. Many of the incidents described herein were retrieved from the dark corners of my mind by this method. In addition, my wife and I spent a week in the National Archives researching and checking dates of various incidents.

The hypnosis process was time consuming, and toward the end it was somewhat disturbing. Finally, I was advised to stop the self-hypnosis by a psychologist in the family. By then I had completed the areas that I wanted to cover and was able to finish the manuscript.

Acknowledgments

In the preparation for and writing of this book I am indebted to many of my friends. I am grateful for their help in expressing their opinions of what I was trying to accomplish and for their encouragement.

To my wife, Don, who helped, advised, and worked with me in putting this in readable form;

Henry E. Brooks, Manchester, Connecticut, for reading early drafts, offering advice in some areas, and confirming the incidents mentioned concerning Battery A, 399th AFA Bn.;

William Hawley, Oxford, Ohio, who responded quickly to my letters of inquiry confirming happenings while a forward observer with an infantry company in combat;

Thomas Palmer, Bradenton, Florida, for his comments describing action in and around Rhineberg, Germany;

Orr L. Reed, Spring Lake, North Carolina, who was of great help in reading and commenting on specific incidents in an early draft;

John Roth, Pine Grove, Pennsylvania, who confirmed certain incidents that occurred while driving our half-track and jeep on the long trip from Rouen, France, east to Halberstadt, Germany, and from Horsica, Czechoslovakia, to Paris and return;

Marvin Sather, Nelson, Nebraska, who furnished the valuable details in some of the happenings, provided photographs, and always responded quickly when help was needed;

Dale Starry, Shippensburg, Pennsylvania, with whom I discussed details of the Battle of the Ruhr Pocket, and provided a valuable insight to a few confused days;

Dr. Lloyd Weldon, a continuing source of encouragement and help in compiling the book, visited on several occasions and sent tapes of incidents in areas that I had requested;

Dr. Kenneth Zierler of Baltimore, Maryland, furnished photographs and the missing details of three occasions;

Lynn C. Atkins, El Paso, Texas, who helped in defining certain terms and in other ways;

Charles V. Chenault, Austin, Texas, for helpful suggestions and encouragement early on;

Dr. Louis Rubin, Chappel Hill, North Carolina, who furnished me a written critique of an early draft that was very helpful;

George Christian, Houston, Texas, who provided many suggestions, changes, and encouragement;

Keith Coulbourn, Miami, Florida, for most valuable assistance in going over the book page by page and suggesting changes where he thought they were needed;

Mary Ann Daly, Washington, D.C., who helped in my dealings with some in the National Archives, Suitland, Maryland, and also with the Audio Visual Center in Washington, D.C.;

Von Tony Krings, Heinsburg-Karken, West Germany, for the details of the happenings on the German side in Karken that day so long ago, and for furnishing photographs and other valuable information including a copy of his book *Eine Jugend Im Krieg*;

J. J. van der Steen, Roermond, Holland, for valuable assistance, photographs, diagrams, and information and happenings on the German side of the line in Holland;

Robert Wilbanks, Houston, Texas, for transcribing from the tapes and helping in many ways early on.

Introduction

This is a story of World War II, the story of a group of men who answered when their country called. No special recognition was received, none was expected. There was a job to do.

Time is running out for us. It has been forty-five years since the war ended. Many of my comrades are dead, many of the others have forgotten what happened to us then. The forty-five years have glossed over the war, given it a polish, a luster, and a fascination that those of us who were there did not see at the time. Now, though, it seems to have been the ultimate adventure.

In this story I have invented nothing. Everything that you will read is true, except that the names of some of my friends and others have been changed at one time or another for obvious reasons.

Most men wish to forget the horrors of war, and as time passes, most do. I think that perhaps I have forgotten most of the really bad things. But there were many other things that happened during the war, humorous and extraordinary events, that seemed to provide a glue and diversion for us, taking our minds off things that were happening around and to us. These are the events that have stuck with me.

Except for a brief background, this narrative begins on June 7, 1941, upon my graduation from Texas A&M College, the nation's largest all-male, all-military school at that time. The story also ends there fifty-seven months later. The forty-nine months between June 1941 and the end of the war were crammed with frenzied activities. In the main, this is a story of the officers and men of the 399th Armored Field Artillery Battalion of the 8th Armored Division and a few officers of the 301st Field Artillery Battalion of the 94th Infantry Division of the United States Army.

During training, we spent ten to fourteen hours a day preparing for combat, which most soldiers never saw. Of the 8,266,373 American servicemen in World War II, probably less than fifteen percent actually saw combat. And some of those saw only a day or two of it. In the training days and maneuvers, we suffered long hours of constant activity in all kinds of weather and usually under pressure. We were harassed, restricted to quarters, transferred suddenly, and seldom knew what the next day would bring.

In Europe, we suffered from cold, anxiety, hunger, fatigue, exhaustion, fear, and frustration. But above all, while we were in combat, we did our job, which was to support the infantry and the tank battalions of our division or those of others when ordered to.

In July 1943, according to an article in *Army Times,* the average age of the officers of the 399th Armored Field Artillery Battalion was thought to be the youngest of any line battalion in the United States Army. I had the dubious distinction of being one of the older captains, and I was twenty-three; our battalion commander was a lieutenant colonel, and he was only twenty-four.

Caissons Across Europe

1 In the Army

June 8, 1941–February 20, 1943

In a world torn by war, the United States was at peace, the Great Depression almost history, and the dust bowl becoming green again. Germany, which had just signed a neutrality pact with Russia, had invaded France and was sitting in the Low Countries, bombing England day and night, waiting for her to capitulate. The German army had chased the British army out of Crete, the British navy had sunk the German battleship Bismarck. *The Balkans were occupied by the armies of Germany and Italy in the spring. The stage was set.*

The World War One artillery piece had stood in front of the American Legion hut in Colorado City, Texas, for as long as I could remember. Gray and weathered, it was sandblasted through the years by ferocious West Texas windstorms. It was a Model 1917, 77mm field piece, the kind that had rained shrapnel on British and French and American troops coming out of the trenches. Nobody had touched the gun but kids like me since it had been captured from the Germans. The gunsight was gone and the breech block wouldn't operate, but the hand cranks worked and I could elevate and traverse the barrel up and down as well as left and right, firing barrages onto an imaginary enemy.

Guns came naturally to me. Guns and horses are a Texas birthright, you might say, and I was just naturally good at them. I was small because I contracted typhoid fever as a child, and to compensate became one of the best bare-back riders in Mitchell County and a crack shot with both pistol and rifle.

I was ten, playing on that German gun, but my dream was that if there was ever another war I would be an artilleryman — not a cannoneer. I would be the commander who told them where to fire the gun.

A little more than ten years later, in 1941, I was still on track with that dream. I was one of 900 graduating seniors at Texas A&M on a hot June 7, the whole corps marching past in olive drab column, guidon flying, the sun glinting off boots buffed to a dazzling polish. The band played "The Stars and Stripes Forever," music that always made the hair on the back of my neck stand up.

Colorado City was still half wild when my father and mother moved there from Cisco, Texas, in 1925. The town had been built about 1879 along the Texas & Pacific Railroad, built while the railroad was being pushed west. The crews ran into a rattlesnake problem some sixteen miles west of Colorado City, and the railroad had to suspend construction until professional snake-killers could clear the way. While they were waiting, Colorado City sprang up. The town was mostly a cattle-trading center with saloons, gambling joints and whorehouses. Storekeepers and merchants came first, then after a few years came farmers, who fenced off the land, and the town calmed down. At first the stores and buildings on Main Street were wooden with false fronts like in the movies. That began changing about 1905, and by 1925 most of the buildings were masonry. The town was quite prosperous until the late 1920s when, after three very dry years, the Great Depression hit.

There was little money for college when I finished high school, but my father said if I would spend a year farming some land he owned thirty miles south of town, he would give me ten acres for my own crop. I lived in an old house on the land, farming and looking after 200 head of livestock, sleeping on the roof of the barn in the summer because it was cooler. That was a long year. By late June my father's crop, barley, was harvested and my cotton was ready for picking by mid-September. When it was all over, I had made a little more than seven dollars.

I told my mother that farming was not for me and I wanted to go to college. Money was still short, but my agriculture teacher told me I might be able to work my way through Texas A&M, the largest military school in the country, and I wrote for a catalog. My mother heard there might be some money in a Daughters of the Republic of Texas student loan fund. I rode my horse to town to find out and ended up with my tuition the first year — seventy-five dollars. When we went to the railroad station, my father, with ten dollars in his pocket, bought a ticket for seven dollars and gave me the rest. It would have to do, he said, till I got a job.

I had been good at drawing in school and at the suggestion of Doyle Williams, my agriculture teacher, I selected landscape architecture as my major. He said I would do well at it, although I didn't have the faintest idea what landscape architecture was.

The A&M campus fanned out in a formal arrangement around the Administration Building, the drill field, where we marched once a week, covering about forty acres between the Academic Building and the railroad tracks. West of the Academic Building were the dormitories, where most of the students lived. These were divided into military units and the cadets drilled nearly every day.

Those who couldn't afford to live in the dorms attended as day students, which meant that they lived in project houses and in an old military barracks on the edge of campus and worked in two- or four-hour segments when classes and labs allowed.

Most of the first year I spiked litter on campus for twenty-five cents an hour. Then I got on with the grounds department, riding around in a truck doing odd jobs. One semester I tended lab rats, a job I liked, but a lot of the rats were dying, I thought. One of them died and fell out of its cage on me. Later I learned that they all had anthrax.

At the end of my sophomore year, about a third of the cadets received an Army ROTC contract. I was one of them. That meant that I would be paid every month and would be given a reserve commission on graduation. On my uniform, I wore the crossed cannon of the field artillery.

We could see the war coming and were excited about it. At the beginning of my junior year, Germany invaded Poland, the war spread during the fall and winter, and by the next year the Germans had conquered France and were bombing Britain. The U.S. was offering to "lend-lease" whatever the British needed, and we were also escorting shipping to England. Everybody at A&M knew that it was only a matter of time before we were part of it.

At the end of the third year, all cadets in the field artillery went to ROTC camp at Camp Bullis, Texas, fifteen miles west of San Antonio, which was run by regular army officers. We learned a little about artillery on a 37mm sub caliber, how to load and fire and sight it by compass. Its shell burst was about the size of a bushel basket, but it was artillery nevertheless. Later, we had a lot more time on the French 75mm, a much bigger gun that had been used in World War One. We felt we were in a glass cage there because the officers were always watching us, looking for leadership qualities.

My senior year went fast. We watched the war in Europe like hawks and knew that we would soon be involved. As graduation neared, we heard rumors, however, that not everybody would get active duty orders and that only a few would go straight into the army. I was only a two-button cadet first lieutenant, two buttons for the round silver insignia we wore, and I thought my chances were slim. Of the 131 seniors in field artillery, only about thirty were to go immediately. But I was one of them.

I was assigned as a student to the field artillery school, temporarily assigned to the 45th Infantry Division at Camp Barkley, Texas, and was to report at 8:00 A.M. on Monday, June 8. From there I was to report to the field artillery school on July 14. I was concerned about getting to Camp Barkley because I did not have a car and it was almost a two-day bus or train ride. James Rominger, whose home was in Breckenridge and near Camp Barkley, invited me to ride home with him where we would spend the night and report in the next morning.

We got our first glimpse of Camp Barkley in the early afternoon of June 8. It was a large complex of two-story wooden barracks sitting on flat land between Abilene and some foothills to the south. They were still building it when we got there, and some of the units were in pyramidal tents with wooden floors, a stove in the middle, and duckboards outside to keep out the mud. There were only mesquite trees, a few clumps of buffalo grass and needle grass, and when it rained there were quagmires. The 189th Field Artillery Regiment was in tents. I was assigned as an extra officer in Service Battery, 1st Battalion of the 189th Field Artillery Regiment.

The officers' mess was a tar paper building with no fans or air conditioning and in June it was an oven. We sat on hard benches, baking like cornbread in the heat, and after the noon meal we listened to the commanding officer discuss problems and other matters concerning the regiment. Colonel Hutchison had many things he wanted to go over every day and instead of passing it through his battalion commanders, he got all the officers together at once. He was a handsome man, tall and lean, with iron gray hair. He was a former school superintendent from Enid, Oklahoma.

One day he announced that all officers would qualify on the .45-caliber revolver the next day. Shooting would begin at 8:00 A.M. The revolver, a large handgun, was a 1917 Smith & Wesson. Developed for the British during World War One, the revolver was a lot better than their Webley. It was new to me, but shooting wasn't.

I had always been a good shot. When I was seven, I carried a slingshot and was good enough occasionally to hit a rabbit on the run. Later, I collected beer bottles for the deposits and bought a .22 revolver for five dollars. A friend of mine had made his own pistol by cutting down an old .22 rifle and putting on a handgrip. He and I used to go hunting in the river bottoms. When I learned how to shoot a shotgun, if I went out with ten shells, I came back with at least nine doves.

I had never seen the .45 revolver before, but I felt reasonably confident that I could handle it. Early the next morning, we jammed ourselves into new GI trucks and rode out to the range. It was a hot day, dry and dusty, and I spent most of the morning listening to the heavy crack of the big revolvers, watching them jump in the hands of the 189th officers. My turn to fire came early that afternoon, one of the last. I was careful and took my time.

Next day after lunch, Colonel Hutchison talked to us about the pistol shoot. He was angry. Of ninety-six officers, only thirty-one qualified. He couldn't understand it. How could officers who had been in the army over a year, and had shot at least once a month, not qualify when a brand-new second lieutenant, an officer who had never even seen a .45 revolver before, could outshoot every officer in the regiment (except Captain Garrison, who had the top score of 98)?

"Lieutenant Hardison," he said, "please stand up."

I stood.

"Lieutenant Hardison shot 97," Colonel Hutchison said, "one behind Garrison. I want to know why in the hell you men can't shoot as good as Hardison, a man with ten days' service?"

That was better than a marksmanship medal, though it got me some notoriety in the regiment.

That summer, the army — still the peacetime army — had a lot of time off Wednesday afternoons and most Saturdays. Camp Barkley was in Taylor County, a dry county. You couldn't buy beer without going to the county line into Nolan County. Social life was severely limited. Meanwhile, I was learning how to be an officer.

Camp Barkley was seventy miles from home and I wanted a car, so I caught a bus home one weekend to buy one. My friend Floyd Quinney, who worked for the Mills Chevrolet Company in Colorado City, had already told me he would have a new car for me when I graduated from A&M. I looked at all the Chevys on the floor, seven of them, and picked out a blue 1941 two-door with a heater, radio, and white sidewall tires. The price tag was $933, which I didn't have. I didn't even have ten dollars.

"That makes no difference," Floyd said with an easy wave of his hand. "You're a commissioned officer in the U.S. Army, aren't you? That's all you need, Richard. Financing will be a snap."

He told them to shine up the car and fill up the tank while he worked it out with the finance company.

A couple of hours later, Floyd came back looking glum. There was a problem, he said. "They don't think your credit's any good."

"My credit's no good? How can that be? Hell," I said, "I don't have any credit."

Floyd nodded glumly. "I know. And that's the problem."

I went home and borrowed my dad's old Plymouth and took my girlfriend to the show. She was the main reason I wanted the car in the first place.

Her name was Don. It was really Anna Don Snively, but we called her Don. I'd known her since I was five and she was three. Her older brother was my best friend, and it wasn't until I got into college and started to date girls that I really started thinking about Don as a woman. She was quite lovely in a wholesome way, her hair brown and swept back in a Betty Grable style. She was a lively eighteen-year-old, smart and lots of fun. When I came home for the summer after my second year in college, we had a summer romance and promised to write when I went back to A&M. I asked her up for the Senior Ring Dance in the spring of 1941 and we got serious. I wanted to marry her.

The next Wednesday in Abilene, I saw a used 1940 Dodge coupe I wanted. It cost $680, which I didn't have.

"Don't worry about it," the salesman said. He took me downtown to one of the banks. "All you've got to do is go in there and tell them who you are. They can see that you're an army officer."

The receptionist pointed me toward a bank officer. I walked up to him, we shook hands, smiling, and he said: "Lieutenant, any graduate of Texas A&M and a lieutenant in the U.S. Army can come in here and get just about what he wants."

I was out of there in ten minutes with the money. I got the Dodge and, over the years, drove it more than 50,000 miles.

Between weekends, life was routine in the peacetime army. We kicked up dust clouds on the roads to the rifle and artillery ranges, trying to whip not very enthusiastic civilians into artillerymen. When it rained, the dust turned to mud.

The 189th Field Artillery went off to Louisiana for maneuvers in July. I was ordered to the field artillery school at Fort Sill, Oklahoma, home of the School of Fire for the Field Artillery. I drove into the old army post late one afternoon. It was Indian country, a post built by Gen. Phil Sheridan in 1873 to control hostile Indians in the area. The Indians were still in the area, men in black hats, women following a pace or two behind, but they were hostile only when drunk. Unlike Camp Barkley, it looked like it had been there forever, with long established permanent buildings. They fired a sunrise gun in front of post headquarters in the morning and flags flew from tall flagpoles all over the post.

In battery officers class eighteen (BOC-18) were fifty-six second lieutenants on the second floor of a barracks in the old post area. The first floor quartered the 1941 West Point Field Artillery graduates. I was put in charge of Section I, not so much to keep discipline in the barracks, but to get the section to class on time and check attendance.

In the three-month course we studied motors, tactics, gunnery, communications, materiel, and military history. Sometimes we went out on night lessons, laying a battery by compass without lights. On one of these — a pitch black night — the instructor asked for a roll call. I called it from memory without missing a name and reported all present. He reported that to his superiors. Later I heard that those in charge of other sections used flashlights, matches, or lighters.

We graduated in November and the officers headed for all points. I stayed at Fort Sill, assigned to the Headquarters, Field Artillery Replacement Training Center. In the fall of 1941, Fort Sill was a good place for a young army officer who had a car. The duty was light. It was fun but hectic, and I was spending all my money on girls and gasoline. Maybe now, I thought, was the time to get married.

I went home to talk to Don. It was the weekend of December 6, 1941. We had talked about getting married and agreed we would after the first of the year, probably in February. That Sunday, December 7, about noon, I picked up Don at home and drove around talking and listening to the radio. Tommy Dorsey's orchestra was playing "In the Mood," sounding smooth, when an announcer broke in.

Pearl Harbor had been attacked by the Japanese, he said. The damage was severe and the loss of life was heavy. I didn't even know where Pearl Harbor was. More dance music came on. Then another announcer said all servicemen should report to their stations.

I felt cold inside, wondering if there was some way we could avoid war in Europe.

"What do you think?" Don said. "I'm scared. Will you have to go? What will happen? And when?"

I had no idea, of course, but I had to say something. "I don't think anything will happen," I said. "Not soon. Probably nothing for six or eight months."

"I don't know," she said. "Everything is changed." We went on talking and finally decided that even though everything had changed, we would go ahead with our plans. When I went home on a three-day leave for Christmas, we were parked downtown, talking about getting married, and Don said she was going to have problems with her mother. "She doesn't want me to get married now," Don said.

"So what?" I said.

"So maybe we should wait."

"Wait? No! We could wait ten years and nothing would change."

"It's a bad situation," Don said.

"We didn't make it a bad situation. It's not our fault. Why should we wait?"

"You're sure about this?"

"Am I sure? No, I'm not sure. I'm positive!"

She smiled. "Okay," she said.

We decided to get married February 13. I went back to Fort Sill, happy; but on January 18, I got a letter from Don. She couldn't go through with it. She wasn't ready, she said, and she was sure her mother and father would object. She wanted to wait.

This was disturbing. I wanted to get married then or not at all. I wrote her a long letter and said so. I told her I'd be home the weekend of January 31 and we'd talk about it. I had always wanted to be a pilot and had given some thought to transferring to the airborne forces then being organized, where promotions would be quicker and life more exciting. I drove home from Fort Sill, arriving in the middle of the afternoon, and saw Don coming out of a department store with her arms full of packages. I stopped and parked and she came and got into the car. She kissed me and seemed happy to see me. I got right to the point.

"Look," I said, "what are we going to do? Get married or forget it?"

"I want to get married," she said.

"When?"

She smiled at me. "Now."

We went right to the courthouse at Sweetwater, Texas, thirty miles away, and I bought a marriage license. We had originally planned to get married in church, but under the circumstances we decided to be married in a private ceremony in a minister's home. We found a minister and he married us at 5:30 P.M. We went back to Colorado City and drove around, making plans. I left her that night and went home, planning to see her the next day before I drove back to Fort Sill.

We decided to have another wedding in her church on February 15. But at 11:00 A.M., Don called.

"Come over here," she said. "There's trouble." She was crying.

I told my mother goodbye and got in the car. Dad was downtown. When I got to Don's house, things were in a mess. Her folks told her she absolutely could not marry me, and that was that! When they found out she was already married, she had to get her things and go with me. There was no other way. We drove downtown and I saw my father on a street corner and told him what we'd done.

"Well, son," he said, "I'm glad for you." He smiled, and we shook hands. He reached in his pocket and gave me all the cash he had, which was thirty-five dollars. We started our marriage on that.

When I reported for duty at the Field Artillery Replacement Training Center in Fort Sill and the personnel officer saw I had a degree in landscape architecture, he detailed me as center beautification officer. I looked around. What was I going to do? There wasn't anything there but dirt and rocks. I learned that $300 was available for beautification so I bought fertilizer and rye grass seed and applied them to the open areas around headquarters and the camp's approaches. Soon we had snow and some showers. The rye grass came up dark green and beautiful. One who noticed it was Major Thomas, post improvement officer at the main post.

One day I got a call. The post adjutant said Brig. Gen. G. R.

Allin had detailed me as post improvement officer. I was transferred to the main post with an office, secretary, staff car, and driver. That was drawing a lot of water for a shavetail.

General Allin said he wanted me to do something about the post cemetery and the old post area, the historic part of Fort Sill. I had the cemetery cleaned up and shrubbery planted. I designed and built a skeet range in an area called the "punch bowl" across Medicine Creek and the "bluffs," high granite bluffs where the Indians once made strong medicine. We fixed the drainage system around the Officers' Club and the baseball field needed a lot of work. Drainage ditches were dug and lined with local blue granite. Every Friday I made a tour with the general in his car, his one-star flag flying on the right-front fender.

One evening Don and I went to the Officers' Club. It was cold and snowy outside but very nice inside. We had a couple of drinks, danced some and looked out through the north group of windows across the swimming pool where we could see the snow blowing. The music was very smooth.

"This is a pretty good life," I said. "What do you think?"

"I like it, too."

I looked at her to make sure she knew that I was serious. "I mean, Don, that I like it a lot."

She nodded and smiled. "I know. And so do I. The people we've met, they're all very nice."

"Yes, they are. I'm glad you like the army, Don, because I like it and I'm thinking this is what I want to do from now on."

We were holding hands across the table and she squeezed mine. "Good," she said.

It was wonderful, I thought, to have settled already on what the rest of my life would be like.

In February my old outfit, the 189th Field Artillery, came to Fort Sill to shoot. I got my staff car and went out to see them. They were quite surprised to see me arrive in a chauffeured staff car. Six months before, I'd been the lowest second lieutenant in the regiment.

In April all that came to an end. An army order was issued saying that officers in my age group were to be assigned field duty. I was twenty-two and a second lieutenant, too young for the job I held. I was sent back to the Field Artillery Replacement Training Center. General Allin wrote Gen. Waldo C. Potter, commanding officer of the center, a letter of commendation. General Allin's secretary said the letter would mean a promotion.

It said I had performed my duties in a "splendid manner," demonstrating "marked qualities of leadership, initiative and professional ability" and so on. (Appendix I) Three weeks later the promotion list came out, and I was a first lieutenant.

I was assigned to Battery C of the 27th Training Battalion. The battery commander, Captain Stone, was a drug store dandy who smiled a lot, always smelled good, and avoided most of his responsibilities. He was supposed to conduct extended field training of the men, but he left all that to me. The men of the battery were finishing their basic training. We were issued two rounds of live 155mm howitzer ammunition and told to go to the west firing range and survey the guns in, then shoot to prove our surveys. The battery was to march out in tactical formation, put the guns in position, survey them in, conceal them, establish communications, and fire two rounds at a given target. This was a five-day exercise, beginning on a Monday.

When surveying in, the guns are precisely located on a map, generally a 1/25,000 scale map made by the Department of the Interior. There is error in map-making, as in everything else, and a survey is made to eliminate as much error as possible.

We were ready to shoot at 9:00 A.M., when four majors showed up in a command car to inspect our work. After they had looked us over, we all went to the observation post. I identified for them the target I had selected, a lone oak tree on a high plateau some 2,000 yards away. I gave the command to fire, one round.

The 155mm howitzer blasted, and through the B.C. scope (battery commander's periscope) I saw the shell burst near the tree. It looked as if it was off in deflection, but I was sure it was off in range. I shortened the range by ½ C (a range factor depending on the distance of the target from the guns, which in this case was fifty yards) and gave the command to fire again.

The howitzer blasted again and the tree disintegrated. Dead on target in two rounds. The majors were happy.

We arrived at the motor pool about 3:30 P.M. on Friday and I was busy parking the five-ton prime movers and howitzers when First Sergeant Outhouse, as I will call him here, arrived in a jeep with a message for me to report immediately to the new battery commander. He said that Captain Stone was relieved the day that we left on the field problem and the new battery commander was Capt. John U. D. Page. I left a lieutenant in charge of the parking and first echelon maintenance and I went with Sergeant Outhouse in his jeep to the orderly room to meet the new battery commander. He was direct and brief and said that he was making changes in the duties of the various officers in the battery. He then said, "I am relieving you as battery executive and am giving the job to Lieutenant Phillips. I have been working closely with him these last four days and I do not know you." This was a lick that I did not need, being replaced by a second lieutenant with less than two months service. Lieutenant Phillips was not taken on the field problem because I felt that he would be excess baggage. He apparently spent his time "brown nosing" Captain Page and it paid off for him. Captain Page said that I would be carried as an extra officer. This arrangement lasted for about three weeks and I became battery executive again. We took on another group of civilians to train in the summer of 1942. Three of them I remember particularly because they were outstanding men. One was from Omaha, the other two from Detroit. One of the Detriot men had served in the Michigan legislature; the other was a prominent lawyer. Drafted into the army in early May, by early June they had made acting corporals.

The ex-legislator told me on a Monday that he and his friend were looking forward to the weekend because their wives were coming for a visit. On Friday, when the first sergeant heard that these men's wives were in town, he detailed one of them as corporal of the guard and the other as charge of quarters, effectively confining them both to the post for the weekend. He did it late in the day and I didn't know anything about it. Don and I happened to go to Fort Sill that night to go to a movie, and I dropped by the battery just to see how things were doing.

I was surprised to find one on guard and the other on CQ. I asked what was going on. "I thought your wives were to be in town," I said to the one on CQ.

"That's right," he said. "They are. They're at the Wolverton Hotel, where they have reservations."

I asked if the first sergeant knew this.

"Oh, yes," he said. "We've called and told our wives that we can't see them, that they should go back to Detroit on Sunday."

I called Sergeant Outhouse out of the barracks and told him I wanted those two men relieved immediately. The sergeant started to give me problems, but I shut him up. We forgot the movie and my wife and I took the two men into town in our car so they could spend the weekend with their wives. Sergeant Outhouse was an old knockdown, dragout, sorry, worthless, no good regular army sergeant, not worth a damn for anything.

There were still a lot of old-army types around.

Sometimes on weekends, when the ranges were open and no artillery was firing, Don and I took a .22 rifle and went hunting for rabbits and crows. In the fall of 1942, I borrowed some shotguns from the detailed enlisted men's list and we hunted doves on the ranges. Once I checked out a Browning automatic rifle with several clips of ammunition and gave the rabbits hell. I would see a rabbit about 200 yards away and shoot once to get him running. Then I would try to hit him with the BAR on its bipod mount, on full automatic. I got one that way. Don shot almost as much as I did but confined her shooting to a .22 rifle and often shot from a prone position on a shelter half. Not a bad shot, either. We made sure we were far enough out in the artillery impact area that no one on the post could hear the BAR firing on full automatic.

By early October, we had a new battery commander, Capt. Porter Grant, and another group almost ready to be shipped out to the various divisions. They had learned to be cannoneers and we were now firing for the field artillery school.

I had been out on the west range more than three weeks, hollering at the top of my voice at the gunners and cannoneers. The howitzers in the battery were fifty feet apart, so the two end guns were 150 feet away from each other, half the distance of a football field. Besides that, I was fifty to eighty feet behind them and by now I had just about lost my voice. The north wind was blowing against me and so it made sense, I thought, to use our new bullhorn, which had just been issued for that purpose. But about that time, the battalion commander drove up, saw me using the bullhorn, and blew his top. "That's no way to handle a firing battery," he yelled. "Use your own voice!"

I put down the bullhorn and started hollering commands again as loudly as I could. The battalion commander was a big man and in civilian life he drove a horse-drawn milk wagon. It was said among the officers of the battalion that the horse pulling the delivery wagon was the brains of the team. He would stop in front of a house and stomp his left front hoof once and the future lieutenant colonel would take one bottle of milk to the house; if he stomped twice then he would take in two bottles. He knew about as much about a firing battery as a pig about Sunday.

That afternoon Captain Grant brought out a new second lieutenant that had just been assigned to the battery. He had been in the army only a few weeks.

"Give him some time on the guns," the captain said. "Let him fire several missions."

I was glad to be relieved, as my voice was all but gone. I gave Lieutenant Smith my notebook with the information he needed and headed for the lister bag, a big canvas bag suspended in the center of a tripod about six feet high with four spouts near the bottom of the bag. I was getting a drink of water in a canteen cup about forty feet farther back when I heard a fire mission come in. From what the recorder said to him, I knew it was a base deflection right shift. Smith gave the correct command to the battery — "Base deflection right two three zero, elevation 187."

Lieutenant Smith needed the bullhorn; the gunners and chiefs of sections could not hear him clearly. I was closer to him than they were and I was having difficulty understanding his commands. The number-three howitzer moved base deflection left instead of right. Lieutenant Smith and the chief of section should have caught the error. The lieutenant waited, looking for the raised right arm of the chiefs of sections to indicate the guns were ready to fire.

Oh, no, I said to myself. He was going to fire. I dropped the canteen cup and turned. "CEASE FIRING," I yelled. But they didn't hear me. I started running toward them. "Cease firing!" I yelled into the wind. "CEASE FIRING!" At this moment, Lieutenant Smith dropped his upheld right arm and all guns fired as one.

I ran up yelling and everything stopped. We saw the shell burst 2,000 yards away, about 100 yards to the left of the block house on top of Signal Mountain. If it had not hit the mountain, I don't know where it would have landed — probably Cache, Oklahoma — but it would have killed a lot of people.

All firing on the range was stopped. I reported that Battery C, 27th Battalion, 7th Training Regiment, had fired 180 miles outside the left safety limit. I had not given the commands to fire, but I was in charge. Now, I figured, was a good time to get the hell out of Fort Sill.

Next morning, Captain Grant told me the 82nd Infantry Division was being reorganized as a triangular division. This was the new army structure with three regiments to a division, and as airborne, too. He had been offered command of a glider artillery battalion and asked if I would like to go with him as a battery commander. I jumped at it. But before it happened, I was transferred to the 8th Armored Division at Camp Campbell, Kentucky.

Don and I packed up, got in the Dodge, and pointed it east.

2 Transferred

February 21, 1943–November 20, 1943

For the United States, the war began on December 7, 1941, with the Japanese attack on Pearl Harbor. The Germans had invaded Russia on June 22, 1941, and were now fighting for their lives. Singapore was in Japanese hands as were the Philippines and New Guinea. Gen. Jimmy Doolittle had raided Tokyo and the navy had defeated the Japanese in the Battle of the Coral Sea and at Midway. The American Fifth Army was fighting in Italy.

I was sent to Camp Campbell, Kentucky, and assigned to the 399th Armored Field Artillery Battalion, where there were sixty-five officers — twice as many as the battalion was allotted. There was nothing to do for many of us and I assumed I wouldn't be there long.

The weather was snowy and cold when I rented one of the dormitory rooms at Bethel College, a Baptist school for girls, in nearby Hopkinsville. Don and I stayed there for ten days, and every night at dinner, which was at 6:30 sharp, we filed into the dining room and stood behind our straight-backed chairs until the president arrived. He was a tall, imposing man with long, silvery hair, a fire-eating preacher who waxed eloquent in prayer before the meal. He returned thanks in a way that covered all bases and included everybody up and down the road, for all the shut-ins, and those who were ill or out of work, while we stood there hungry as barracuda, waiting for him to finish. When finally he said "amen," we all sat down as one and began eating.

Toward the end of February, the division moved to Camp Polk, Louisiana, which was at least warmer than Camp Campbell. The enlisted men and most of the officers boarded troop trains which transported them to Camp Polk. Those of us who had cars were given a few extra days to get there. Don and I packed up the Dodge and headed south. Despite the war, these were light-hearted times for young, newly married men and women in the service. We hardly ever thought about the war itself. We didn't read about it or talk about it and we never worried about it. We thought only about what truly mattered, about doing our jobs right, about bills, about the car needing a new tire, and about the sorry food at the Pig Trail Inn. The unmarried men also thought some about women and whiskey, but nobody thought much about the war itself or getting killed, though many of them would be killed later in the war.

The nearest town to Camp Polk was Leesville. Before the war, it had a population of 3,000. It still had about that many natives. But the army had added about 300,000 troops to the area, swamping the town with soldiers. When we arrived I went to the U.S.O. and was given a list of rooms available, and found one for two days in a private home next to the railroad tracks. All night long, the trains clattered through, keeping up an unbelievable racket, whistling and spinning the drive wheel against the rails and making a terrible din when they coupled up. It was like living in a switchman's shed. In a few days Don found a comfortable room in the home of a banker, who rented rooms to servicemen.

The battery commanders and staff officers kept to themselves, leaving extra officers like me alone. The extra officers went to headquarters every morning and signed in, then sat around reading field manuals and trying to look busy. It was an awkward time for us.

The commander of Battery A, 2nd Lt. Henry E. Brooks, was a pleasant exception. He and I got to talking one day and I told him I didn't like hanging around battalion headquarters all the time, and since I didn't know anything about some of the weapons that I had seen, I asked him if he would mind if I checked some of them out and worked on them in his battery gunroom.

Brooks was from Manchester, Connecticut, and had an easy way with people. "Sure," he said with a smile. "Why not? Which ones are you most interested in?"

I told him I would start with the Thompson submachine gun, then go to the Browning .50-caliber machine gun and then the M-7 self-propelled howitzer.

"Hey, hold up," he said with a grin. "That's a course and a half already." He laughed. "But seriously, you can use the gunroom anytime you want to."

I went by battalion headquarters and signed in. Then I went to the Battery A gunroom in the motor park, checked out a Thompson submachine gun, and with a manual I began field stripping it, which means taking it apart and learning how to put it back together again — in the dark! When I finished that one, I studied another weapon, then another. For two weeks, I worked alone like that, then on Tuesday of the second week, I heard a door open behind me. I was caught up in something complicated and didn't look to see who it was. Whoever it was stayed there for a long moment, nobody saying anything. Then the door quietly closed.

Suddenly, my curiosity got the best of me, and I went to the window and looked out. It was Maj. Roger M. Lilly, the battalion commander. He was walking away. I had noticed him earlier when the door to his office opened and we were all sitting around in headquarters building. He scanned us as he went in and out and occasionally came over to see what we were reading. But he hadn't said anything to us. He was about my age, but much more intense. He was all muscle, bone, and brain — a West Point graduate who was hard as nails and a natural leader.

A couple of days later, I was working on a big .50-caliber machine gun and had it pretty well torn apart on a table. I heard the door open again, and once again I didn't look up.

A voice behind me asked: "How long have you been doing this?" I turned around to see who it was. It was Major Lilly.

"About two weeks, sir . . ." I told him.

He nodded. "Why?"

"Well, sir," I said, "These guns are new to me and when I get to where I'm going, I may need to know something about them."

He looked at me straight in the eyes, nodding seriously. Then, without a word, he turned and walked out. The next day, about 11:00

in the morning, a runner came down and told me to report to Major Lilly at battalion headquarters. The major had dark-brown hair and cool eyes. He looked at me for a few seconds, tapping the desk with a pencil. Then he smiled slightly.

"You're the new adjutant of the battalion," he said.

I tried not to show any feelings, but I couldn't help myself. I grinned from ear to ear. This was wonderful. This was not only something to do but also recognition. My duties would be to see that the reports that needed to be submitted were submitted and, in general, I would be the chief administrative officer of the battalion. It was a good job that called for the rank of captain. About six weeks later, Major Lilly sent in a list of names of officers for promotion to captain, including Henry Brooks, John J. Collins, Matthew A. Oliver, Marvin Sather, George Salisbury, and me. Most of us would go through the war together and become close friends.

John Collins of New York City was tall and thin, with light curly hair and a reddish complexion. He combined a slick, big-city personality with a lot of warmth. He was also extraordinarily bright, and could get to the heart of a problem as quickly as anybody I have ever known. Before he joined the battalion, he had been an instructor in gunnery at the field artillery school.

Marvin Sather of River Falls, Wisconsin, was the commander of Battery B, a six-foot blond with blue eyes, a handsome man with an open face and a ready smile. He was well liked and a good officer.

George Salisbury was short, muscular and strong, having spent his life on the family ranch in Carbon County, Wyoming, riding every day and working cattle and sheep. He had big bones. One of his wrists would have made two of mine and when he bought a watch, he had to buy extra links in the chain. George always spoke his mind, and when I asked him a question, I always got a direct answer.

Hank Brooks, commander of Battery A, was a quiet and efficient officer who took his job seriously. He had dark hair and a medium build. We became close friends.

Matthew Oliver of New York City was tall and red-haired with an angular build. He was somewhat of a loner and had few friends.

I pinned on my silver captain's bars on June 8. Major Lilly was promoted to lieutenant colonel on the same order.

About six weeks later, Colonel Lilly stopped at my desk and said: "Tex, come in here. I want to talk to you."

I stopped what I was doing, got up and walked into his office, and stood in front of his desk. "Yes, sir."

"I've got another job for you," he said. He gave me a long look. "I want you to take over Headquarters Battery and straighten it out." He looked at me and frowned. "You'll see what I mean when you get there." He gazed out the window for a moment, then glanced sharply back at me. "The orders won't be cut till in the morning," he said. "Why don't you get over there this afternoon and nose around a bit?"

Headquarters Battery, nerve center of the battalion, consisted of several sections each headed by a staff officer and assisted by non-commissioned officers. The sections were S-1, personnel; S-2, intelligence; S-3, operations; communications, with telephone and radio; three FO (forward observer) sections, each with a tank and a half-track; two liaison sections; and two air sections, each with an L-4 airplane.

In addition, there were three other sections headed by battery officers: supply, maintenance, and kitchen. It was a group of 138 men, eight officers and a number of NCOs, including two master sergeants and five technical sergeants. The top kick and the battalion sergeant major were of master sergeant rank.

When I walked in, I saw immediately what the problem was. Discipline, or the lack of it. Men were walking around with their sleeves rolled up, no hats, dirty uniforms. I walked into the barracks without being announced. It was the middle of the day and it should have been vacant, but several men were lying around. I walked over to the motor park. It was a mess. Several vehicles were in various stages of repair, nothing being done, no officers around; in fact, I found no officers anywhere.

Headquarters Battery had some good NCOs. Most of them had received their stripes under Lilly, so they had to be good. The first sergeant was William F. Hughes, Jr., of Florala, Alabama, one of the very best top kicks in the army. He knew his job and knew how to get others to do their job.

My style is generally low key — a soft voice backed up with authority — and that's how I went into this assignment. The next morning when orders were cut, I appeared in crisp khakis and told Sergeant Hughes to call a meeting of the section chiefs in my office.

"When do you want the meeting, sir?"

"Soon as possible," I said.

"It will take a few minutes, Captain. Several of the men are in the motor park."

"OK, as soon as you can."

Ten minutes later everybody was there, standing around in the office. "Men," I said, "I was here yesterday. I walked through the area to get a fix on things." I looked around from face to face. "As most of you probably realize, this battery has problems. When I went in the barracks yesterday afternoon, I found nine men there, lying around. Goofing off. I don't want any more of that crap." One of the non-coms caught something in his throat and coughed several times. I waited for him to get through. "There's more than enough things to do. You know that as well as I do. I want everyone in this battery in proper uniform at all times. And in case you need me, I will be available." I gave them my phone number at home. "You men didn't earn your stripes for nothing. You are good soldiers, and I want you to continue to be good soldiers."

One of the problems we had in the battery was gambling. I didn't know this at first. Gambling was a problem because some of the NCOs had been gambling with the new men, the fillers, and cleaning them out. I realized this when some of the new men came to me for approval of Red Cross loans. I could tell that resentment was high and morale and dissatisfaction was evident. So I ordered a stop to it.

A few days later, Private Johnson brought things to a head. Johnson was a big man with an attitude problem. He was brought into the orderly room by the MPs with a report that he had been fighting in town, drunk in a sleezy Leesville bar. When I heard about it, I was almost glad. Sometimes you need a clear-cut case like this to make a point.

Johnson was not a good soldier. He was surly, slow, and glowering. He was in disarray and stinking. I had checked the manual of courts-martial to make sure what my authority was. For fighting I could have had him tried by a special court or a summary court; I could also simply impose battery punishment. I explained these options briefly to him. He didn't know what to do so I told him that the simplest, from his viewpoint, might be battery punishment. This meant that I would impose some physical punishment, I said. He looked glum.

"But there would be no deduction from your pay," I added.

He brightened. "Okay," he said. "I'll take battery punishment."

I ordered him to get his entrenching tools (a shovel and pick) and a shelter half. I had arranged for Sergeant Hughes and his section chief to be in the orderly room when he reported. We then went out between the barracks. "Hand me the shelter half," I said. He handed it to me and I spread it out on the ground. "There," I said. "You will dig a hole that size and four feet deep. And on your own time."

It took him about a week to dig the hole, doing it on his own time. I was attending night classes when Private Johnson dug the hole most of the time, but I noticed him once. He had stripped to the waist and was methodically digging while a circle of men watched grinning at him. When he finished the hole, Private Johnson reported to me. I called in Sergeant Hughes and the three of us went out and looked it over. "Okay," I said, "now fill it in." He showed no emotion. "And when you're through," I said, "report to me again."

He spent about two days filling in the hole, and when he reported to me, I checked it again and promptly arranged a transfer for him. Before noon the next day he was gone. By then, the Johnson incident had left its simple message, that if anyone screwed up, they would be quickly and surely punished, then shipped out.

One day a private came to us from the 82nd Airborne. He wore jump boots and had a bad habit of butting in front of others in the chow line and in the supply room. Besides that, he wore a good conduct medal and was lording that over the other men. I don't like bullies and I called him into my office and told him to turn in his jump boots and pick up some combat boots like everybody else. About then, his service record came through and when I read it I realized that he was bad news. I read parts of it to Sergeant Hughes, and said, "I don't think our paratrooper really deserves that good conduct medal."

Sergeant Hughes said, "No, he sure don't." The sergeant, a quiet man but as hard as a nail and trim as a wildcat, said as he left the orderly room, "I'll be back in a few minutes."

I heard a ruckus in the mess hall and looked out the window to see the paratrooper fly through the swinging screen doors and down the ten back steps to the ground. Soon Sergeant Hughes walked into my office and tossed a piece of khaki shirt with a good conduct medal on it.

Despite my order against gambling, I knew that it was still going on. I hadn't seen any gambling, but I'd heard the men grumbling that they were still losing their pay. According to the stories, one of my best NCOs continued to gamble with the men. They played anywhere they could — in the barracks, in the latrine, in the woods. He was an excellent soldier in all other respects and a close friend of Sergeant Hughes, so I told the sergeant to tell him to stop gambling or he would be shipped out like anyone else. "It's not just gambling that's so bad," I said, "hell, it's disobeying a command." I looked Sergeant Hughes in the eye and said, "I won't have that."

Sergeant Hughes was gone for a while, then reported back that he had relayed the message.

"You think he'll stop gambling?"

Sergeant Hughes didn't answer immediately. Then he shook his head. "I don't know."

"Well, if he doesn't stop, he will be transferred."

"I know. But I don't know if that matters to him."

One Saturday at the motor pool, I chanced upon them, the sergeant and three of the men, all on their knees with dice and a pile of money in front of them. They saw me and froze. I walked over to them. "Having a good game?" I asked pleasantly.

The sergeant stood up and the three men followed suit. "Yes, sir," he said, eyes fixed on the horizon.

"That's good," I said. Then I turned and left. I had discussed the matter in detail with Colonel Lilly and he was fully aware of the cirsumstances. Late that afternoon he stopped by my orderly room and asked how things were going and I told him that gambling was still a problem. He said, "Enough is enough," and the next day he was gone. I regretted losing him as he was the best NCO in the battery after Sergeant Hughes. Later he made first sergeant of an infantry company and distinguished himself by winning a Silver Star.

The men now knew how serious I was about gambling. To balance it out I tried to do what I could in other ways. Division was very strict on leaves for officers and furloughs for enlisted men. The longest an officer could get was ten days. An enlisted man could get fifteen days. In the past, division had given enlisted men from three weeks to a month off. They had thirty days coming every year and I thought that should continue. I told each of my NCOs when they went on furlough to call the Red Cross in their hometown and say they had personal problems. When the Red Cross called me, I would give them more time. We did that until the division caught up with me and raised hell. But by treating the men that way and being firm and consistent with discipline, we got the battery running like a Swiss watch.

That fall, I was detailed as a member of a general court-martial. We were trying enlisted men for desertion and other crimes. None of them were ever acquitted. They were sentenced to from ten to fifty years for desertion. I think most of them were out of jail before I was out of the army, thus they avoided combat. The court went on for two nights a week for six months. At night, I was either on the court or in officers' school.

The summer was hot and dry and we worked hard. The days were full of heat and dust and tension, long columns of vehicles moving through demanding maneuvers. We went to the training area in column, then into position, camouflaged the vehicles and established communication and observation posts, all under strict combat conditions as the division staff imagined them to be. We left with the sunrise and returned about dark and washed the vehicles under lights. Then we ate and the men went to bed, and the officers went to school. There was constant pressure on the battery commanders to have a hot meal ready at 6:30 A.M. and move out at 7:30 A.M., clean up the area, cover the sump, mark the route to a new position, establish communications — day after day, fourteen hours a day, six and seven days a week.

The division artillery commander was not noted for his common sense. One of his ideas, for instance, was to have everybody at officers' school wear wool uniforms — even in summer.

He ordered a division artillery review one hot, muggy, dusty Saturday morning and the artillery battalions of the 8th Armored Division Artillery marched past with guidons flying. The colonel, who had a sharp eye for irrelevant detail, noticed that when the batteries passed the reviewing stand that the tops of some guidon staffs in some batteries were higher than others. This might have been because some men were taller than others, or carried the guidon staff at a different angle or level, but that never occurred to him. He ordered that all guidons be brought before him. Then he had them stood up on the sidewalk. The staff was supposed to be seven feet tall. When he had them measured, a few were a little over seven feet and a few were a little under. The guidon staff carried by my battery was of chrome and it was a half-inch short. For that he confined me to quarters for a week. But the colonel himself had awarded that very guidon staff to my battery for excellence!

The old army died hard.

Don came out to see me every night and we ate at the officers' mess and spent some time together. By this time, she was working at South Camp Polk, heading the war bond section. She had a staff car with a driver, an office and secretary. She had more people working for her than I did for me and her salary was better than mine.

That summer, reading about Guadalcanal, Midway, North Africa, and the Battle of Coral Sea, we wondered what was ahead for us.

But whatever it was, we were ready for it. We didn't talk about serious things. Nobody did. All those things had been settled long ago and passed on to us unquestioned. We were a nation undivided then and didn't question everything that happened. The most important things — patriotism, honor and courage, fighting and dying, doing the right thing at the right time, and life itself — were taken for granted because we were young and we thought that we would never die. Fidelity? I didn't even know what the word meant. But I knew what it was. It was being true to one's mate, and Don and I never talked about such things because it was never in question.

Summer was drawing to a close and we were glad. It had been a hard one for all of us. We knew what was ahead in November. We were going into the field for six weeks, the thick piney woods of East Texas, with few roads and numerous trails. The division maneuvers were to start November 20 and continue until January 4. We would fight a mock campaign in a part of East Texas from Jasper north to San Augustine.

3 Camp Polk, Louisiana

November 21, 1943–October 30, 1944

By November 1943, the U.S. Eighth Air Force and the RAF were bombing Germany day and night. The Russians had re-taken Savastopol and the U.S. Fifth Army had broken out at Anzio. On June 6, 1944, the American and British forces landed on Normandy beaches. Marines invaded Saipan, Guam and Tinian, and the first V-2 rockets began to fall on London. The U.S. First Army reached the West Wall in Luxembourg while the Third Army was on the west bank of the Moselle River. There was a lot of fighting to do.

We hit the road November 21, a long olive-drab column of tanks, half-tracks and self-propelled artillery, trailing trucks of the support units. The division moved slowly, like a big olive caterpillar out of Camp Polk, and for ten hours down the narrow asphalt roads to an area southwest of Yellowpine, Texas. It started to rain and we went into tents and slickers, put chains on the jeeps and trucks, and kept trying to conduct a maneuver, but it was cold, hovering around forty degrees during the day, freezing at night. By December 20, it was sleeting a lot of the time and we had the worst snowfall old-timers in the area could remember — eight inches one night. Ice formed on everything, the limbs of trees as well as power lines, breaking them down.

The maneuvers (D Series) were exercises in combined arms, tanks, and infantry supported by artillery. We would go into position, survey the guns in, lay wire, and establish observation posts in support of the tanks and infantry. Military maneuvers are like real war in the unexpected screwups, the unintentional humor, and the never-ending battle with the elements. This maneuver was designed primarily for unit commanders, division staff, and battalion commanders and their staffs. Those of us at the battery level didn't know what the hell was going on most of the time, and in that respect, too, it was very much like war.

We worked night and day, and it was tough; tough on equipment, too. Trucks and half-tracks were torn up in what must have been record numbers. Vehicles were constantly getting bogged down in the rain-soaked ground, and it was almost impossible to drag them out. More than one of the battalion's half-tracks were pulled apart.

One wet, soggy, cold, red-ass day, Captain Sather of Battery B had a half-track stuck down to its axles in the mud when Colonel Lilly arrived in his jeep.

"Sather," the colonel said, "pull that damned half-track out of there and get going!"

The tall, good-looking captain just looked at the colonel for a long moment. He was mad as hell at the driver of the half-track and had been chewing him out. Now it was the colonel eating him out in front of God and everybody.

"I don't know, sir," he said, "but I think it's going to take a tank retriever to get us out of here. I don't want to tear it up with an M-7."

The tank recovery vehicle, which is equipped with a crane, is called on when all else fails. But Colonel Lilly didn't think we had reached that point yet. He could operate any vehicle in an armored division, and he was proud of that.

He shook his head and said, "Hell no, Sather, get an M-7 over here and I'll get the son of a bitch out."

The M-7, a self-propelled 105mm howitzer, is like an M-4 medium tank but without the turret. It has one-inch armor on the front, half an inch on the sides and back — enough steel to stop a rifle bullet or machine gun fire but not tank or artillery shells. The M-7, a real workhorse, is relatively fast, too, with a top speed of about thirty-five miles an hour. We used to call it "The Priest" because the .50-caliber machine gun was on a ring mount that looked like the pulpit where Catholic priests deliver their homilies.

An M-7 was brought over and the driver got out. Colonel Lilly, who fancied himself a hot M-7 jockey, got in and backed up to the half-track. The chief of section hooked two one-inch tow cables to the half-track, then Colonel Lilly gunned the M-7. The engine was roaring, the track spinning and throwing mud, then suddenly it lurched forward and we saw with a sickening sensation what had happened. The M-7 had yanked the half-track in two; the front end of the half-track, the front axle, wheels, bumper and winch all tangled with the cables on the ground. Now Sather had two problems.

Nobody said a word. We all just stared at the mess. Then Colonel Lilly, red in the face, muttered something unprintable, climbed down from the M-7, and got into his jeep and roared away.

One of the battalion commanders decided that his tanks, half-tracks, jeeps, and trucks didn't look sharp enough. They had been painted with a flat paint the government had spent hundreds of thousands of dollars to develop. A lusterless paint reflected no light, thus offering an enemy no shiny target to shoot at. But the battalion commander discovered that if he went over his vehicles with used crankcase oil, it would leave the paint as glossy as patent leather shoes. This was a violation of regulations, but the division commander, a parade-ground general, liked it and ordered that all units go over their vehicles with used crankcase oil. So we did.

We were in the piney woods of East Texas, the situation non-tactical, and Colonel Lilly bucked the order down to the battery commanders without comment, except to say that we should get this done as soon as we could. We drained the oil from two tanks, drivers and mechanics got buckets and rags and they smeared the dirty oil on the sides, the hoods and doors of all the vehicles till every inch was covered. This comedy lasted two days, and at the end of it the men were as oily as the vehicles. There was no laundry on maneuvers, so the men lived that way, their clothes dirty and oily and full of dust, for the next two weeks. The tanks and jeeps and trucks were even dirtier, if that was possible.

Another brilliant idea occurred to the division surgeon. A West Point graduate and a medical doctor, he decided that all the cooking utensils of the units should be blued like new rifles. Having read an article on how to blue cooking utensils, he made copies of it and sent them around to each of the units. We were to gather about a cord of wood and build a roaring fire, then throw the pots and pans into the fire and wait until they cooled off. Then we were to put coals on top, and after a while the utensils were supposed to be blued. But when we dug them out of the ashes, the pots and pans weren't blued, they were browned. A lot of units ruined all of their utensils. We were lucky; we ruined only about half of ours.

We had problems with our garbage, too. Each unit was required to dig a sump, three feet by four and four feet deep. All of the kitchen garbage was thrown in the sump and it was covered with dirt, then the dirt was to be stomped down. When the unit pulled out, the sump was closed and a sign erected, giving the day it was closed and the unit number. People at division headquarters would check later to see how well the units were taking care of the garbage. If they found a deficiency, the sign on the sump told them who to chew out and raise hell with.

Battery C of the 399th closed a sump on December 8, but it was later opened without authorization by wild hogs. The hogs scattered tin cans, papers, and other debris all over the area. Someone from division headquarters checked the bivouac and decided the sump had been opened by hogs because it had not been dug deep enough. Too much garbage had been thrown in and not enough dirt put on top. The staff officer wrote a hot letter to Colonel Lilly, and Captain Salisbury, commander of Battery C, got burned.

Having worked all his life with cattle and sheep in Wyoming, Salisbury probably had a better understanding of animals than most, and he took what the hogs had done personally. The next sump Battery C closed was different. The cooks and KPs dug a trench around the sump in a circle about twelve feet in diameter. Off of that, they dug a small trench about eighty feet long into the underbrush where Salisbury could hide. He had gasoline poured into the trench, into the one circling the sump, and into the sump itself. Then when Battery C moved out, Salisbury stayed behind.

The hogs were lurking about as usual, and as soon as the half-tracks and the last M-7 pulled out, the hogs, veterans of two or three maneuvers, came running straight for the sump, rummaging around and rooting at the garbage.

Salisbury, watching from cover, gave them a little time to get into it, then, when eight or ten of them were in the circle, he tossed a lighted match into the trench. The fire ran down the trench and into the sump, engulfing the hogs, and they, squealing, ran off in every direction.

By that time, we'd been in the field for weeks and most of us hadn't bathed at all. It was too cold. I was nasty and dirty and smelled like a goat, and I shaved only when I couldn't avoid it.

After each problem, the officers attended a critique at division headquarters. One of them in December was held in a sort of open-air bowl, where at the north end of it was General Grimes' caravan. It had a platform in front about thirty feet across and ten feet wide. When all the high-ranking dignitaries were seated, General Grimes, eyes sparkling and smiling brightly, emerged from his pad. He swept the audience and his big smile faded into a frown.

"When I was a lieutenant," he announced gravely, "I shaved every day." He looked around darkly and saw me, then said, "And I expect you to do the same." He gave us another baleful look. "I know it's cold. But that is no problem." He shook his head and turned his mouth down. "If the water is frozen, break the ice and shave your face." He gave us all a slow, frowning look and added, "And that is an order."

The temperature was about thirty degrees as we sat there in the bowl, a brisk wind blowing in from the north. When he and the others finished their critique, General Grimes returned to his caravan, and I noticed, when he opened the door, that steam came out of it.

Camp Polk was looking pretty good by this time. The night before we were to pull out of bivouac, we were given the route back to camp. It wasn't the most direct route from East Texas, which was about one hundred miles away, because some of the Louisiana roads were substandard and some of the bridges were too weak to hold our tanks. The designated route was for us to cross the Sabine River near Bon Wier, Texas, proceed north for miles, and then turn southeast into Camp Polk. Looking at a road map, I noticed that trucks could cross to Highway 63, northwest of Burkeville, Texas, and go directly to Camp Polk. There was a secondary road intersection along our proposed route that would lead to Highway 63. Our convoy was a number of miles long, and even though we were leaving at 6:00 in the morning, we wouldn't be getting into Camp Polk until around 6:00 in the evening. It would be long after dark by then.

After breakfast, I arranged to have the men in headquarters battery issued K-rations, packaged food meant to be eaten cold. Then I button-holed Sgt. Peter Polus, mess sergeant, and told him to pull the kitchen truck out of the column at a crossroad twenty miles down the road where I would be waiting. Two hours later, I met him at the crossroad and told him to take Highway 63 to Louisiana Route 6 and on to Camp Polk.

"When you get there," I told him, "light all the furnaces and water heaters in our buildings and in battalion headquarters." I also told him to have a hot meal ready for the men about 6:00. He saluted smartly and I got in my jeep and caught up with the convoy.

It was a rainy, bone-cold day. The rain began to freeze and was mixed with sleet. By 4:00 the freezing rain began sticking to the vehicles, and an hour later they were covered with ice. The freezing rain and sleet kept coming down, and by 6:30 when we rolled into the motor pool at North Camp Polk, I was miserably cold — we all were. Wet and chilled to the bone, we parked the half-tracks, jeeps, and trucks in their usual places. The night was cold and dark and mean. The men fell out and formed two ranks, standing at ease, sleet slashing in from the north.

I noticed lights on in the Headquarters Battery area and also in Battalion Headquarters. "Good!" I thought. "Sergeant Polus has done his job." Sergeant Hughes reported that all the vehicles were in and the men were dismounted and waiting for orders. I told him to take the men to the barracks, feed them, and put them to bed.

Maj. C. D. Meadow, battalion executive officer, was standing nearby, and he had another idea.

"What's this about taking the men to the barracks?"

I told him what I had told Sergeant Hughes.

Major Meadow was short and overweight with a small mustache, beady eyes, and a penchant for picking at nits. Behind his back, we called him Snuffy because of his resemblance to Snuffy Smith, the comic strip hero, particularly in profile. He wagged his head back and forth. "You're not leaving here," he declared, "until every damned one of these vehicles is washed, greased, and first-echelon maintenance is performed."

First-echelon maintenance is washing the vehicle, greasing it, checking tire pressure, engine oil and so on. Under normal conditions, first-echelon maintenance is expected. But conditions now were hardly normal. I just looked at Major Meadow. Finally, I said in my most reasonable tone of voice, "Major, these men have been in the field for six weeks. There is hot food in the mess hall and the barracks are warm.

It's freezing out here and the vehicles are covered with ice. All the water pipes have been drained since November, and the hoses and faucets are frozen." I held my gloved hands out, palms up. Ice was even on my glove. A few officers and men standing within earshot looked from me to him. He could have backed down gracefully if he had wanted to. I was not trying to face him down or embarrass him. In fact, I was trying to give him a position he could fall back to with dignity.

Speaking softly, I continued, "Is that an order, sir?"

"Yes," he said harshly, "that is an order."

I then said, "I will not order my men to wash these ice-covered half-tracks, trucks, jeeps and tanks in this snow storm."

He stiffened as if he'd been hit across the back with a piece of pipe. His jaw quivered, and his voice, when he spoke, was reedy. "Nevertheless, Captain," he said, "that's what you're going to do."

I was astounded. At first I thought I must have misheard him. But then I realized, because of the way he stood there glaring at me, that I had heard him right.

We were both silent for what seemed like a long time. Many of the drivers had colds and the walking flu. They were chilled now, and it didn't take a degree in medicine to realize that getting wet, as they would have to do in washing down the vehicles, was the last thing they needed. Also, if my unit started trying to wash and service the vehicles, Major Meadow would have ordered the other batteries to do the same, compounding the problem.

He sputtered, as somehow I knew he would. He was an older man, about thirty-five, and had a lot of old-maid ways about him. His little eyes got round, his nostrils flared, and he said, "I'll have your ass for this, Hardison. You'll be court-martialed. You realize that? I'm going right now to Colonel Lilly and prefer charges against you."

I said nothing. I couldn't. I was disgusted. I asked myself how this had happened. But I had no idea how it had happened and it didn't matter now because there was no backing out for either of us.

He jumped in his jeep and headed for battalion headquarters. I decided to wait and see what was going to happen. Sergeant Hughes had heard the whole thing, and so had several officers and men.

In five minutes, I saw the headlights of a jeep flash on at battalion headquarters. A minute later, a jeep was moving toward us, coming pretty fast. I figured it was North Africa for me. When the jeep reached us, it skidded to a stop. By then, it was snowing heavily. Colonel Lilly jumped out of the jeep and walked up to me.

"Why are these men standing out here in this sleet and snow?"

"Sir," I said, "I'm awaiting orders from you."

"Captain Hardison," he said, "take your men to the barracks, feed them, and put them to bed."

I relayed the order to Sergeant Hughes, who snapped me a sharp salute, turned, and gave the order to the men.

I felt a sudden flush go over me as I realized that it could have gone either way. I had apparently won the first round, but the fight with Major Meadow was just beginning.

As we marched to the battery area, I noticed that all the other batteries' barracks were dark. I went into Headquarters Battery mess hall for a cup of coffee and to warm up, and I was sitting there drinking coffee with two of my officers when Colonel Lilly walked in. We all stood up.

"At ease," he said, and ordered a cup of coffee. As the coffee was being poured, the men began to drift in.

Colonel Lilly took a sip of the hot coffee, steam curling up, and said, "I want to tell you something, Tex. You've got a fine outfit here." He took another sip of coffee and said he had cut out of the column at 4:00 P.M. and had been pleasantly surprised that his office was warm. He had stopped in and had a cup of coffee, he said, adding that it was the only unit in the division that had sent somebody on ahead. "Yes, it's a damn fine battery and I compliment you."

That was the only compliment he ever paid me. But it wasn't just for warming things up and for the coffee. Headquarters Battery was the best on road marches, it had the best kitchen, and the best discipline in the whole battalion, and they all knew it.

We spent a month in Camp Polk, then went out on maneuvers from February through April. Ten new divisions had been brought in, swelling the population of the maneuver area to about 400,000. The maneuver area was extended to include western Louisiana as well as eastern Texas. The war problems were more complicated and we had a lot to do, everything done as if in war. The battalion was to occupy and organize tactical positions, which included Headquarters Battery establishing communications by radio and telephone to the firing batteries and to two observation posts. This survey was to pick up from a control point set by division artillery, firing charts were to be established for each battery, the guns laid by compass, and aiming stakes set out. Men unloaded 100 rounds of ammunition at each gun, and everything was concealed under netting or trees.

Meanwhile, my private war with Major Meadow had heated up. He caught me on everything he could, which may be one of the reasons Headquarters Battery stayed so sharp. When he inspected the kitchen, for instance, he checked in the most out-of-the-way places, running his hand along the top of doors, for example, or reaching in the cupboard and getting the pot on the bottom and running his hand around in that, looking for grease. He popped up at odd moments to see if anyone was goofing off and entered the orderly and supply rooms suddenly and without notice. Anything he found the slightest bit awry, not only with Headquarters Battery but also with any of the others, he wrote up and presented, sometimes three and four pages long, at the next battery commanders meeting. There wasn't much I could do except go along with it. Captain Sather took another route: avoidance. He always had a lookout and when Major Meadow approached, the lookout warned Captain Sather, who conveniently disappeared. Because of his rank, Major Meadow had a natural advantage over us. But because he was so much older than we were, because he was overweight and out of shape and seemingly impressed by himself, wearing his major's insignia stuck out in relief from his helmet at least a quarter of an inch, for instance, while the rest of us had our insignias merely soldered on — because of all that and perhaps in the arrogance and intolerance of youth, we made fun of him. In the field, where things were changed, there I got revenge.

We fought our sham battles during the week, but on Sunday, the situation was usually non-tactical, which meant that we could walk around, build fires, and take a nap if we could find a place to do it. Major Meadow took a nap every Sunday afternoon in the command tent. He and Colonel Lilly shared the same tent. But Colonel Lilly didn't need a nap in the afternoon. Which gave me an idea.

I waited until Major Meadow went into his tent and gave him about twenty minutes to get his boots off and begin really sawing logs, then I set off tear gas upwind of his tent. Lieutenant Russ, who helped, set off smoke canisters in another area.

Watching from the bushes, I could hardly keep from laughing as Major Meadow came charging out of his tent in his drawers, blind, mad and sputtering. Then we sounded a gas alarm and hollered: "Gas! Gas! Gas!"

Everybody grabbed their masks and put them on and waited for the all-clear signal, which was usually as soon as Major Meadow went back into his tent.

I pulled off the "gas attack" week after week, and everybody knew what was going on, including the major. On Sundays, when it was time to put up their tents, the men made sure they were not near his.

Meanwhile, maneuvers went on. It was sleeting and snowing a lot and it was hard to get a bath and a shave. 2nd Lt. William H. Hawley had grown a beard about a quarter-inch thick and he smelled awful because he hadn't had a bath in several weeks. Since the situation was non-tactical, he decided to shave. They had a fire going, made of pine knots, and officers and men were sitting around the fire talking about women and whiskey. Bill went to a half-track and got a five-gallon water can, poured his helmet about half full, and put it on the fire.

Whooooom! The helmet blew up. It burned the hair off the legs of three men sitting around the fire and ruined their pants. They were all sitting around wondering who the fool was that put gasoline in the water can when word came for Lieutenant Hawley to report to Colonel Lilly. The lieutenant went directly over to battalion headquarters and got chewed out thoroughly by Colonel Lilly for not wearing his helmet.

Part of the property of Headquarters Battery was a new bugle, which had never been used. Late one afternoon Sergeant Hughes said to me, "Captain Hardison, we got three new men this morning and one of them is a bugler." I asked him if we had brought our bugle and he said, "Yes, the battery clerk has it in the field desk."

I told Sergeant Hughes to take the new man and the bugle in a jeep and go somewhere well away from our area and see if he could play it like it was supposed to be played. About an hour later he returned, and reported that the bugler was exceptionally good. The area that we were in was uneven, and near the kitchen truck was a rise in the ground. I told Sergeant Hughes to have him go there and sound taps at 10:00 P.M. and reveille in the morning at 6:00 as long as the situation was non-tactical. The sound of the bugle at night was hauntingly beautiful as the notes drifted through the woods.

In the field, we covered a lot of ground in half-tracks and M-7s, using light observation airplanes to spot for us overhead. One day I heard that Lt. Frank Argenio was flying into Camp Polk. Argenio, one of our liaison pilots, was short and dark with curly hair and laughing blue eyes. He had some business in camp, so I arranged to fly in with him. Mostly, I just wanted to fly. I'd been taking flying lessons with him whenever I could find the time and I thought I was getting pretty good.

About 9:30 A.M. Argenio and I climbed into his L-4, which was essentially a Piper Cub, a narrow two-seater with the pilot seat in front and dual controls. I took the back seat, and Argenio buckled himself in front. He flipped the switches and a ground crewman turned the propeller. The engine caught and in a minute we were moving across the grass and into the air. When we got a little altitude, Argenio let me have the controls. I was doing figure eights, making easy turns and feeling good, when the airplane fell off on the left wing, turning and diving — and we were not that high. I yelled at Argenio and beat on his back until he took over, gave it some gas, and pulled out of the spin, just clearing a clump of tall pine trees. I decided that experience would last me for a while so I took a jeep back to the maneuver area.

Nearby, the 49th Armored Infantry Battalion was maneuvering and some fighter planes from the Alexandria Army Air Field were "strafing" the infantry. They were P-39s, Airacobras, a hot airplane in those days but somewhat experimental. Bell Aircraft Corporation built the P-39 with the engine behind the pilot, which made the aircraft more maneuverable and permitted it to be more streamlined. The plane was armed with a 37mm cannon, the first one in an American fighter, and four machine guns. Unfortunately, the plane was underpowered and hard to handle. And because the center of gravity was behind the pilot, it would flip over on its back under certain conditions. Most of the P-39s were shipped to Russia, where the pilots reportedly loved them.

I was watching them zoom through and "strafe" the troops as I drove up to the battalion. They came screaming down from about 3,000 feet, diving like silver arrows. There were four of them. As they came in, the infantrymen hit the dirt, and after its pass, each airplane would pull up and twist once, then climb, level off, and head east. The fourth one came screaming down like the rest, but apparently it went up at too sharp an angle. It flipped over and began to spin. Then the nose turned down and the airplane plowed into the ground, making a tremendous crater. Another 400 feet of altitude and he might have made it.

The pilot was a twenty-two-year-old second lieutenant. When the airplane hit the ground, the engine came loose and rammed him against the cannon. We found his watch 400 feet away. Some of his buddies showed up shortly. They were all second lieutenants and didn't seem to be bothered by what had happened. They stood around the crater and smoked cigarettes, joking. I left.

Next morning, I got a call that one of our airplanes had cracked up. It was Argenio. He stayed in camp the day I flew with him, and the next day, he flew back — or he tried to. He got into some fog and lost his bearings, then cracked up the L-4 in front of Combat Command A's reviewing stand. He was pulled from the wrecked airplane and rushed to the post hospital. When I got to Camp Polk, he was unconscious. That afternoon, he died.

In the field, maneuvers were still going full blast. About midway through, we drew a complicated field problem. We had to reconnoiter, find positions for the batteries, and survey them to get set up for firing. The battalion was in an assembly area seven miles away. It was to move up and prepare to fire as soon as possible. Colonel Lilly was on reconnaissance ahead of the battalion. I was forward. The survey officer and the communications officer were also ahead of the battalion. The battalion was to be brought up by Major Meadow.

Though the weather was sunny and dry, lots of rain had fallen for the past two or three weeks and the ground was saturated. The route chosen included a place where it was narrowed by a gigantic mud hole covered by water. We could go around it on the right, but not on the left. At the mud hole I got out of my jeep and saw by the tracks that a tank had been bogged down there and apparently been hauled out by a tank retriever. I found a long pole and poked it into the mud hole. It was nearly five feet deep, with a foot of water on top of the mud. From a distance it looked like a shallow pool of water with a hard bottom, the kind you could shoot right through. I stationed a guide fifty yards in front of the mud hole and told him to direct all vehicles around it on the right.

But I knew that Major Meadow would never go around the hazard. He would go right through it. After all, he was Maj. C. D. Meadow, the battalion executive officer, and no private soldier was going to tell him what to do. The column would be coming along pretty fast, so I parked behind a hummock about a hundred yards off and sat down to watch through my field glasses. On my battery radio channel, I called my motor section and told them about the mud hole. I told them that if Major Meadow got stuck to bypass him and leave him for service battery and the tank recovery unit.

A few minutes later, I saw a cloud of dust on the road. The battalion was coming along about twenty-five miles a hour, fast for an armored unit, the dust boiling up from the half-tracks. Through my field glasses I could see them as if they were fifty feet away. Major Meadow was in a half-track, leading. I watched as the guide waved him around the mud hole. I saw him as he reached over and tapped his driver's helmet, signaling him to go straight ahead. The driver did, right into the mud hole. The half-track plowed in and stopped dead in its tracks, as if it had hit a concrete wall. Muddy brown water flew high into the air and fell in a heavy, dirty wet sheet on Major Meadow, his driver, and the others in the half-track. As I watched through my glasses, I could see that he was wet to the skin and looked like a drowned rat. But since he was the battalion executive officer, each vehicle commander threw him a snappy salute as they passed him by some six feet away.

My motor section passed him by and I pulled around and led Headquarters Battery on to our positions. We were unloading, setting up the command post tents and the survey table, when Colonel Lilly walked up.

"Where's Major Meadow?" he asked.

"He's down the road about three miles," I said, "in a mud hole."

"In a mud hole? You didn't pull him out? Why?"

I looked at him with a straight face, barely suppressing a smile. I could have gotten Major Meadow out of the mud hole and Colonel Lilly knew it. I had the horses. Major Meadow's half-track weighed around eight tons, an M-7 eighteen tons, and the tanks thirty. But it would have taken me more time than I had to pull him out. The main problem in pulling him out was to keep the vehicles lined up. If the tank got a little off center, it might twist the lighter frame of the half-track. "I thought, sir," I said, "that we should wait for a tank retriever in Major Meadow's case."

A tank retriever was built on an M-4 tank chassis. It had no turret as such and was equipped with a strong winch working through an A-frame. The cable goes to the front of the vehicle that's stuck and the winch pulls it straight up, then the retriever moves forward with the vehicle. It takes five or ten minutes. Service battery would get him out, I said. Meanwhile, the firing batteries arrived and went into position. And finally, service battery rolled up. The last vehicle in the outfit tied a cable onto Meadow's half-track and hauled his ass out. He was about an hour and a half late getting in, red-faced and mad. But he didn't say a word to me.

Toward the end of the maneuver, he came out to inspect my battery and discovered several discrepancies. The toilet paper was not covered by a tin can, for instance. He sputtered and fumed about that, as if he had found a German spy or something. The sign pointing to the latrine was not absolutely straight, he claimed, and the sump was too close to the kitchen truck.

But all this was merely prologue to the really big discrepancy: the slit trench.

When Major Meadow checked the slit trench, I was busy with a communication problem. He summoned me on the double and I dropped what I was doing and reported to him. "Yes, sir," I said.

"Come here. I want to show you something," he said.

He was leaning over the slit trench, which was about eight feet long, two deep and one wide. I leaned over with him to see what he was talking about. I thought there were snakes in it from the way he was acting. He pointed. "You see the walls of this slit trench down there?"

I looked down at it, wondering what he had up his sleeve. "Yes, sir," I said.

"Does the wall appear straight up and down to you? Or is it dug at a slant?"

I studied it a moment. "It's dug at a slant, I would say, sir. But it looks okay."

He grinned and frowned at the same time, a grisly sight. "It looks okay, does it? And do regulations call for a slit trench that's straight up and down or one that's dug at a slant?"

Usually when Major Meadow gleefully pointed out an error, it was enough to act contrite and pledge that it would never happen again. This seemed to please him, usually, and he went away and forgot about it. And so did I. "We'll do better next time," I said.

He wagged his head slowly. "No, we won't do better next time. We'll do better this time. This is a non-regulation slit trench, Captain. Cover it up and dig another one. Right now."

I didn't like his getting at me through my men. I said, "It's adequate like it is. It's only a place to piss and crap, and all of the men are busy."

He puffed up, sputtering. "That's it!" he said. "I have had it with you!" He turned on his heel, climbed into his jeep, and roared off in a cloud of dust to see Colonel Lilly. I knew what would happen. He would report that I was insubordinate again. I regretted that, but I was tired of the game by now, tired of avoiding a showdown with him and tired of his bullshit. In a few minutes, Colonel Lilly drove into the battery area. He got out of his jeep and just stood there for a minute looking at me, one foot tapping the ground.

"You know, Tex," he said finally, "it's a hell of a note when a battalion commander has to come out and referee fights between his executive officer and the Headquarters Battery commander."

"Yes, sir," I said, "I'm sure that it is."

"I'm tired of it," he said, "and I want it stopped."

I said, "Well, I do, too. That old man has been on me ever since East Texas. He's on my back from daylight till dark. If he'll get off my back and leave me alone, I'll leave him alone."

"Okay," he said, "but if this shit doesn't stop, I'm going to have to get rid of one of you or both. That clear?"

"Yes, sir," I said.

And just like that, as the maneuver ended, so did the silly feud between Major Meadow and me.

The battalion went into bivouac between north and south Camp Polk, waiting for the 11th Armored Division to move out. They were going to France. We were going to take their place. In late March, we moved into South Camp Polk to reorganize, polish our training, and see that our equipment was in shape to go overseas. We were next.

Some of the first sergeants seized on this hiatus to try to get rid of some undesirable men, in their opinion, in their batteries. They wanted to give them section eights, an undesirable discharge. A section eight board consisted of a medical officer and two line officers. They interviewed the soldier and found out what the facts were. Generally, the first sergeant brought the charge and if the board of officers agreed, the man was discharged. I was in charge of the section eight board and we found nothing wrong with most of the men who were brought up on section eights. One man from Battery B said the first sergeant didn't like him and he didn't like the first sergeant. He admitted that he was awkward, but that was all. We looked him over and decided he was all right. He didn't get a section eight, and neither did any of the others. They were all being railroaded and we didn't go along with it.

One man went to Colonel Lilly and said he was afraid of the Germans and wanted a transfer. He was from New York City, a short fat corporal with black hair, a big nose, and a bad complexion. He didn't look much like a soldier and he wasn't. Colonel Lilly decided he wouldn't be worth taking and shipped him out. I would have taken him with me if I had taken nobody else. We had a lot of men who didn't want to go overseas. Some of them were Air Corps soldiers who were no longer needed and had been sent to us late in training. They sucked up their guts and did their jobs.

About that time, Major Meadow was transferred to the field artillery school at Fort Sill. I regretted his leaving. By then, we were getting along well, and because of his expertise in technical aspects of the artillery, he would have been a big help to us later on.

The rest of us went on with our jobs, getting ready for action. I taught battalion classes in aircraft identification, flashing airplane silhouettes to classes ranging up to 200 men.

On June 19, 1944, a few days after D-Day in Europe, I got word from home that my father had died. I got emergency leave, and Don and I climbed into the Dodge and headed for Colorado City. We rolled in about mid-morning on June 20.

We found my mother composed and calm, surrounded by friends at my grandmother's house. I went to the funeral home and talked to the people there. My dad was a complex man, largely unfulfilled, but a good man. He had a high temper, and cussed like few that I have ever heard. He never drank but he smoked hand-rolled Prince Albert cigarettes one after the other until he died.

The funeral was scheduled for 10:00 in the morning on Saturday. I spent Friday seeing Dad's friends and trying to dispose of his business as best I could. When we went to the funeral home that evening, six or eight of his life-long friends were there. He had been laid out in a casket in the raised area in the back of the room. I spent two or three hours visiting with them and other people who came in. I didn't look at him because he had wasted away so. He had always been a rather handsome man, I thought, with good features and dark curly hair.

After a simple service the next day, we buried him in the old Colorado City cemetery on rising ground two miles east of town. A typical West Texas cemetery, it had been there since 1880. The streets were gravel. Cedar, mesquite, and a few elm trees grew there. Lone Wolf Creek flowed to the north. Some graves had large monuments, others only funeral home marking tags. A hot June wind whipped across the rise of ground as we said goodbye. I felt bleak.

Three days later, I sold my father's feedmill and arranged for a friend of his, Pete Ainsworth, to sell his cattle and horses. Then I had to go. I had been ordered to the field artillery school officers advanced course at Fort Sill. It was designed to train battalion operations officers, or S-3. It was heavy on gunnery, surveys, logarithms, and the sort of thing I hadn't thought about since college. It was tough early on, and I had trouble getting into it. But help came from an unexpected quarter, Major Meadow, who had been assigned to the field artillery school's department of gunnery. Though we had fought each other in the 399th, he helped me through the early rough spots of the course.

I finished the officers advance course, reported to Camp Polk, and was made battalion intelligence officer, S-2. My responsibilities were to assign and brief observers who would accompany the tank and infantry units, keep track of them and see that they were rotated, write and distribute an intelligence summary at regular intervals, assimilate data that came in and write shell reports, handle prisoners, and report information gathered from them.

We were getting more new men, most of them former ASTP cadets. They were good men but they didn't know what was going on and we didn't have time to train them. The battery commanders and first sergeants tried to put them in slots where they could function without much training.

In late October, we boarded trains for Camp Kilmer, New Jersey. I was on the battalion staff now and had no direct responsibilities to a battery. I rode in the caboose much of the time and talked with the train crew. I watched with amazement as we rolled through New Jersey on tracks that were ten feet above the ground. We were up on the level of second-story apartments, rolling slowly past buildings eight feet away on either side. I saw a family having dinner, a man seated at the table in his undershirt, his body covered with hair. It seemed as if I could almost reach out and touch them as I went by, and I wondered how people could live like this with a railroad so close. It was another world, a long way from the open spaces of Colorado City.

Atlantic Crossing to England

October 31, 1944–December 16, 1944

President Franklin D. Roosevelt was re-elected to his fourth term. On December 15, the western front was stable from the North Sea south to the Swiss border. The next day, the German Fifth and Sixth Panzer Armies and the Seventh Army attacked the American First Army on a narrow front in the Ardennes Forest of Belgium.

At Camp Kilmer, where the air was full of coal smoke and cinders, we got our shots and practiced boarding lifeboats on a mockup of a ship. Everybody wanted to go into New York. I wangled V.O.C.O. (vocal order, commanding officer) leave and went into the city with George Salisbury, Marvin Sather, and six or seven others. We ended up at Roseland Dance Hall and I found myself sitting at a table with half a dozen women the others had picked up. The women were short, buxom Italian girls looking for a good time. After a while, some of the fellows left with girls and suddenly I realized I was alone with five of them, including two who were dog drunk and stirring up a row. Deciding that the safest thing was to beat a quick retreat, I took off.

A couple of days later, Sergeant Hughes of Headquarters Battery said, "You know, Captain, we ought to go into New York." I said okay. So he, Master Sergeant Davis, Warrent Officer Mace and I hailed a cab and went to town, ending up in a Greenwich Village joint called the Nineteenth Hole, where we had a few drinks. When we started to leave, I paid the tab with a $100 bill. I was about half shot and wasn't watching the money. Sergeant Hughes was watching it, though. He saw that the bartender had cheated me on the change. Sergeant Hughes was normally the most self-possessed of men. But this suddenly made him very mad. He grabbed the manager by the front of his shirt, pulled him half across the bar, and told him he would stack the furniture in the place if I didn't get my right change. He had brought the manager's face up close to his own. I had never seen Sergeant Hughes like that before. He was snarling like an animal through clenched teeth. "And you know something," he growled deep in his throat, "I'll start stacking this place with you."

I looked around and Sergeant Davis was gone. He was running down the street, Mace fifty feet behind him. Meanwhile, in the restaurant, the manager, being held by the neck, got one hand free. He poked the cash register and it opened, then, his eyes bulging, he fished around for the proper change.

"Here," he said in a strangled voice. "Take it."

Sergeant Hughes took the money and threw the man down. The sergeant counted the money and handed it to me. "That about right?" he asked.

I counted it. "Yeah. That's it."

We left, strolled down the street, and hailed a cab. Then on a whim we had the driver circle the block and go by the bar again. Cops were everywhere, so we headed back to camp.

We read that in Europe the Third Army had bogged down for lack of gasoline. First Army had taken Aachen and was trying to clear the Hurtgen Forest. Ninth Army was moving into the area of the Roer River north of Aachen.

A few days later, we got orders to board ship. We pulled out of Camp Kilmer in trains late in the morning, olive drab duffel bags slung over our shoulders. I took a foot locker, a Val Pack and duffel bag. The enlisted men had only a musette bag and all their clothes and gear in the duffel bags.

The ship sat low against the dock and looked damned small, I thought, for crossing the Atlantic. I read the name on the bow, *George*

W. Goethels. It was November 10, and cold. The men were in GI overcoats. The first man I saw on the ship was Lt. Lloyd Weldon. We called him Moose. He was part Indian and was standing at the head of the gang plank.

"HOW!" he yelled.

That got a laugh. I wrestled my duffel bag up the gang plank and found my way to the stateroom I was to share with Hank Brooks and two other officers. We got settled and went to bed. During the night, I woke up startled. The ship was shaking, the engines were running, and tugs pushing us out of the harbor.

The next morning, I got up early and went up on deck. I couldn't see land. There were ships all around us: two destroyers, several corvettes, a frigate or two, and several tankers and other troop ships. In all, I counted thirty-eight ships in the convoy.

Just before dark, a voice on the ship's public address system said: "Now hear this! Now hear this! The officer in charge of the garbage will dispose of the garbage off the side aft."

Later: "Close all ports and baffle doors."

And still later: "There will be no smoking topside."

After we ate, there was nothing to do. Some played poker. Some did nothing but play poker. Some of us read, though there wasn't much to read. Sometimes, we just sat around and talked. And thought. By now I was looking forward to combat — somewhat apprehensive but not afraid.

The sea got rough and a lot of the men got sick. It was miserable below decks — hot and stuffy and smelly. The men were crowded into big compartments, sleeping on bunks made of metal pipe with canvas stretched across them. Sergeant Pollock, the supply sergeant of Headquarters Battery, was in an area just big enough for a man to stand up in. He was short and fat. He got sick when he first saw the boat and didn't get out of his bunk until we landed in England. After breakfast, I went to the windward side of the ship to get the wind in my face and keep from becoming nauseated.

Topside one day, I was watching the ships in the convoy. There were two tankers off our port side abeam. When the waves broke over the bow of the ships, water and foam covering the decks, the ships looked like submarines, only their bridges showing. For a long moment it seemed as if the ship might stay down. Then it bobbed up again, the water, caught by the wind, flowing off in a wild spray. The seas must have been running thirty feet.

The crossing was rough on the enlisted men. They were down in the hold, crowded three stacks high and with barely room enough to stretch out. The ventilation was bad and it was hot. When one of the men got sick, the environment suddenly got a lot worse. A lot of the men were former Air Corps cadets who had been cut when the Air Corps had all the pilots it needed. There were some army specialized training program men who had also been cut and sent to the Armored Field Artillery. One of them was Pvt. James B. Keegan.

Keegan was a bright, open-faced young man, a bit on the chubby side, who, because he had been washed out of the Air Corps through no fault of his own, despised officers.

He was mad because he thought the officers were getting much better treatment than the men. He had gotten hold of a dinner menu for the officers' mess listing ripe olives, celery, and several other appetizing items. It sounded better than it was. Officers might have had an olive and a chunk of celery, but neither of them was ripe. It wasn't the Waldorf, in other words, and the food was pretty much the same that the enlisted men were getting, but it wasn't served quite the same way. That was the main difference. We were seated at tables and were eating off plates and drinking out of glasses and glass cups. Keegan and the other enlisted men below decks used their mess gear, and Keegan didn't like it a bit.

Using the ship's mimeograph machine, Keegan started an underground newspaper and wrote all this about the officers' mess. He also complained bitterly in an editorial that officers were sleeping in well-ventilated cabins.

Keegan's newspaper had come to the attention of Col. Henry W. Holt, division artillery commander, who liked the newspaper not a bit. He told Colonel Lilly to see who had written it and find out what was the matter with him. In turn, Colonel Lilly told me to check it out.

It wasn't hard to find out what was going on. I soon discovered it was Private Keegan who had been using the ship's mimeograph machine, so I went down into the hold to see him.

When I found him below decks, I held out a copy of the little newspaper. "Is this yours?"

He drew himself to attention and gave me a tight look. "Yes, sir," he said. "It is."

"At ease, Keegan." I sat down on a bunk and gestured to another bunk for him. He sat down too and we were across from each other, face to face. "I read your paper," I said, "and thought it had some good things to say."

"Is that so? Thanks."

When I read the yellow sheet, I saw that it was not all bad. One article was funny and one had news of a general nature. Only the article about the officers was vicious. He had the red-ass from way back and I knew his feelings. "You've got some writing talent here," I said, holding the paper up.

"For whatever that's worth," he said.

I went along with it. "I think I know how you feel," I said. "You feel like it's not fair, right?"

He gave a half-hearted laugh. "That's an understatement, sir. Why should you get fancy food while we eat slop for the hogs?"

"Wait a minute, Keegan. We had two olives a few nights ago. Is that what you're so pissed off about? If it makes you any happier, our meals are the same as yours, slop, you call it, but it's a damn sight better than nothing and it's better than sitting around eating K-rations. Come on, Keegan, grow up." This was probably the first time he'd had a face-to-face talk with an officer and I got the feeling that it wasn't going the way he thought it should. "What you're really pissed off about is privilege."

"And what if I am?"

"This is the army, Keegan. You think you got the shitty end of the stick, but not everybody can be a general. You're a private, I'm a captain, those are the facts of life. I get it a little better than you, the majors and colonels and generals get it better than both of us. And we've both got to live with it. Do you understand me?"

"Yes, sir."

I went to the ship's office and told the clerk not to allow army personnel to use the mimeograph machine without my okay, and I left the number of my cabin with him.

By the time we sighted the coast of England, I heard that he was working on another edition of his newspaper but it was never published.

Ten days out, nearing the coast of England, we heard a lot of racket one night. A siren sounded through the ship and the voice came on the PA system.

"Dog down all the hatches! Close all companionway doors!"

I was topside and didn't like the sound of that. People started slamming hatches all over the ship. I went down the companionway steps three at a time, into the hold. Colonel Lilly and the battery commanders were in life jackets, everybody tense. The doors were bolted shut. It was hot and we were very quiet. No wisecracks. No smartass remarks.

We wondered what the lookouts had seen. A periscope? We had no way of knowing. A sub could send the *Gen. Goethels* to the bottom of the sea in minutes. Only the destroyers and corvettes on the edge of the convoy could fight back. We felt helpless. Half an hour later, the "all clear" sounded. I went back to my state room, wondering what might have nearly sunk us.

The siren went off again a couple of nights later. The naval voice started hollering for everybody to dog down the hatches, and people started running like rabbits in every direction. Then the depth charges started going off, a dull *whoomp* in the water that made the ship shake like a wet dog, and a white geyser shot up in the air.

I wanted to get outside to see more of the action but the companionway doors were all dogged down. I was stuck inside the big steel doors listening to the *whoomp! whoomp!* of the depth charges, feeling the ship shake, and wondering if a torpedo would come smashing into the bulkhead and what would happen if it did. As far as I could see, there was no way out.

The depth charges went on and on and then the shooting stopped and the alert ended. It was all over. We could relax. The latrines were soon full. After an incident like that, they always were.

Early in the evening a couple of days later, the voice on the speaker informed us that we were off Lizard Head. Lizard Head? Where is that? I had never heard of Lizard Head. We would be landing sometime later that night, the voice said.

When I woke up, something had changed. I lay there and wondered what it was and finally I realized that the ship was still. We had stopped. We were somewhere in England.

I got up at dawn and went topside. Outside was a cold gray city, a rock-lined harbor with the land rising gradually behind it into low hills. The tide was out and the water was about fifteen feet below the tops of the rocks. The sky was overcast, a light mist falling. The houses were of stone with slate roofs. Here and there were some ruins, jagged walls, and heaps of gray stone rubble. They had obviously been bombed.

A navy officer passed by. He was in a hurry, but when I hailed him he stopped. He was smoking a cigarette and he blew the smoke out. "Yes?" he said.

"Where are we? Nobody tells us anything."

He took a drag on his cigarette and blew out the smoke in a thick cloud, then he said, "This is Plymouth. We'll pull in to the dock in a couple of hours. Later today, you'll disembark and load onto trains."

"And then?" I asked.

He shrugged and grinned. "For you? I don't know. But we head back to the States."

Late in the afternoon, the ship pulled into a pier, the dockhands snubbed the big hausers onto the docks, and the gangplanks went down. The pier was concrete, gray and empty. Railroad tracks ran to within eighty feet of the ship. Beyond the tracks were warehouses.

The men slowly filed up the companionways, big duffle bags slung over their shoulders. After two weeks in the hold of a troopship, they looked pretty ragged. The trains had pulled up directly across from the pier. Passengers on these European cars did not enter from the end like American trains, but from a dozen or so little doors on one side.

The sergeants started cramming the men into the tiny compartments and I went off to talk to the conductor. He was a paunchy man of about forty-five, wearing a full uniform: ribbons and brass buttons and a cap on his head. At first, I thought he was a general and almost saluted him. He was quite cordial and I asked him where the train was going.

"London," he said. "The train is going to London, but how far you're going, I don't know." He got off at Exeter in Wiltz.

Exeter is a big town, but we could see little of it because the lights were low. By the time we pulled out forty-five minutes later, it was raining steadily and the temperature was in the low forties. Finally, we stopped at a small station near Tidworth. Flashes of lightning lighted up the gray night sky. About the time we disembarked, a sudden flash illuminated houses across the railroad tracks constructed of plaster with thatched roofs. One of them had the date 1607 above the door.

While we were waiting, Brig. Gen. Charles Colson arrived to take us where we were going to be stationed for a while. Colonel Lilly, Maj. John Collins, Maj. Matt Oliver and I got in the general's car and we drove to a tent camp on Windmill Hill, where the 11th Armored Division had prepared a good meal for us. They were moving out.

Our new home for a while, Windmill Hill, was part of the massive Tidworth Barracks compound, well known in British military history and the home of famous regiments. We unloaded and moved into our assigned tents. Windmill Hill was a collection of dingy green tents stretching as far as the eye could see, the countryside rolling and green. Company-grade officers, lieutenants, and captains were quartered there along with the non-coms and the men. Field-grade officers were quartered somewhere else. The tents had wooden floors and four cots each. In the middle of the floor was an oil stove, but to stay warm at night you had to sleep in all your clothes. Outside, there were duckboards to keep you out of the mud. Tidworth Barracks was home for six weeks, right in the middle of the English winter. It wasn't Siberia, but it wasn't Miami either. We were always cold.

On Tuesdays, battalion commanders and intelligence officers went to division headquarters for a briefing in the war room. It was a big room with a map of the western front stretching across one wall. At the briefing, Colonel White, division G-2 or intelligence officer, briefed us on the military situation. The week before the Battle of the Bulge, which started on December 16, the situation map showed a concentration of the 6th Panzer Army in the Eiffel.

Colonel White said it was strange, the concentration of six or eight armored divisions in such a relatively small area. "My guess," he said, pointing generally to that part of the map, "is that they are refitting after the beating they took in Russia."

We got our airplanes on December 9. The L-4s came in two big boxes. We took the airplanes out and sent them to the field to be assembled and made good use of the crates they came in. Nailed together, they made do as an officers' club. We rigged up a bar with some whiskey and installed a stove and found a non-com to run it. It was a good place to drink and we used it for another job we had at night, censoring mail.

I cut very little of the letters. We were supposed to cut out anything that told where we were or what we were doing. One of the men wrote home that he was stationed forty miles from England's tallest cathedral. That sounds innocuous, almost like a casual remark of a tourist. But England's tallest cathedral is Salisbury Cathedral, and a clever enemy would know almost exactly where we were. So I cut that out. A master sergeant wrote to his family that it would be a while before they heard from him again because we were leaving in the morning for France. I cut that out because that broke rules about revealing our location. A sergeant in Headquarters Battery wrote that we were leaving in the morning and would be in the fighting going on in Belgium or Holland. I cut that out, too. Same reason.

Lt. Bill Hawley was mess officer and we had brussels sprouts just about every meal. I ate so many brussels sprouts that I began to feel like one. If that were not enough to put me off brussels sprouts forever, discovering how the English grew them would have been. It had to do with our latrines. They were big and could handle forty men at a time. The waste went full strength into buckets.

One day I noticed a wagon being pulled up at the latrine by a team of handsome Clydesdales, their manes flying in the wind. It was an odd wagon, made up of a barrel about five feet in diameter and ten feet long. You could smell it in the next county. The two Limeys driving the team sat on a bench above the barrel wearing full leather suits with white shirts, ties, and derby hats. They were picking up the "honey buckets" from under the toilets and the urinals and pouring the waste into the barrel. I learned that they dumped this stuff on the fields of brussels sprouts as fertilizer. I haven't eaten a brussels sprout since.

At Tidworth, we started some advanced training. I went to school for S-2s, learning the latest doctrine on combat intelligence including uniform and insignia identification. I taught a battalion school for the enlisted men in the observation sections. These were the men who would accompany the forward observers, artillery officers, when they went to the front. I taught them the elements of observation. For example, I told them to be on the lookout for enemy activity such as trucks and troops. Measuring distances is tricky, I pointed out, so I told them how to compare objects at a distance using their fingers held at arm's length. I showed them silhouettes of German tanks, half-tracks, and other vehicles at various distances and coming from different directions.

North of us were some airfields of the British Bomber Command. They had been fighter airfields during the days of the Battle of Britain, but now they were loaded with heavy bombers, Lancasters, Sterlings, and Halifaxes. One day, I had a group of men in the field talking about calculating distances when we heard an airplane coming. It was a Halifax, terribly late because it was 11:00 in the morning. They were night bombers and the airplane should have been home by daylight.

This bomber had been over Germany and was shot up. The rudder had been almost shot away and the machine guns in the back turret were tilting crazily and only two of its engines were running. We expected to see him plow into the ground any minute, but he kept on going, disappearing over a low hill.

Off duty, there wasn't much to do at Tidworth Barracks. A couple of days after we got there, Brooks and Sather and I heard about a USO show at the Tidworth House, so we got a jeep and went in to see it. On the way back, a military policeman pulled our driver over for no reason at all. When he realized that the jeep was full of officers, he must have figured that he needed to justify pulling us over, so he began nit-picking about everything he could think of: where we got the jeep, who gave us permission, where did we go with it and whether this was authorized — just a whole bunch of irrelevant stuff. It was cold and late and suddenly I'd had my fill of it. I popped off right back at the MP, telling him with all the military command I could muster that he had gone too far, that he was getting in deeper all the time, and that this was silly, the whole damn thing. "Why can't you show just a little elementary common sense?" I didn't yell but my voice had gone up at least an octave.

The MP's face froze and he glared at me. "Now I need to see your ID."

I showed him mine, he took it and said, "Now you'll have to follow me back to the provost marshal."

I was fuming. We all were. But there was no way out. Military life was a dream come true except for the chicken shit like this. We followed him back to headquarters, where we waited while the provost marshal was summoned. He finally came in and sat down heavily in an arm chair behind his desk and listened to the MP first, then us. When he'd heard it all, he said, "Is that it?"

The MP said that was it.

The provost marshal shrugged and waved his hand. "Dismissed," he said, adding, "And I was waked up for this?"

Not long after that, I was sitting around battalion headquarters studying shell reports when the phone rang. Division Artillery was on the line and wanted to talk to me. It was Lt. Col. Edwin Burba, the executive officer of division artillery command.

"Tex, come on up here," he said, "I've got a job for you."

I grabbed a jeep and the driver burned rubber to Division Artillery headquarters. Colonel Burba was waiting. He was about thirty-three, five-foot-eleven, with straight brown hair and a straightforward way of talking.

"On Saturday night," he said, "we want to have a dance for all the enlisted men in Division Artillery."

That included three armored field artillery battalions — the 398th, the 399th and the 405th — as well as the Division Artillery Headquarters Battery.

I gave him a blank look, wondering what that had to do with me. "Yes, sir," I said finally.

"You will be in charge of it," he said.

I just looked at him.

"This dance is going to be your responsibility. You'll need to have a band, drinks, refreshments, and a hall."

He had an afterthought. "And women, of course."

I just looked at him, dumbfounded. Where I came from in West Texas, it was almost against the law to dance. Before I'd gone into the army, I'd only been to a few dances in my whole life. Now, I had to round up about 400 girls and put on a dance for 1,500 men.

Colonel Burba said he would help. He would arrange to get beer and drinks and he would see that the division dance orchestra was available that night. That was a start. Nevertheless, I would have to see that the orchestra and the drinks and the girls were there on time.

Not only that, I had to stay around and keep the fighting and loving down.

But what could I say? I said, "Yes, sir."

I jeeped back to battalion headquarters and sat down to think. I had to scrape up 400 English girls. I didn't know even one. I got back in the jeep and drove to the Tidworth House. If I was going to get 400 of them by Saturday night, it was time to meet some girls.

The USO people at the Tidworth House told me there was a land army barracks near Andover. A British women's service army was near Salisbury and there were WAAFs, the women's auxiliary of the Air Force, at Winchester. In some of the other little towns nearby there were more land army girls and some other English women who drove trucks. They were in the ATS, Army Transportation Service. Around our area, ATS was known as "Action, Traction, Satisfaction." Other units preferred "Army Tail Service" and "Any Time Soldier."

Tuesday morning, I got a jeep and drove to Andover to the land army. A short-haired sergeant in a shapeless OD uniform finally promised twenty-five girls. Downtown, I walked into a bank and up to the girl behind the information desk. She had dark hair and large, blue eyes. I spilled my problem out to her and she thought a minute.

"Let me work on it," she said.

She gave me a number to call in the morning. When I called, she said she had found thirty girls. I lined up another twenty-five from the land army barracks east of Andover.

At the ATS barracks in Winchester, I ran across a tough-looking woman first sergeant. She looked like a horse someone had put a uniform on, but she turned out to be helpful.

"It's been bloody months since we've had a dance, love," she said. "Our girls are horny and a dance will help."

"How many have you got?" I asked.

"Well, I can probably fix you up with a hundred."

I grinned. My total was rising. "Sure," I said. "I'll take them all. The trucks will pick them up on Saturday afternoon at 5:00."

Wearing out rubber between Salisbury, Winchester, and stops in between, I had lined up 458 girls for the dance. I got back to Colonel Burba and told him how many trucks I needed. I also told him I wanted a detail of senior non-commissioned officers. He gave me a quizzical look.

"They'll be in charge of the convoy of trucks going after the girls."

He gave me another puzzled look.

"I don't want any problems."

He nodded with sudden comprehension.

I put an officer in charge of the Andover, Winchester, and Salisbury contingents, with non-coms driving the trucks. On Saturday afternoon at 3:00, they roared off to get the girls and they were back by 6:00 P.M. The girls piled out of the trucks — big girls and little girls, fat girls and skinny girls, pretty girls and homely girls. The tough woman first sergeant had been right. They were ready for a dance! The men were ready, too. The hall was bigger than a high school gymnasium, neither hot nor cold, with a stage for the orchestra, a kitchen with coffee and beer and chairs, and benches along the sides. By 7:00 the division orchestra, made up of old Tommy Dorsey and Glenn Miller and Russ Morgan musicians, was reeling out nice arrangements of "Don't Sit Under the Apple Tree" and "Skylark" and "Bye Bye Blackbird," and a sea of heads was bobbing up and down. By 9:30, with all those bodies so close together, the whole room was pleasantly warm.

I was watching the dance when Colonel Burba grabbed my arm.

"Tex, I want you to end this at midnight."

I said, "Yes, sir."

The GIs and the girls got along fine. No fights, no problems. The five hours passed like a shot and at midnight I decided to let it go on a while longer. Colonel Burba was probably sleeping anyway, I thought.

But at 1:00 A.M., I looked up and there he was.

"Captain Hardison," he said sharply, "I told you to end this dance at midnight. Why didn't you do it?"

I said, "Well, sir, it's going so good and everybody's having such a good time." I gestured around at all the dancing couples. "And I suspect, sir, that this is the last dance some of these men are ever going to have. If you want me to, of course . . ." I didn't finish.

He looked at me for a minute, then relaxed.

"Okay. I know what you mean, Captain. But I think as soon as you can, when the next number is over, you better stop it and take the girls home."

When that dance was done, the girls and the GIs filtered out of the hall together, most of them a little tipsy, but feeling very good. Some of the men stood around waiting and smoking cigarettes as the girls piled onto the trucks, giggling and squealing. There was a loud chorus of cheers as the trucks pulled out. The girls waved out the back until they were out of sight.

The next week, Hank Brooks and I went to London, which was only two hours away. We boarded a train and rolled into Waterloo Station at 6:00 P.M. on a Saturday afternoon. It was cold and drizzling. Stacks of mail bags were piled on the platform. Outside were hacks and people milling around. Newsreel theaters were everywhere. People went to them to kill time.

We looked for a place to sleep, but London was full of soldiers and sailors and airmen, all looking for a bed. We finally found a room on the top floor of a small hotel. It had no elevator. We didn't know what to do, so we just walked around and went to a pub or two, talking to soldiers who were stationed near London.

Groping around in the blackout, we found a place that served oysters and ordered some. One they served me fell out of the shell onto the bar and the bartender just slid it over to me, through the germs and dirt and all. I didn't order any more oysters in London.

We walked back to the hotel through streets as black as tar. During the night, we heard some explosions in the distance and figured they were V-2 rockets hitting, but when we looked out we couldn't see anything. Sunday morning, we got up early and went back to Tidworth Barracks, but I was back in London for another look the next week.

ENGLAND
LONDON
Tidworth
Plymouth
Weymouth
HOLLAND
St. Odilienberg
Rhineberg
2
Kirchhoven
1
BELGIUM
Soest
3
Dortmund
Hamburg
Bremen
Halberstadt
4
Langenstein
Hann Munden
BERLIN
POLAND
PRAHA
Pilzen
Rokycany
Klencl
5
CZECHOSLOVAKIA
Furth in Wald
Winterberg
GERMANY
LUXEMBOURG
Reims
Rouen
PARIS
Raucourt
Neuburg au Donau
VIENNA
AUSTRIA
EUROPE
1944–1945
Chaumont
Route of the EIGHTH Armored Division
Area Map 1 Kirchhoven
Area Map 2 Rhineberg
Area Map 3 Soest
Area Map 4 Halberstadt
Area Map 5 Czechslovakia
SWITZERLAND
N
W
E
S
FRANCE
Bordeaux
ITALY
JUGOSLAVIJA

5 England

December 17, 1944–January 5, 1945

In the Ardennes Forest, the U.S. First Army was fighting a desperate defensive battle in snow-covered fields under a heavy overcast. The U.S. Third Army captured Metz and a few days later its 4th Armored Division reached the encircled Bastogne. The Russian Army occupied Warsaw.

We jumped on the London train early Saturday morning in the middle of winter, Jim Russ and I. Russ was ammunition supply officer on the division artillery staff. The train was dingy from hard use during the war and the country outside looked grim. We rolled steadily through the gently undulating countryside, much of it obscured by fog. We passed an airfield where some shot-up Wellington bombers were in for repair, fragile looking with most of the fabric off the fuselages. Finally, we rolled into Waterloo Station. I didn't know where we would stay, but I knew I wasn't going back to the hotel we were at the week before.

We grabbed a big squarish London cab. "The Savoy Hotel," I told the driver. He was a small, wizened man with a gray mustache. He nodded cheerfully and we got inside the cab, still trying to translate the pounds and shillings in our pockets into dollars and cents. When the cab pulled up to the Savoy, the driver turned around and I held out a handful of English coins and let him pick what he needed.

The Savoy was an imposing building. It had been London's finest hotel for a generation, a gathering place for high-ranking officers and London's elite. It didn't have a reservation for us and no room, but the desk clerk was helpful, nevertheless, calling the Strand Palace across the street, where they had a tenth-floor room with a double bed and sitting area and a small bathroom adjoining. It wasn't the Savoy, but it was a hell of a lot better than the Tidworth tents. We showered and went out.

London had been in the war a long time and looked battle-worn. It was December, traditionally a time for Christmas display, but the stores were barren, with few ornaments and decorations up. At one large department store, the windows, which were blown out by the blast of a rocket or buzz bomb, had been covered with plywood. Even when stores still had windows, nothing was displayed. The people looked threadbare, making the best of it with old clothes. The city was full of British soldiers with nothing to do. They walked around or hung around on corners. A light mist was falling and it was cold. By the time we got back to the hotel dining room it was 7:00 P.M. and I was lonesome and blue and a long way from home.

In the dining room, a string orchestra of six old men was playing Viennese waltzes. When the waitress came over to take our order, Russ told her he would like a bottle of Scotch. It was not easy to get Scotch by the bottle. But she got a bright look on her face and took off, then came back a minute later with a smile and a big bottle of Scotch.

"There you are, gentlemen." She plumped down the bottle and we sat there drinking until suddenly Russ got up and talked to the leader of the orchestra. The man looked puzzled and started shaking his thatch of silvery hair from side to side.

Russ came back looking mad and disappointed.

"What'd you say to him?" I asked.

"Just wanted him to play 'Turkey in the Straw,' " Russ said. "They never heard of it. So I told 'em, okay, then play 'The Yellow Rose of Texas.' And they never heard of that either. Can you believe it?"

Soup came first, then salad, then a British brigadier with a beautiful girl on his arm. He was a fine-looking man, six-feet-two and about forty-five years old. I thought she must be his daughter, but

Russ didn't think so. He thought the brigadier was dating a young girl and he started making remarks to me about it. I could tell by the way the British officer glanced at us that he'd overheard Russ, but he ignored it. I finally got Russ out of the dining room and up to our room. We finished off the Scotch and decided to go out and see London at night.

I wanted to see Picadilly Circus. I'd heard about all the whores and homosexuals there and it wasn't too far away, so we walked. It was a big circular block whose buildings had been built out to the sidewalk, with no street going in. The Circus was almost shoulder to shoulder, people walking both ways and even out in the street itself. The lights were dim, no vehicular traffic at all. We just walked around looking, taking in all kinds of people in the street. They were mostly girls, lots and lots of girls, most of them young, bare-headed, and wearing overcoats. There were a lot of British servicemen, too, but not many Americans.

While we were stopped in a doorway, we saw an Air Corps lieutenant walking toward us. At the same time, a girl was coming toward him in a full-length fur coat. She had long brown hair and good legs and a swing to her walk. She was a hooker.

When she and the Air Force lieutenant were about eight feet apart, she let her coat fall open. My eyes must have jumped out of their sockets. She didn't have anything at all on underneath. Just the fur coat, and that was it. The lieutenant grabbed her arm and off they went. I was impressed, too. I'd never seen anything like that in Colorado City, or anywhere else.

We started walking again and after a while we came to a corner where an old man was selling newspapers. He was hollering something but I couldn't figure out what it was. I kept watching him and pretty soon I noticed something funny. The only people buying papers from him were girls. Attractive girls. I moved in a little closer and finally figured out what he was hollering.

"Papers! Papers! Condoms! Condoms!"

Folded up in each paper, I realized, was a contraceptive. I just stood there gaping until Russ gave me a nudge. We started on back to the hotel.

On the way, we heard a loud explosion. People started running in every direction like scared chickens.

We were about half a block from the Savoy. We found out a V-2 rocket had slammed into the Thames River behind the hotel. The explosion, or the concussion from the explosion, had blown out most of the windows facing the river. It hadn't hit that far from us, maybe 250 to 300 yards. Nobody was hurt — just scared.

In a minute, I realized that we didn't know where we were. We were trying to find our way back to the hotel, but the fog was so thick and the lamps so dim we couldn't read the street names on the lamp posts. Besides that, we'd had about a dozen drinks. I clambered up a lamp post to read the name. We were only a block from the Strand Palace.

The next morning, clear and chilly, we were tired of walking and decided to hire the first means of transportation we saw. That was a fine-looking horse-drawn hack with two Limeys up on top in silk hats and good-looking suits. I wondered why they were driving around like that. Russ didn't stop at wondering. He went out and tried to pull them down, but they ignored him.

I buttonholed a man on the street. "What's the matter with those hicks that they won't take a fare?" I asked.

He gave me a long pitying look. "Well, chum," he said, "them's the Queen's Messengers. They're on official business."

Finally we found a cab and driver parked by a curb. The driver was small, like the car he drove, and had a cheerful Cockney accent. For a price, he agreed to show us the town: Ten Downing Street, Parliament, Buckingham Palace, Westminster Abbey, Hyde Park, and all the rest.

"Hop in, guv," the man said, and we were off to Parliament. We swung through the London sights like somebody thumbing through a pack of picture postcards. The Houses of Parliament were dark and dingy, but there was Big Ben right where it was supposed to be. The driver made a fast turn into Downing Street, where Winston Churchill lived. It was a narrow street with surprisingly small houses. No. 10 Downing was no bigger than the rest. Then we went to see the king, or at least where he lived. British soldiers in red tunics with tall bearskins, a platoon from one of the king's regiments, marched around the outside of the palace, stiff as broom handles, and people were standing outside the gate trying to get a look at them. It was a different kind of soldiering. We paid off our cabbie and got our stuff from the hotel. It was time to go back to Tidworth, out of the Strand Palace and back into tents.

Tidworth was cold, dreary, foggy, dark, rainy, drizzly, and unpleasant in the extreme. I was cold from the time I got off the train until I left. Tidworth was also busy. The firing batteries were bore sighting their howitzers in preparation for action. Bore sighting a howitzer is exactly the same as bore sighting a deer rifle. The sight and the bore of the rifle must be absolutely parallel. If not, the further the range, the further off the shot will be. The gunners would center the bore of the howitzer on a cross at, say, 100 feet, and the sight would be centered on a cross above the first one. In the battle of Kursk in 1943, the Germans rushed their best tank, the new Mark V, against the Russians without bore sighting most of the tank guns. They couldn't hit a damned thing and they lost most of their tanks to the Russian T-34s.

Along with bore sighting, the men were going through intensive training. Some of them who had joined us just before we left Camp Polk had had very little training, if any, and the battery commanders were struggling to make cannoneers out of them.

Meanwhile, Capt. Marvin Sather of Battery B was getting ready in another way. He had decided that the army was wrong in determining how many vehicles, primarily trucks, weapons carriers and jeeps, that an armored field artillery battery needed. His eye had fallen upon a large ordnance depot across the road. Inside its fence there were hundreds of trucks, half-tracks, and tanks. Sather thought he needed another three-quarter-ton truck, a jeep, and a two-and-a-half-ton truck. Captain Salisbury wanted a three-quarter and a half-ton. Captain Brooks wanted a jeep and a three-quarter-ton truck.

They picked a foggy morning to go shopping. This was a fog that would have made pea soup look like branch water. Sather, Brooks, and Salisbury showed up at the depot with a party of drivers, and while Sather was chatting with the guard, the drivers picked out what they wanted and roared off through the fog with a dozen trucks and jeeps. They didn't stop until they got to the woods north of Windmill Hill, where they painted out the army numbers and replaced them with the same numbers some of their legal vehicles had. They loaded them on the boat that went with the advance party to France, and Colonel Lilly didn't find out until the last shot had been fired.

In Europe things were touch and go. The Germans had attacked through the Ardennes and advanced rapidly, surrounding the town of Bastogne. General Eisenhower had committed all of his reserves, which were primarily the 101st and 82nd Airborne Divisions. The 101st was embattled, and though General Patton's Third Army was attacking toward the Bastogne bastion, things were critical. We were to be rushed in there to man roadblocks because it was thought the Germans would pull out of the Bulge and hit again around Saarebourg, Saarbrucken, and Saareguemines with these troops and with those opposite the U.S. Seventh Army.

Back in England, we knew little about all this. We simply knew that the Bulge was going on. It wasn't even called that. On our radios — in my half-track we had four radios, including two shortwave sets — we could pick up the British Broadcasting Corporation. It was the only news we got.

The batteries fired for a week on Salisbury Plain, the rounds throwing up mushrooms of dirt on the dull green of the artillery range. We had been alerted. We were going to France as soon as the firing batteries came back. Meanwhile, I was in S-2 school again, burnishing my skills as an intelligence officer. The batteries fired for five days and came back the day after Christmas.

We pulled out of Tidworth at daylight on December 28, heading south in a column of batteries. The weather was getting colder and it was raining and sleeting and the roads were freezing. In that rolling part of England, the roads run up and down, making right-angle turns around buildings and snaking through the towns. That's tricky for tanks to maneuver on. In a small town south of Salisbury, an M-7 from Battery C took a corner off a drugstore without even slowing down. We kept moving, all night, rumbling through little towns whose names we never knew. The people living there were used to armored columns rumbling through at night. They slept through it all. At dawn we rolled into the seaport town of Weymouth. The people who lived there were just getting up, opening their windows and getting some fresh air. A lot of them waved at us and gave us the "V" sign. A sergeant on an M-7 waved back and yelled. The column moved onto the docks.

Down on the beach, the LSTs (Landing Ship, Tank) were waiting. Long, low vessels with flat bottoms, they were designed to put tanks ashore. The bow drops down and forms a ramp for the vehicles. On the beach, the LSTs were lined up and waiting for us like whales. We backed our vehicles on so they could easily be driven off when we landed.

By 3:00 in the afternoon, the battalion was loaded aboard three LSTs and we were on our way. I went up to the bridge for a look around, but it was crowded with naval officers looking important, so I didn't stay. Around 11:00 P.M. that night, I went back. There was no one there except an ensign, who was steering the ship. The LST was blacked out except for a small red light shining over the compass, which was pointing 180 degrees, south. The ensign said we were passing the Isle of Wight and we were headed up the River Seine to Rouen.

"You know," he said, "I'm awfully glad I'm not in your shoes and going where you're going. In the navy, we have a hot meal every day, sometimes three, always a dry place to sleep. It's not like the army," he said, "out there in the cold, in iron vehicles and in bad weather, exposed to bullets and shells and bombs. I don't envy you guys."

I asked him if there had been any trouble on the channel crossings like this one.

He nodded, keeping his eyes straight ahead. "A few nights before," he said, "one of the ships was sunk and a regiment was lost." He looked at me without expression. "About 3,000 men drowned."

We passed through Le Havre the next morning. The harbor was littered with sunken ships, their superstructures jutting up from the black water. The LST picked its way through the harbor, slowed down to pick up a river pilot for the tricky, winding trip up the Seine, and pressed its blunt bow into the mouth of the river itself. The Seine was the pathway to Paris, but we weren't going to Paris.

Moving along like a barge, the LST took three days to reach Rouen, stopping at night because the river was so narrow. These were pleasant, uneventful days. We passed villages, women and children waving from the banks. Many of the bridges across the Seine had been blown up and its steep banks were occasionally littered with the wrecks of airplanes and armored vehicles, mostly German. By mid-afternoon of the third day, we were on the outskirts of Rouen. It was snowing.

6 France

January 6, 1945–January 31, 1945

The U.S. First and Third Armies' counteroffensive in the Ardennes Forest (Battle of the Bulge) had become a killing ground, and the counteroffensive was chewing up the German army. In the Pacific, the U.S. Sixth Army had landed in Luzon and was advancing on Manila. For some time, the United States had been bombing Japan with B-29s.

The snow got heavier as we moved up the river toward Rouen. The river made a turn to the right and dead ahead was a beach about 300 yards long, 30 wide. Behind it was a bluff with a big building on it. A road had been cut between two bluffs and led from the beach up a steep incline to the street. The LST ran up on the beach and opened the big doors in the bow. Our tanks and trucks and half-tracks inched up the incline to the street, where the battalion guides were waiting, and formed into a column.

We left Rouen in a column of batteries without ever really seeing it. After an hour-and-a-half down snowy, icy roads, we pulled into the village of Bazomesnil and stopped at a chateau, a big rectangular building with multiple chimneys, many out-buildings, small houses, and barns.

The troops pitched tents; some of the officers bedded down in the chateau, which belonged to a retired French artillery colonel of World War I. We spotted a quonset hut nearby that looked as if it could probably bunk from seventy-five to one hundred men, but the French colonel refused to let anybody in. When finally someone asked him why, the colonel, a dignified man with a neatly trimmed gray moustache, stared for a minute.

"Monsieur," he said, "the Boche lived there."

Despite his feelings, Battery C moved into the quonset hut. It was warm.

I found a room on the top floor of the chateau. It was cold. No heat, no stove.

The next morning, I got a better look at our temporary home. It had been built in the eighteenth century and was quite ornate. It had extensive gardens, a large forecourt, a service court, and formal garden off each end of the house. The house, facing south on an elongated meadow of about fifty acres, had been planned by somebody who knew what he was doing. It was picturesque and beautiful, but cold as a deep freeze. We stayed three days. The alert came on the morning of the third day.

The weather had grown very cold and it was sleeting and snowing when we pulled out. The column had moved only a few miles down the road when I saw a sign, "Compegne." I remembered it from reading about World War I, and as we passed through, we could still see evidence of the terrible fighting there in the summer of 1918. On January 8, we passed through Soissons, heading east. It got colder and colder as the day went on. There was a light snow mixed with sleet, and the roads were icy. Off to my right, I saw a large monument, erected in 1926 by the Battle Monuments Commission, a tribute to the Americans who had died near Soissons. The column crept down the frozen roads. I dozed off in our half-track, and when I woke up, we were coming into a town.

It was Rheims. I didn't need a road sign. I knew it by the big beautiful cathedral in the distance. After a while, other buildings began to take shape. On the right, they were jammed against each other — shops, stores and houses, two and three stories high. On the left was a walk about ten feet wide. Beyond that, a two-foot stone wall, and past that a canal. It was mid-afternoon and people were moving back and forth along the walk, some of them walking even in the street. Our convoy was moving east very slowly.

I noticed a man on the walk digging in his britches. In a minute, he came out with it. Without looking right or left, he started to urinate on the sidewalk. People near him jumped out of the way. He just kept right on, not a bit bothered. People were walking around him on both sides and he just kept on, paying no attention. I watched in amazement, wondering what would have happened if he had done that in Colorado City. In France, nothing happened. He finally shook and replaced his instrument, then walked on.

Presently, the column began to move, edging forward at tortoise pace. Soon the road coincided with a canal, and a canal barge was moving slowly, almost alongside us. It was a low vessel with a black hull and a white-painted cabin. A young man came out of the cabin. When he opened the door, a cloud of steam rose from the cabin because it was so warm inside.

"Lucky bastard," I thought.

In a minute, an attractive young woman with dark hair came up carrying a baby about a year old, obviously his wife and child. I wondered why he wasn't in the army defending his country instead of letting someone else do it for him, someone like us. Up ahead, the lead vehicles started up and the half-track I was in started to rumble forward. The canal barge family watched us silently as we moved slowly on.

We rolled through Rheims, past its magnificent cathedral. It towered before us as it had for centuries, lofty and gray and magnificent, but we had no time to admire its architecture. The column snaked to the left around the cathedral, then pressed straight on for miles, moving past houses and shops dingy from years of war, on out through the outskirts of the city. The country began to roll and a heavy blanket of snow covered it, sticking in the branches of the trees and bushes. It was still lightly snowing and very cold.

I heard the mutter of a heavy machine gun ahead. From the sound of the gun, it was ours, a .50 caliber. I thought it might be an air attack, but I could see the gun firing up ahead and it was obviously not firing at aircraft. Instead a line of tracers was stitching a path in the snow. I found out later that a rabbit had jumped up and started running across the field, and a gunner on one of the half-tracks had cut down on it. The gunner was bored. We all were, bored and cold.

Slowly we moved forward toward Pont-a-Mousson and Raucourt.

A solid sheet of ice covered the road and the temperature hovered around zero. The fully tracked vehicles slipped dangerously on the road and sometimes only a tree kept them from sliding over the steep banks. Men walked half the time, guiding the vehicle, relieving each other when the cold had numbed their limbs. Twenty-seven hours later, thoroughly numb, we reached Pruney and stopped for the night, establishing our headquarters in the schoolhouse.

For sleeping quarters, I was assigned a room in the home of a villager. I was billeted in a small upstairs room with a short bed. My roommate, Maj. Matt Oliver, got the bed, and I unrolled my bedroll on the floor because there wasn't enough bed for both of us. I didn't want to sleep with him, anyway. Pruney was a very small village, just the schoolhouse, two or three stores combined with living quarters, a cafe and a railroad station about as big as a large truck.

The first morning there, I got up and went over to the mess tent to get something to eat. The cooks were busy dishing out eggs and steaming hot coffee. There was no place to sit, so I stood there in the snow eating out of my mess kit. Outside was not much colder than headquarters. The schoolhouse where we had established battalion headquarters was like Antarctica except for its one big room, which had a fireplace.

I looked around and saw a surprise: the latrine. It was like none I'd ever seen before. The floor was a concrete slab raised four inches above an adjoining slab. This raised area was about eight by sixteen feet and enclosed by a wall six feet high. Each side was cut up into stalls four feet square. These were divided by a wall in the center: boys on one side, girls on the other. In each square was a hole the size of a baseball, with two footprints pointing to the front. You put your feet into the footprints and your backside was theoretically aimed at the hole. From looking around, I could see that people before me hadn't been all that accurate.

These were to be our accommodations for a week. Six hundred men in a facility built for a hundred children. To improve our sanitation, each day Private Remitore burned out the excrement of the previous day. He would pour a gallon of gasoline into each of the eight holes and then drop a match on the gasoline. On the second day in Pruney, 1st Lt. Bun Baldwin came to answer the call of nature. He took off his tank suit, two pairs of wool trousers, lowered his long-handled underwear, and perched himself on the footprints, endeavoring to do things the French way. He did not see Private Remitore and Remitore did not see Lieutenant Baldwin on the other side of the center wall. Then Remitore tossed a lighted match into his side of the pit.

Whooomp! The flames jumped out about four feet from all of the holes except the one Lieutenant Baldwin was perched over. From that one, the fire jumped only about fifteen inches before reaching his exposed bottom and private parts. He let out a bloodcurdling "*Yeeeeowww!*" and grabbed his pants and ran out into the snow, his pants and underwear smoldering. Private Remitore, surprised, found the lieutenant sitting in a snow bank. Others were surprised also. Two housewives were walking by when this happened; they just looked at Lieutenant Baldwin then started running. I arrived soon after Bun was removed from the snow bank by medics and asked Remitore if he had anything against Lieutenant Baldwin.

"No, sir," he said, shaking his head. "I seen him standing around outside, but I didn't know he was wanting to take a dump."

For the rest of the week in Pruney, Private Remitore took a man with him to scout the stalls before he touched a match to the gasoline.

Walking around the edge of Pruney, I found the remains of a World War I trench system. There were rusty pieces of barbed wire, some metal stakes with loops that had held the wire, a rusty old helmet and a belt buckle. The trench was deep, a good six feet.

Back at battalion headquarters, I got word from Combat Command B that S-2, the intelligence section, would have maps ready for us the next morning at 10:00. I was to go to Combat Command B headquarters and pick them up. Their HQ was in a chateau owned by a champagne merchant near the village of Bacannes. We drove up to the front and entered through a tall wrought-iron gate with iron figures on top. There was a large forecourt made of a dark-red earth material similar to iron ore or crushed limestone. The front of the building was white, with vertical columns and tall narrow windows.

I reported in and found out from the CQ (charge of quarters) that the maps wouldn't be ready for an hour-and-a-half. I waited in a warm, empty bedroom at the end of the hall, a room about twenty-five by forty feet. Off the bedroom was a bathroom as long as the bedroom was wide. The ceiling was mirrored and the floor was of white tile. Two bath tubs were enclosed and sunk into the floor, and across from them were a pair of bidets. The male bidet looked like a urinal with a faucet handle. There were two marble commodes enclosed in an opaque glass closet with gold door knobs. Down the hall I found a ballroom, fifty by seventy feet with a twelve-foot ceiling and a floor of inlaid wood. A large chandelier hung in the center of the room, an expanse of glittering glass about fifteen feet in diameter. The ballroom opened north onto a formal garden. I was still exploring when the maps were ready.

About an hour later, I jeeped back to the 399th through the sleet and snow. We had been put on alert and also been notified that the officers' liquor ration was to be picked up in Rheims before 4:00 P.M. For some reason, Colonel Lilly sent the battalion alcoholic, Lt. Jack Daniel, on that assignment. He went off with a driver at 2:00 P.M. for the ten-mile drive to Rheims.

The batteries were loaded up and in line ready to move out. It was still snowing and so cold I had the shakes. I got out of the jeep and went to the schoolhouse, hoping to find a fire. The big fireplace had had a fire in it for two or three days, but now no coal, no ashes — nothing. It was still warm, though, and I crawled into the fireplace and partly lay down, luxuriating in its warmth, and went to sleep. A commotion outside woke me up. I crawled out of my fireplace and went outside to see what was going on. Jack Daniel had come back from Rheims with the liquor ration, drunk as a fiddler's bitch. He got out of his jeep and tried to throw Colonel Lilly a salute, fell down, and didn't get up. He didn't even move. His driver, Private Twig, got out of the jeep and he went down, too. The jeep must have come home like a horse.

Colonel Lilly shook his head. "Jesus Christ!" he said as he stomped off. Two minutes later, he had both of them loaded into a half-track like a couple of sacks of potatoes.

We moved out slowly at 11:00 P.M., heading east. All night we rolled over icy roads in a heavy snow, the chill seeping through the GI woolens. In the morning, we stopped to try to get something to eat. Near Verdun, where the great battle of World War I had been fought, we started down a long hill covered with ice. At the bottom was a big house, with barns on the left and a walkway between the house and barns. As Battery A was coming down the hill, the driver of the M-7 tried to brake it to get around the left turn at the bottom of the hill, but the track locked because there was so much ice on the road and he lost control. The M-7 went straight through the Frenchman's house without even slowing down. It ran over the frozen manure pile and the frozen beet pile, too, but by that time, the driver had gotten control of his vehicle, pulled it to the left, and gone on up the hill to join the column without missing a lick.

Hank Brooks, commander of Battery A, went to the house to see if anybody had been killed. Nobody had. We inched forward on the icy roads toward Pont-a-Mousson.

I was detailed to go on ahead of the column and find our billeting party. I left my half-track and got Larry Quist's jeep. It was snowing intermittently, the temperature about eight degrees. The driver headed east. I climbed into Quist's bedroll, boots and all, in the front seat of the jeep, drifted off and woke up in Verdun. On our left was a quarry, and beyond that a knocked-out tank, one of ours. The town was cold and stark, the streets deserted. Verdun has been a garrison town since the days of Charlemagne, but there was no sign of the famous forts. It was an ordinary French town, shot up to beat hell.

We pushed on through the city and turned south, crossing the Moselle River at Pont-a-Mousson and turning east to Nomeny, then north to Raucourt. The 160-mile journey from Pruney to Raucourt took forty hours because of the ice and snow.

I met Larry Quist, battalion reconnaissance officer, and went to look at the billets. Headquarters Battery had been assigned a farm house and barn area. Since my bedroll was on the fender of my half-track, Larry let me keep his, and got in the jeep and went to meet the battalion on the road. It was about 3:30 and beginning to get dark, and the battalion would not arrive till early in the morning, so I decided to meet the French family, try to get warm and get some sleep.

I was somewhat reluctant to knock on the door and talk to these people, but I was cold, so I found the door on the back side of the building and knocked. It was soon opened by a woman and I was invited in with gestures. There I met her husband, who had gray hair, and daughter, about twenty. They pointed me to a chair near the tile stove and I sat down. They were also seated, the girl on a box near another door. I began as best I could to talk to the old man; the woman and girl said nothing. But it was difficult, none of us speaking the same language, and I felt quite ill at ease. I had placed my carbine near the door and my musette bag was near my feet, and in an effort to break the ice, I opened the bag and removed three cans of 10-in-1 rations. I put the cans on the table and in sign language suggested that the woman prepare the food for all of us. I was pointing at her and the food and making chewing motions with my mouth and nodding and soon we were all nodding and grinning. She got busy and the old man spoke to his daughter, who left the room and returned with a bottle of red wine.

Soon the food was hot and we were drinking the wine and feeling rather good about things. When we had finished eating and drinking, I tried to indicate that I needed to go to bed. They looked from one to the other, not knowing what I meant. So I drew them a simple picture of a bed and a very tired soldier. They smiled and nodded their heads. The old man showed me where I could sleep. Using body language like a mime, he apologized for the accommodations. My room had been hit by artillery fire. No windows, most of the roof gone, the floor covered with snow. It had taken a solid shot. But it was the best he could do, he said with an expressive French shrug. I got Quist's bedroll and came back up and spread it out on the floor. And slept.

The battalion came in at 1:00 A.M. As they were getting settled, Quist came in and wanted his bedroll back. I told him to get mine off the fender of my half-track and lay it alongside his. I'd get out of his and into mine. The wind whistled in from the north because the room was open in that direction. Next morning, half frozen and jumping up and down to warm up, we went looking for a place for battalion headquarters.

We soon found a house. The roof had been shot off and the upper story was in sad shape, but the rest of it was all right. The bottom floor had three good rooms and we took them over. The room toward the front of the house became Battalion Headquarters and a room in back was assigned as message center. The room in front was about fifteen feet square, and had a big stove. Someone had to be in Battalion Headquarters at all times, so I moved in there, next to the stove, and slept there three nights. Colonel Lilly had been sleeping in a schoolmaster's house, which had no heat, so he moved into Battalion Headquarters and I moved into an adjacent hallway with about three feet of straw on the floor.

Lieutenants Sears, Weldon, and Baldwin were bedded down in one room of a nearby house. It was cold, a couple of feet of snow on the ground. Baldwin went to a nearby town and came back with an old wood stove, which had been shot full of holes. He took some pieces of tin and some stove bolts and patched the holes, but they had no stove pipe, so the three of them went scrounging and Sears came back with a piece of downspout off a barn. With the downspout and some grapefruit cans, they made an elbow and ran the smokestack out the window of the house.

When they got ready to fire it up, they couldn't find any wood. Everything was covered with snow. With two axes, they started to work on the stable, chopping out several big oak beams and other floor timbers.

The old Frenchman who owned the house ran out waving and hollering and wringing his hands, but nobody knew what he was saying and didn't give a damn anyway, so they just went right on chopping. When they finally got it cut up, they carried it inside and started a fire. The stove got so hot, it was jumping up and down when the solder melted out of the downspout and the smokestack came crashing down. The smoke from the stove filled the rooms and spread all through the house. It wasn't ordinary smoke. The timber they had chopped up for wood had been in the stall more than a hundred years and the stench of burning horse piss that impregnated their uniforms was so bad that for several days they were left pretty much to themselves.

At Raucourt, we were on the old German border, about fifteen miles from Germany. Our mission was to defend certain roads coming into France from the east. The area we were in had been part of Germany from 1870 to 1918.

Raucourt was a small farming village with houses, barns, outbuildings, and two stores. Rural France was different from the United States in that the farmers banded together and lived in small villages. You rarely saw a house or farmstead by itself. People lived in town and farmed their land when they could. With the snow two feet deep, the temperature ranged from about twelve to fourteen degrees above zero during the day, to about ten to twelve below at night.

Shortly after we got there, Colonel Lilly decided he wanted me to be in charge of the security of the battalion; to organize and establish a perimeter defense and to get a guard set up. I started to work.

Down the road, the 36th Tank Battalion had set up its own perimeter and we coordinated our security with them. The job kept me up from four to six hours at night. The first couple of nights, the guards were lax. I found two of them asleep and some were not at their posts. They knew there were no Germans nearby and they saw no reason for being out in the snow. They got in houses where they could look out on where they were supposed to be. That bothered me.

I talked the guard situation over with Colonel Lilly and Major Collins. I told them I would like to shake the outfit up if I could.

Colonel Lilly looked at me sharply. "How?"

"Well," I said, "I'd like to get an engineer up here and place some explosives around and about, and then tonight or tomorrow night, start setting them off one at a time."

Colonel Lilly smiled. "Go to it."

Next day, I went down to the 49th Armored Infantry Battalion, which was at Louvigny, two towns north of Raucourt, to talk to Captain Look, the S-2 officer. Battalion Headquarters was in a large house in Louvigny. He said he couldn't help, so I headed outside. Just as I stepped through the front, there was a terrific explosion in a jeep six feet in front of me and a man on fire came flying out of it. When I got out the door, I saw that the canvas top of the jeep had been blown off and the soldier was lying on the ground. His overcoat was on fire and he was trying to get up.

I couldn't figure out what in hell had happened. The only thing I saw in the jeep was a round tube about three feet long and an inch-and-a-half in diameter. Captain Look and some other officers came charging out of the house to see what had happened.

Captain Look had found a Panzerfaust, a German anti-tank grenade, and he'd put it in his jeep with the rocket part of it leaning up against the windshield between the seat and the driver's seat. The driver had been fooling with it and somehow pulled the trigger. It fired. It could have killed several people, including me, but it went over the top of the building and came down in a field about 300 yards away. The driver was sent off to be treated for burns and I went to the next town, still looking for an engineer.

I found one and he arranged for a sergeant with several pounds of plastic explosives to come back with me. He and I placed several charges, one in each battery area, and then ran a small wire from each charge to the church, where we put the detonator. All this we did in broad daylight, but it was snowing so hard nobody noticed. We had it all done by 2:00 and the sergeant returned to his outfit.

At 10:00 that night, it was still snowing. You couldn't have seen a tank move. Most of the battalion was in sleeping bags and the guards were doing their best, as usual, to stay out of the cold. I went down to the church and pressed the plunger.

Blam! The first charge went off. Troops started scrambling out of their sleeping bags. Men piled out of the billets.

In quick succession, I set off the other four charges. The place was like an anthill somebody had kicked. In minutes, the battalion was wide awake, everybody looking east for gun flashes. It shook the outfit up, and the soldiers began to take guard duty seriously.

The next night, the temperature about ten below, I was walking around checking on security. Off to the northeast, in the area of the Saar Moselle Triangle about twenty miles away, I could see flashes of artillery. Passing a barn, I noticed some horseplay in progress in the loft and called up to them to be quiet for a minute.

I said, "A couple of you men come over here and have a look."

They did, and they could see the flashes. Everybody got quiet and they could hear the rumbling of the guns. When I came back an hour or so later, they were quiet.

Next morning, a sergeant from one of the batteries came to headquarters and said he'd found fifteen or twenty rifles stacked in a vacant building nearby. He was going through the outbuildings, some of which were occupied by the French, and once in a while found one vacant. It was in one of these that he had found the rifles. He said he was afraid to handle them because they might be booby-trapped. I went over and looked at the stack of rifles. They were M-1s. A few hand grenades lay around, too. They looked like they might be booby-trapped. I called the engineers.

The sergeant was right. If anybody had picked up one of those rifles, he would have been blown to pieces. There was more than five pounds of plastic explosive lying under the debris around the rifles. Picking up any one of the rifles would have set it off.

The engineers cleared up the booby-trap. I took a rifle and the engineer and the sergeant took one. Some of his men divided the rest. We were armed with carbines as personal weapons and I was glad to get an M-1.

The same sergeant was prowling around in the barns the next day and found four bodies. They were Germans, frozen stiff. He had talked to the Frenchman who lived there and he took him outside and pointed to some shapes in the snow. They were like logs, fifteen bodies, also German. We didn't fool with them. I didn't want to go out and examine them because the area had been mined.

The second Sunday we were in Raucourt, a chaplain came boiling up in a jeep with his Christian flag flying. He was a tall, angular, rather homely man with thin, clean hands. He had a portable pulpit with him and an assistant to help set it up. Someone gave him some coffee and he asked us to put out the word to the batteries that he would have a church service in the schoolhouse in thirty minutes. He didn't say anything about communion. Some of the men began to drift over, about forty men out of 600. I was one of them.

As I went in, I noticed 2nd Lt. Sam Blatman of Wilmington,

Delaware, standing around outside. Sam was Jewish.

I said, "Sam, come on in, you might as well get in on this."

He said, "I'd like to go to church, but I don't know about this."

"It won't hurt you," I said. "It may not help you any, but it can't hurt you."

Sam came in and we listened to the sermon. The chaplain didn't preach on money, tithing, or love your enemy or anything like that.

On the way out after the service, we heard an airplane, a distant hum of engines. Then we heard a whistling sound. Sam, who had been on Guadalcanal and was bombed by the Japanese, knew instantly what it was. He let out a yell.

"Those are *bombs* coming down!"

We couldn't see a thing. The clouds were thick and there was a flurry of snow. There wasn't a hope of seeing the airplane, but we could hear that whistling, louder and louder and louder.

Wham! Seven 1,000-pound bombs landed south of the town, one hitting within 200 yards of a B Battery M-7 on the perimeter.

I went in and told Colonel Lilly I was going to go have a look at the crater. I wanted to see if I could tell what kind of bombs they were. I stomped off through the snow, feet sinking in as I went, and finally found the hole. It was about forty feet across, eighteen feet deep. Chunks of gray clay had been blown clear out of the hole and as far away as fifty yards. Some of the chunks were as big as a car.

When I climbed down into the hole, it was still hot and smoking. I hoped there were no delayed action fused bombs there. What I was looking for was fragments. If I could get the right fragments, I might identify the bomb from a manual. Digging down in the clay, I found pieces of an incendiary bomb, half of two of them. They were Allied — I recognized them instantly. They were Allied because American and British incendiary bombs were hexagon-shaped and fourteen inches long. German incendiaries were round and shorter. I plodded back through the snow with my bomb fragments and got on the phone to division.

"We've just been bombed by friendly aircraft," I complained. A staff officer asked me how I knew it was a friendly aircraft since I couldn't see it. I told him I had identified the bombs. He asked how and I told him.

"Well," he said, "okay, we'll report it."

He didn't seem to give a damn whether we'd been bombed or not. Later, I found out what happened. A British pilot had gotten lost and dropped his whole bomb load, then his crew had bailed out.

Despite the rumbling off in the distance, and the British airplane, life in Raucourt was relatively quiet. The town was accustomed to war. Lorraine had been German territory until World War I. The Americans had captured it shortly after the successful St. Mihiel offensive late in the summer of 1918. The house next to the one we were billeted in had two stories, the bottom floor a pillbox. I looked at it one day without going in. The top of the pillbox was about four feet from the ceiling. The date on the concrete was 1914.

It was on a cold, dreary, foggy morning in Raucourt when a messenger arrived from division with a packet of papers, one of which was addressed to me. The letter, more than half an inch thick, had originated in Calcutta, India, five months earlier. It had been endorsed by the commanding officers of the English and American headquarters, including General MacArthur's adjutant, and was further endorsed down through the channels beginning with Supreme Headquarters Allied Expeditionary Forces, Third Army, and on to 8th Armored Division.

The letter claimed that I had left Calcutta without paying The Grand Hotel the sum of 139 rupees. The correspondence contained a copy of the bill with a signature, my army serial number, and a demand for immediate payment. The endorsement from 8th Armored Division contained a threat: "Pay this damn bill now and don't do it again."

But I had never been to Calcutta. In fact, I had never been west of El Paso, Texas. I thought about the bill for a while and responded that though I had never been to Calcutta nor had I incurred such a bill as was included in the correspondence, I was prepared to leave immediately for Calcutta and get the mess straightened out. However, I wrote, in order to accomplish this, I would need six months temporary duty, a letter authorizing transportation and lodging, and further would desire a leave of fifteen days while passing through the United States on my way to Calcutta.

I signed the letter and Colonel Lilly endorsed it. I heard no more about it.

We went on marking time in Raucourt, the weather colder than a well digger's ass. Usually, the food was cold when we ate it. We ate standing up in the area of Headquarters Battery and the kitchen truck was in an open air storage area. From time to time, I noticed several carts and wagons and farm implements in the area, but they were coated with snow and I didn't look at them closely. Some of them were loaded with logs, and in some places there were stacks of logs against a fence.

After lunch one day, the weather warmed up suddenly and a warm rain began falling. It melted the snow in many places, including one where we ate. I discovered that the wagon I'd been eating off of for a week was not loaded with logs. Piled on it were the bodies of twenty German soldiers — frozen. I had been eating with my mess kit on the chest of a corporal. The stacks of logs against the fence were frozen corpses, too.

It soon stopped raining and started to snow again. For once, I was glad.

The 8th Armored Division was on full alert the entire time we were in Raucourt. In late January, CCA was given the mission of reinforcing the 94th Infantry Division trying to penetrate the Siegfried Line in its switch position some twenty miles north of us. Several of our F.O.s and crews took part in the attack and capture of Berg and Tettingen.

7 First Contact

February 1, 1945–February 15, 1945

Charles B. MacDonald, office of the chief of military history, USA, sets the tone of the Siegfried Line Campaign in The U.S. Army in World War II *like this: "As a kind of temporary stalemate settled over this part of the Roer plain, the battlefield was a dreary spectacle. The sun seldom shown. A damp grayish mist predominated. Sodden by rain, gashed by shells and tank tracks, the beet and cabbage fields were dismal and ugly. Drab at the start of the fighting, the villages were now desolate."*

The 8th Armored Division was relieved from attachment to XX Corps, Third Army, and reassigned to Ninth Army and XVI Corps. We packed up our gear, cranked up the vehicles, and rolled north toward Holland. It was a bitter cold day in February.

We moved slowly and steadily over 170 miles of roads as slick as a skating rink, through country that had been bitterly fought over. In the Ardennes, the devastation was enormous, most of it done by our artillery. The tops of hundreds of trees along our way had been shot off as if someone had taken a sickle and mowed them down. Stumps were sticking up, some four feet, some twenty feet. The dark carcasses of knocked-out vehicles lay strewn along the route. The villages had been badly shot up, but life was going on; people were going about their business, cutting wood and feeding animals.

We headed west of Metz to Longway, Orlon, and through the ruins of Bastogne where the 101st Airborne Division and other attached forces had recently stood off the German panzers for so long.

We moved on through Huflienz, Liege, Maastricht, and on to Groot Welsden. The march took a full three days. Some of the units went on to nearby villages, Sittard and Heerlen. We were put up in an unfurnished attic in Groot Welsden. The man who owned it, a sixty-five-year-old Dutchman with a bit of a paunch and gray hair thinning at the top, wore gold-rimmed spectacles and spoke some English. One of his sons was in his late twenties, he said, and lived with him. The other was off working somewhere in the resistance. He had some beef hanging in his attic and seemed apprehensive that we might take it, but we didn't.

In Groot Welsden, we were getting closer to the war. On February 7, we were assigned to support the 35th Division in their assault crossing of the Roer River. Colonel Lilly and I went on reconnaissance. We jeeped down to Geilenkirchen and Heinsberg, then turned north to the little German farming village of Kirchhoven, which was about a mile west of the Roer River. It was occupied by an infantry company of the 35th Division. Most of the civilians had been evacuated, but those who were left were going about the daily business of scratching out a living, the war within earshot.

The Roer River, which ran between Holland and Germany, was rising. Across the river was the German army, though we couldn't see anything of it. Colonel Lilly told his driver, Corporal Fisher, to head for Groot Welsden.

The next day he ordered Headquarters Battery and the base piece of Battery B to move into Kirchhoven. When a battery goes into position, it usually forms a six-pointed diamond, with the base piece in the rear of the formation. This is the gun used for registering. There may be fifty yards between the base piece and the gun at the forward point of the diamond. The rearward gun is used to register the battery so that there will be none of our shells falling on our own people when firing a close support mission.

Headquarters Battery and Battery B's base piece would slip in and take up positions at night. Late in the morning, Colonel Lilly, Maj. John Collins, the executive officer, and a few others besides myself, jeeped over to Kirchhoven. As we went east, I noticed a big billboard on the left of the road. It had been put up by the British, who had been in the sector. It read: "Attention! The road you are on the next four miles is under direct German observation. Be careful!"

My scalp tingled a little when I saw that. It would have been pretty damned hard to hit a jeep or a half-track moving along at thirty miles an hour, but if you were in a long truck column, their artillery could blow you to bits.

One of the towns on the way to Kirchhoven was Heinsberg, an old town of about 15,000 population. Now, though, the town was deserted. It had been leveled except for jagged snow-covered fragments of houses jutting up against the gray sky. Aircraft and artillery attacks had reduced it to piles of rubble. On the north side of town, rubble had been bulldozed aside to make a road. Everywhere, the smell of death was in the air.

On the northeast edge of town, the road turned sharply north and went on for two miles, then forked like a "V." Our route was to the left, then north a mile. We came to the tiny village of Lieck, passed through it, and rolled on to Kirchhoven. The road to the right went to the German positions in Kempen, and three-quarters of a mile farther was the town of Karkin, on the Roer.

The west bank of the river was at ground level; the east bank, the German side, was much higher, from twenty to sixty feet, forming bluffs along this part of the Roer that extended several miles both ways.

In Kirchhoven, we found a house across the street from the schoolhouse and got settled. It was not as cold as it had been in Lorraine, but it was still cold. Afternoon temperatures were about twenty-five degrees, often dropping to zero at night, with some snow on the ground and intermittent flurries as we moved up.

The rest of Headquarters Battery and one gun section from Battery B were to come up after midnight. The sky was overcast but visibility was not bad because of the full moon, light filtering through the clouds and reflecting off the snow.

That night, Sergeant Hughes was leading Headquarters Battery to the new location in Kirchhoven. He had not been over the ground before the battery marched, but the battery commander had given him a marked map and had gone on ahead to Kirchhoven.

Leading a column of eighteen half-tracks, six trucks, six jeeps, and three tanks, Sergeant Hughes got as far as Heinsberg, but after he turned north and came to the "V" in the road, he took the right turn instead of the left. The column went on about three-quarters of a mile before he began to get uneasy, thinking perhaps he'd made a wrong turn. He stopped the column and walked on ahead.

He had gone about 200 yards when a shape suddenly loomed in front of him — a sentry. Sergeant Hughes walked up to within four feet of the sentry. "Which way is Kirchhoven?" he asked.

The sentry said nothing and Sergeant Hughes took a closer look. Wearing a coal-scuttle helmet and a greatcoat that reached nearly to the ground, the sentry was a German soldier.

Sergeant Hughes knew he was in trouble. He was in a nest of Germans. His carbine was slung over his right shoulder with the muzzle pointing up. He quickly unslung it, trained it on the German, and pulled the trigger.

Nothing happened. The carbine was on safety.

The safety button on the carbine is on the forward part of the trigger guard, and just in front of it, about three-quarters of an inch away, is the magazine release button. Trying frantically to get the carbine off safety, he pushed the magazine release button and the clip fell out of the carbine. That left him with one round in the chamber.

The German hadn't moved, but now he turned around and walked away. And so did Sergeant Hughes, leaving his twenty-round clip in the snow on the road.

Sergeant Hughes backed up the half-tracks, trucks, and tanks for three-quarters of a mile to the proper road junction, took the left fork, and went on to Kirchhoven.

If he hadn't stopped the column when he did, the battalion would have been out of business for some time. We would have lost the S-3 section (operations), the wire section, the communications section, maintenance section, kitchen truck and the cooks, two liaison sections, three F.O. sections, and a lot of other vehicles. The German sentry standing alone on the snow-covered road had probably been listening to the column approach. He probably had little back-up and didn't know what to do. He was also probably scared to death.

Plans were changed at Corps level, and Combat Command B was to relieve the 137th Infantry of the 35th Division. Our job was to attack across the Roer and secure a bridgehead near Kempen. The battalion's mission was to support the 36th Tank Battalion and the 49th Armored Infantry in their assault.

By February 8, though, a valve on the dams sixty miles upriver in the Hurtgen Forest had been blown open and the water came sweeping down in a huge wide current that swelled the Roer way over its banks. From a river twenty yards wide, it became a broad water barrier of at least 300 yards. There was no way we could cross it in its flooded stage. The attack was put on hold for a few days, until the excess water could run off.

This left us with Headquarters Battery and part of Battery B in Kirchhoven and the rest of the battalion still back in Holland. For ten days we sat there, not altogether unhappy because we were a long way from the division brass and Colonel Lilly was in a good humor.

The first day in Kirchhoven, I set up an observation post in the steeple of the only church in town. From that vantage point, I could see Karken, about 3,000 yards north, very clearly. Kempen was about 1,500 yards east of Kirchhoven. North of Karken, across the Roer, I could see St. Ludwig's College on a bluff about sixty feet high. The college was a cluster of tall gray buildings on high ground rising from the bluffs. I kept watching one building in particular, a four-story structure. I was sure its top story was full of field glasses, telescopes and telephones. I knew they were watching us with as much interest as we were watching them.

Watching was all we did for a while. We were on German ground for the first time and it was fair game. I started to nose around. I went through the schoolhouse across the street and was amazed to find that the third-, fourth- and fifth-grade children were taught military map reading. I noticed a rolled up screen in one of the rooms and pulled it down. There was a military map of Kirchhoven, the same as the one I had in my map case, except it was as big as the wall. They were teaching eight-year-old children to read maps, interpret symbols, and calculate heights by contours — all things we didn't learn until we were in ROTC in college.

Kirchhoven was primarily a farming village with three north-south streets and eight more crossing them. North of where we had set up, a Dutch-type windmill ground grain. In one building, we found a small factory with fifteen sewing machines that made uniforms. Checking through the other houses, I found some forty German civilians still there.

It had been a prosperous community, with decorative hedges, and many of the houses made of brick and sidewalks of stone. Windows were curtained and the houses had fine furniture and crockery, stoves, and electric heaters. The bins were full of coal, potatoes, and apples;

the shelves loaded with preserves, fruits, and vegetables.

The men helped themselves to this bounty. Soon, elegant crockery replaced battered mess kits and many of the men had commandeered bicycles.

Kempen and Karken, though, were still full of German soldiers and we suspected they might be returning to Kirchhoven at night. The infantry told me a few German combat patrols had been passing through, but nothing to be worried about. Nevertheless, we established outposts in the woods to the east of us and manned them during the daytime.

The wire section went out to lay phone lines to the outposts and encountered a billy goat problem. When men of the wire section crawled through snow-covered grass and bushes, a local billy goat ran up and gave them a butt. One lineman got butted three times. What worried them even more was that the German lines were only 400 yards away and the goat was black, standing out against the snow like a beacon on a dark night.

At night we pulled the men in from the outpost, but left the phones. The Germans often went to these outposts and called us on the telephone. But they never said anything. Later, we took out those phones and put in sound-powered phones.

The sound-powered phone was an advanced telephone for its time. You didn't have to ring a switchboard. All you had to do was whistle into it softly or talk and it would trip little gadgets on the switchboard and the call would go through. It was a lot more secure than a ringing telephone.

The second day we were in Kirchhoven, a shell came in about 2:00 P.M., striking between Battalion Headquarters and the ground where Battery A was to go into position. 1st Lt. Frank Gillespie was walking in the road looking over Battery A's future gun position when a shell landed about fifty feet from him. I went off through the snow and found the shell hole. A 105mm round had scooped a crater out of the black German dirt, throwing chunks all around. I figured it had been fired from some woods about a mile and a half on the other side of the Roer. From the shape of the shell hole I was able to get good data as to the size of the shell and the direction from which it came. I telephoned the information to Division Artillery.

Judging from that shell crater, the Germans had a pretty good idea where they were shooting. I was worried about the German civilians in Kirchhoven. Ever since we'd gotten there, I had suspected they were giving what information they could to German soldiers at night. German patrols were coming in and staying for an hour or two and leaving. The infantry had listening posts, one or two men well hidden, and they would sometimes see fifteen or twenty German soldiers pass by at night, their long greatcoats and coal scuttle helmets hard to miss against the snow.

We had come up from Third Army and our move had been a reasonably well-kept secret. Ninth Army was pulling a lot of troops from First Army and Third Army, getting ready for a big offensive. Ninth Army wanted very much to keep the Germans in the dark about how many new divisions had been brought in, so we were not allowed to move our half-tracks and trucks during daylight.

But after we had been there a day, we were welcomed by Axis Sally. She said she wanted to greet the 8th Armored Division, newly arrived from Third Army in the area of Kirchhoven, Roermond, Posterholdt, and Heinzburg.

I figured German civilians had told them about us. I had an idea, too, that the Kirchhoven people still had some telephone communications with the German forces across the river.

At Battalion Headquarters, Colonel Lilly and I talked about the civilians. I suggested that we run them off, just get them together and start them walking.

Colonel Lilly thought it over a minute and nodded. "Round 'em up, Tex."

I sent off a detail in jeeps to round them up. By 1:00 P.M., the whole remaining population of Kirchhoven was out on the road. There were about fifty of them — old men, women, and youngsters. They had all kinds of carts piled high with all the personal belongings they could haul, and the carts were hitched to some kind of animal, horses or cows, except in one case an old man pulled a cart himself. They looked dejected, but I didn't feel sorry for them. I just wanted them out of there.

I told them they were going to a rear area, and headed them off down the road toward Heinzburg. I didn't know where they were going and I wasn't sending them anywhere in particular. I just wanted them out. They stood there without saying a word. I was getting ready to move them out when a jeep drove up and a major from the 35th Division jumped out. He was madder than hell, his face red, his lower lip trembling.

"Captain," he snapped at me, "why have you got these people lined up on the road?"

"I'm sending them out of here," I said.

"You're not sending them anyplace," he said. "You're in the 35th Division sector and we don't have any place to put these people west of here."

"Major," I said, "these people are seeing German soldiers at night and I don't like it and Colonel Lilly doesn't like it, and we don't want 'em here." I let that sink in, then added: "We're to relieve you tonight at midnight."

By now his face was even redder. He wouldn't budge. Until we relieved them, he said, the civilians wouldn't move. "These are General Baade's orders and they will be obeyed."

I backed off. Arguing with a major is one thing. I didn't want to get into a controversy with a general. The major went out in the street and in perfect German told them to get back in their houses, then got in his jeep and roared off, still mad. I kept the Germans standing there for a minute. Then I told them we weren't going to tolerate their seeing German soldiers from Kempen and Karken, feeding them and putting them up in their houses at night. If we caught any of them fraternizing with the German soldiers, it was going to be too goddamned bad for all of them. Further, I told them I would personally shoot any son of a bitch that I caught with a telephone or radio. I meant it, and I think they knew it.

They returned to their homes, most of them on the east side of the main road running north through Kirchhoven. I didn't see a single one of them any more while we were there.

This was my first experience coming down hard on groups and individuals. It was a case of doing what the job demanded, and I found that it was not difficult for me to do.

ROERMOND
German Artillery positions
Maas River
Flooded Area
International Boundry
Melick
Heide Woods
Roer River
St Ludwigs College
St Odilienberg
Posterholt
Montfort
Karken
Orsbeck
GERMANY
HOLLAND
Kempen
Kirchhoven
International Boundry
Sgt. Hughes stopped by
German sentry at this point
Route to and from Kirchhoven
HEINSBERG
Flooded Area
AREA MAP 1
KIRCHHOVEN
N
W
E
S
Front line along East bank of
Roer River except where shown
Indicates bluffs along east bank
of Roer River
Graphic scale one mile
German Field Artillery positiones
7 FEBRUARY 1945

8 Kirchhoven

February 16, 1945–February 25, 1945

Charles MacDonald describes the period in The Last Offensive *like this: "All plans were complete in expectation of a D-Day on 10 February (Operation Veritable) when, on the eve of the attack, the Germans destroyed the discharge valves on the Roer Dams. Not for about twelve days would the water in the reservoirs be exhausted. . . . Downstream (from Duren) along most of its length, the Roer poured over its banks and inundated the valley floor . . . (creating) inundations of 300 to 400 yards. The ground on both sides of the flooded river was soft and spongy."*

By the time the last of the German civilians had melted away, it was mid-afternoon and getting dark. The weather at night was still frigidly unpleasant, with snow flurries and low clouds, and I felt the chill coming on. I went on in to Battalion Headquarters and made some notations on the maps and wrote some reports and went to bed.

At 2:00 A.M. a corporal was shaking my shoulders. I stuck my head out of the sleeping bag like a turtle.

"Captain," he said, "you better come out. Something funny's going on."

I always slept in my clothes, so all I had to do was pull on my boots and jacket. As we went through the door, I realized that it was very quiet.

I said, "What's happening?"

"Well," the corporal said, "I don't know, but I don't like it."

There had been mortars firing to the southeast and every once in a while a machine gun tuned up and started working. He didn't know whether it was the Germans or ours.

"I can't tell one from the other," he admitted.

I listened for a while and heard both German M-42s and our light Brownings firing. They were not near us, but the corporal was right. Something was happening.

I decided that it would be a good idea to find out what was going on and I wanted to talk with the infantry company commander. He was several hundred yards south of us on the main street of Kirchhoven. I called for a volunteer to accompany me and Cpl. Morris Pottish, from New York City, slung his carbine on his shoulder and we started down the street. It was then 2:30 A.M. and snowing lightly. After we had walked about 300 yards, we saw an American soldier lying on the sidewalk next to a building. We went closer and saw that he had an M-1 pointed at us. The only sounds were the distant chatter of the machine guns and the occasional *crump* of the mortars.

Corporal Pottish and I continued down the street to the infantry unit's command post in the basement of a three-story building about 500 yards from our own position. It was the CP of Company C of the 1st Battalion, 137th Infantry Regiment. The only light in the room was a flickering candle set squarely in the center of a table. Around the table sat the company commander, a captain, a lieutenant, and four men, all unshaven, their faces occasionally touched by the light of the candle. They were quiet, waiting for the field telephone to ring, wondering when and where the Germans were going to attack.

The company commander said they had a listening post in the edge of the woods near Karken. At 1:00 A.M., a German combat patrol had come through, headed toward our end of town.

"How many?" I asked.

"Our man counted thirty-six."

"What were they armed with?"

"Most of them had burp guns. Maybe one or two had machine guns."

That shocked me right out of my boots.

"You mean, they were headed toward our part of town?"

He looked at me calmly. It wasn't his problem.

"Yeah, they ought to be getting there about now."

That was a hell of a note. Here we were, Pottish and I, 500 yards from our area, and most of the battalion was asleep. Our sentries were armed with carbines and would be no match for a combat patrol of that size. There was nothing to do but turn around and go back, and I didn't like that one damned bit. We started walking, eyes straining for shapes in the darkness.

We never saw them. They seemed to have melted away. As soon as we returned to the Headquarters Battery area, I ordered the officer of the day and the sergeant of the guard to alert the battery. We posted men at the windows with grenades, machine guns, and carbines. And we waited. Nothing happened. After two hours, with everything quiet, I crawled back into my sack and went to sleep. An hour later, I woke up to the rattle of machine gun fire. The patrol had gone north of us and was coming out south of Kirchhoven when it ran into some of the men of the 137th Infantry. The confrontation developed into a minor fire fight of about fifteen minutes. Nobody on our side got hit, so I went back to bed.

I'd been in the sack for about an hour when it was time to start another day. It was a cold, snowy dawn with nothing much happening. I thought over the night before and decided I was not going to walk down that street anymore not knowing who was in front of me or behind me. I asked Lieutenant Weldon, the battalion communications officer, to install a telephone line to the infantry company command post. Within an hour, we had telephone communications with the infantry.

The highest point in Kirchhoven was the church steeple and from there I could see what the Germans were doing. The church was a rectangular building set on slightly higher ground than the surrounding area and facing west. It was made of dark red masonry and its steeple, in front of the auditorium, was on the far west side, its rectangular base standing a good five stories tall. The steeple itself went up another two stories, to the weather vane at the apex.

From the steeple, our view was northeast, taking in mostly the house tops of Kirchhoven and the snow-covered woods on the edges of town. Across an expanse of level ground, I could see the church steeple in the town of Karken.

The stairs in the steeple went a third of the way to the top. To get the rest of the way up, it was necesssary to climb a ladder to a landing, where I saw a louvered window. With some of the louvers removed, I could look to the east and the north where the Germans were positioned.

Then with the help of Sergeant Hughes and two men, we built another landing about eight feet above the first one. Above that, in the very top of the steeple, hung a large bell, about four feet in diameter, and from it, hanging in the center of the steeple, was a bell rope. The landing we had built was strong enough for six people to stand on, and it made an excellent observation post.

I brought up a chair so I could sit with my field glasses and look east across high-pitched roof tops to St. Ludwig's College, which reared up out of a patch of woods, and the town of Kempen, and another fair-sized town, Orsbeck, to the southeast of Karken. Orsbeck was on the east bank of the Roer and on bluffs higher than Karken. I began to methodically search the whole area with my glasses, sweeping the towns, the college, the river, looking for activity. Something stopped my eye in Karken — a big house. German soldiers in their long field coats were coming in and going out of it. They were crossing the river in motor boats and row boats, two or three boats an hour. They would tie up the boat and go into the big house. After a while, some of them would come out, get into their boats, and cross the river again. It had to be a command post. It was probably the regimental CP of the unit on our side of the river.

While I was watching, the sky opened up and the sun came out, throwing dazzling light on the snow and making a beautiful winter scene, with snow a foot and a half deep on the ground and blanketing the buildings and fir trees around us.

Looking at Kempen through the glasses, I saw a flash in a window. I had to laugh. It was a German soldier looking at the church steeple through glasses as I was looking at him. The house was on the northwestern part of Kempen. I knew it had to be either a company command post or an observation post, and I recorded the location on my map. I also circled the house in Karken where the soldiers were moving in and out. Something should be done about that activity, I thought.

Meanwhile, it was 3:00 P.M. and getting dark. The sky had closed in again, assuming its customary hue of gray, and it was beginning to sleet a little. I climbed down out of the steeple and warmed up a bit in the church office, where we had a stove, and went back to Battalion Headquarters.

Colonel Lilly was there studying some maps and I told him what I had seen. I told him about the house with all the activity around it and said I would like to get at it with some artillery. He shook his head.

"Tex, you know we can't shoot artillery up there. We're not even supposed to be in the Ninth Army."

"Sir," I said, "I know that, but nobody said anything about shooting mortars."

He looked at me and a grin started across his face. "No, they didn't."

I said, "How about me getting a mortar up here and shooting them with it?"

"You think you can hit them?"

"I can hit them."

"Okay, go ahead."

Service Battery had two 81mm mortars on the tank recovery vehicle and were used primarily to fire smoke shells when retrieving tanks. I called Capt. Willis F. Gausman, battery commander, on the radio and asked for a mortar and crew and all the high-explosive shells he had. I had decided to work over both of the German sites I had marked on my maps in the afternoon. Gausman said he had a ration truck leaving in about an hour and he would put a mortar, ammunition, and crew on it.

With my map of Kirchhoven spread on a large table, I started to work. The 1/25,000 scale map of Kirchhoven and vicinity was very detailed, even individual trees in some cases, as well as canals, mills, houses, and churches. Fortunately, I had all this data on one map. I located the mortar away from our battalion area because I didn't want the Germans shooting at the mortar and hitting in the area of Headquarters Battery.

Next morning at first light, I got busy, locating the mortar some distance north of our CP at a site I could pick up on the map. With transit and three men from the survey section, we ran a survey from a road junction north of the mortar site. In locating the mortar precisely, it was necessary to run a survey with several angles and legs. Doing this eliminated whatever error there might be on the map and correctly established the mortar's location. The traverse wasn't a long one, maybe 600 yards, and I had all the data I needed by 11:00 A.M.. I cranked the field phone and called Corps Artillery for a "metro message."

This is of value to artillerymen when they're shooting from maps as distinct from shooting observed fire. The metro data provides the density of the air, temperature, temperature of the powder, wind velocity and direction, and humidity. All of this has a bearing on the ballistics of an artillery or mortar shell. When you get a metro message, you look at certain tables and get a factor — a little plus and a little minus, some one way and some another — and finally a net factor, the K factor. It might be plus or minus, right or left, 100 yards, 200 yards, or whatever. With my K factor, I had cold dope on the German soldiers going in and out of the house in Karken. We ran a telephone line from the mortar to the observation post in the church steeple and another from the steeple to the battalion command post. It was time to shoot. I laid the mortar and set the elevation, then started for the church. A couple of other officers wanted to go along, 2nd Lt. Raymond E. Verlinder from San Antonio, Texas, and Warrant Officer Bill Pieper. Pieper, from Dallas City, Illinois, was assistant battalion motor officer attached to Service Battery and had delivered the mortars the night before. They followed me up the ladder to the steeple and sat down on the bench. I showed them the target and explained what I was going to do.

I cranked the field phone and got the mortar crew. They were ready to shoot, they said. I rechecked the setting with them, then called Colonel Lilly and told him we were going to fire in about five minutes.

I had just hung up when I heard some commotion and saw a soldier coming up the ladder. I asked him what he was doing there.

"Well," he said, "I brought a truckload of 30-caliber ammunition to the 137th and I saw you going into the church and I thought I'd see what was going on here."

"We're about to shoot some Germans," I said.

Then I heard some more noise and another soldier clambered up the ladder. He was just following his buddy, he said. There was room enough for all of us, so I told them they could watch and explained what we intended to do.

I phoned the mortar crew and gave the command to fire. I could visualize the round being dropped down the barrel, then zooming out on a high arcing flight toward the house in Karken. While it was on its way, I was searching the area with my field glasses. My glasses were not fixed on the building and I didn't see the round explode. A mortar shell makes little smoke. You have to see the flash of the explosion. I didn't see it and ordered another round at the same setting. But when it was time for it to hit, I didn't see it either.

"Goddamn!" said Lieutenant Verlinder.

I thought he was flacking me because I'd missed. Before I could say anything, a shell came by the church from the east, really moving on. It had been laid on the steeple direct from somewhere around St. Ludwig's College about 3,500 yards away. At that distance, shooting at a steeple is like shooting at a string with a .22 pistol at thirty feet. It would be very hard to hit. They came close, though. The shell sounded like a train going by at a hundred miles an hour. Several more followed, falling all around the church.

That was all our visiting soldiers needed. The first one was standing close to the bell rope and when the first shell came by, he leaned back and caught the rope and down he went like a fireman, hitting the bottom running. With that, the big old bell began to peal and nearly burst our eardrums. The route of the first guest was closely followed by the second and the bell kept pealing.

The church bell was still making a hullabaloo as the two soldiers jumped into their trucks and with engines roaring, headed for the rear. When the bell stopped ringing, the telephone started. It was Colonel Lilly.

"What in God's name are you doing up there? You shot two mortar rounds and you've already gotten seven big ones back! Get the hell out of that steeple before you get killed!"

He had an afterthought. "And stop ringing that goddamn bell!"

I hung up the phone. I was ready to go. A shell had just hit in back of the church and killed a cow. I was looking right at it when it happened. Then I heard two more go over. That was fourteen! We stirred up a hornet's nest. We hustled down the stairs and out the front door, heading for the CP.

Colonel Lilly was waiting at the front door.

"Well, you stirred 'em up."

I nodded. "Sure as hell did."

"Where did the mortars hit?"

"I don't know," I said, "I didn't see 'em."

"Goddamn!" He asked, "Are you blind?"

Lieutenant Verlinder, sitting in the corner, said, "I saw them explode, sir."

Colonel Lilly turned around to him. "Well, where did they hit?"

"They blew up in the house," said Verlinder. "I saw them through the window. Both of them went through the roof and blew up in the house."

Von Tony Krings, Heinsberg-Karken, West Germany, states in his book, *Eine Jugend Im Kreig,* that the mortar shells exploded in Colonel Landau's quarters in "Wolfhanger-Muhle" and that eight soldiers as well as Colonel Landau were there at the time. Colonel Landau was the commanding officer of the 1218 Volksgrenadier Regiment of the 176th Infantry Division. The individuals mentioned above were in the downstairs kitchen drinking coffee and none were hit.

The mortar rounds had certainly stirred up the Germans. Colonel Lilly had one more question.

"Why did you ring that goddamn bell?"

With a deadpan face, I told him about the visitors in the steeple.

"Why didn't you run them out?"

"I didn't have to, sir, they left of their own accord."

It was decided not to shoot the mortar at the Germans anymore. Colonel Lilly figured it wasn't a good trade to fire two 81mm rounds and get back fourteen rounds. The Germans knew where Battery B had its gun and they were shooting at it. They put five rounds in the Battery B area, though none of them hit anything.

Shelling the house had upset the Germans and I expected them to jump us during the night. Colonel Lilly agreed, so we began organizing a reception committee. We removed some of the .50-caliber machine guns from the half-tracks and put six of them in buildings facing the east and another one in a building facing north. If the Germans attacked us that night, they would be facing some hot fire power. Sergeant Patrick of Oak Ridge, Tennessee, was placed in charge of this detail, manning one of the guns himself. He had worked out an early warning system, too. He and his men had strung some tin cans with rocks in them on a wire line. If anyone stumbled across the lines in the dark, it would rattle the cans and alert the gunners.

At about 2:00 A.M., Sergeant Patrick heard some rattling and cut loose with his gun, sweeping an area about waist high. When he started firing, the other five joined in like a string sextet. It caused a hell of a din for about a minute. Then they quit shooting. When the clatter of the .50s died down, they could hear a lot of hollering and screaming, but they didn't go out to investigate. The area was full of mines.

The next day was much like the others, cold and overcast with occasional snow flurries. At 11:00 A.M., a flight of B-26s came in from the north and was flying parallel to the front, maybe a half mile inside the German lines and just below a layer of broken clouds. The guns opposite Karken at Orsbeck began firing at them, and the planes took evasive action, but one of them was hit. It began to burn and turned left, heading for a cloud. It was the wrong way to turn. If he had turned right and flown ten more seconds, he could have bailed out over us.

By mid-afternoon, it had begun snowing again. It snowed steadily for about an hour and a half, then quit, but the snow clouds continued to hover over us as if they were ready to dump some more. In this weather, the Germans were quiet and there wasn't much to do. I wondered where the mail was. We had been moving fast and we hadn't received mail for more than two weeks. On slow afternoons like that, I began to think of home. Around 6:00 we had mail call in the dark. I got nine letters from Don and one from my mother. Nearly everybody got a letter.

One of them was a death message. About 8:00 P.M., while I was still reading my own mail, an NCO came in and said, "Captain, Corporal Fletcher got a letter from his mother-in-law. She wrote his wife had died."

I went and talked to Corporal Fletcher. He was from Kansas City and a good man. When I found him, he was sitting and staring at a lamp, with a few friends around him. It was sad, I thought, that he had to be sitting in a cold, sorry, no good, red-ass German town on the Roer when his wife died. "I'm sorry," I told him.

There wasn't much anyone could say. There was really nothing I or anyone could do. I stayed for a while without saying anything. When I left, he was still staring at the lamp. I went to bed, feeling down.

The next thing I knew, a non-com was shaking my shoulder.

"Captain, could you come out here? Something's fixing to happen."

I groaned and tugged on my boots, sleepily buckling the buckles. They would always alert me because one of my jobs as S-2 was the security of the battalion, and since I had been Headquarters Battery commander for a year, I knew all the men in the battery.

Outside, the chill penetrated like a razor blade. Sergeant Hughes, the first sergeant, was waiting. He had been talking to Corporal

Fletcher and it had upset him, he said, and he hadn't been able to sleep. So he had gotten up and gone outside. He said, "Look up to the north."

I walked around the corner of the house and it looked like dawn was breaking in the north. The clouds were white as if someone had snapped on a giant electric light bulb.

North of us was the British XXX Corps. Something was happening that I had never seen before. The clouds were lit up for miles. I asked Sergeant Hughes what the Germans were doing.

"Well," he said, "they've been messing around shooting mortars and every once in a while they'll shoot a flare."

Now and then they would cut loose with a machine gun.

I said, "I guess they're expecting an attack, but I don't think there's going to be one tonight. I haven't heard anything about it."

We stopped to listen and we could hear mortars firing. We were facing east and from our left to our right we could hear them as clearly as if the tubes were across the street. Then the first shell exploded and drifted down and fell through the clouds. They were parachute flares, hundreds of them, falling through the clouds with smoke drifting away from them as they burned.

There was no wind, and the flares sank straight down toward the snow, turning it a dazzling white. Most of the flares were white, but at intervals a red one or a green one would appear. By the time the last one dropped through the clouds, the first was burning out on the ground. They settled down one by one, making pools of light all over the snowfields. It was one of the most beautiful sights that I have ever seen. Herr Krings states in his book that the flares that night were the result of a coordinated effort of all of the units from Posterholdt south beyond Karken. This was a joint effort of the infantry and artillery.

The Germans had lighted up six miles of the front at the same time that night — no small job of coordination. They clearly believed an attack was coming soon and they had hoped to catch us out there naked in the light of the flares. When the last of the flares had burned out, I shucked my boots and crawled back into the sack. Dawn was coming.

Next morning after breakfast, I was waiting for a second cup of coffee to cool when a corporal from Headquarters Battery came in and said there was an old man who wanted to see me. I told him I didn't know any old man around here.

"He doesn't know you, either," the corporal said, "but he needs to talk to somebody and we thought you'd be the best one to speak to him."

I got up and went outside. The man was in his sixties and bundled up against the cold in a heavy dark coat. I recognized him as the miller from the north side of town. His face was red, maybe from the cold, maybe because he was mad. He spoke no English and we talked through an interpreter, Capt. Ken Zierler, our surgeon. He was sore as hell because every day when he cranked up his mill to grind flour for the few Germans who were still in Kirchhoven, the soldiers across the Roer would start shooting at it with artillery. He wanted me to do something about it.

I said, "What do you want me to do?"

"Shoot at them," he said.

He said he could tell me where the Germans were.

I said, "I would like to know that, but I can't guarantee you we'll blast them the next time they start shooting at you."

He told me where the German guns were and I marked it down.

"Look," I said, "when things start happening around here, there's not going to be anybody shooting at you. In the meantime, instead of you grinding grain in the daytime and letting those people east of the river see your sails turning, why don't you grind at night?"

He pulled his hands out of his overcoat pocket and shrugged. "There's not much wind at night, but I'll try."

He thrust his hands back into his pocket and walked off, a dark figure against the snow. He ran his mill at night until we left three days later.

That afternoon, things were quiet and George Salisbury and I were prowling around Kirchhoven seeing what we could find. We came out of a house just in time to see two men approaching, riding bicycles.

We couldn't believe what we were seeing. They had on long-tailed coats, striped pants, starched white shirts, black ties, and tall silk hats. Top hats in the middle of a war! They looked exactly alike. They looked like they were going to a royal ball, except that they were both in need of a shave and they had M-1 rifles slung over their shoulders.

I went out and stopped them. "Where in the hell are you going?" I asked.

One of them grinned. "We're a contact patrol. We're going to Posterholdt."

I had to laugh. "You're really dressed for it."

They'd found the clothes in a German's house. On down the road they went, coattails flapping in the breeze, pedaling their bicycles furiously.

Maybe they were right. On this day, if you were going to Posterholdt, that was the way to go. The road was high and the distance between the Roer and the road at this point was less than a thousand yards.

Every day, a patrol went down the road to Posterholdt to check with the first platoon of Company C, 137th Infantry. There were no phones and every night there would be a small fire fight. The Germans were constantly probing at them. No Americans were killed, but every night, they'd kill one or two Germans.

The two on the bicycles had a sense of humor and plenty of guts. They could have been picked off any time.

9 From the Roer to the Rhine

February 26, 1945 to March 3, 1945

As the 35th Infantry Division headed northwest to gain maneuvering room for the XVI Corps, General Anderson alerted a combat command of the 8th Armored Division (Brig. Gen. John W. Devine) to cross the Roer on February 27 and take up the fight to the north. At the end of February and in early March, events proved conclusively that "the battlefield belonged to armor." American units recorded advances of seven to ten miles all along the front.

On February 26, we were ordered to relieve a battalion of the British 7th Armored Division in and around Montfort and St. Odilienberg, Holland. We rolled in late the next afternoon cold and hungry, met the British, got a hot meal, and went to bed.

That night, the Germans shot some "screaming memes" in our direction, but they were off and did no damage. One round hit close to Battalion Headquarters, but failed to explode. I took a look at it lying in the road. It was a mean looking thing, twelve inches in diameter and three feet long, with a rocket motor on the back of it. It was dangerous and we put up barricades to keep tanks and other vehicles from running over it and setting it off.

In the morning, Colonel Lilly and I drove to the CP of the British Armored Division Artillery Battalion, whose area we were taking over. The lieutenant colonel in command was a tall, gangling, awkward-looking man with a red mustache that dominated his face. He was wearing a heavy, coarse uniform and a tam.

The British colonel told Colonel Lilly that we would need to go to St. Odilienberg to be shown their forward observation posts. Colonel Lilly said, "All right," the British colonel said, "Right-o," and I jumped into the back seat of the jeep.

The Limey colonel shook his head. "Captain," he said, "we are not going up there in a jeep. We would not get 500 yards. Those German bastards in those woods over there would get all of us."

We were going to go in a British tank that was around the corner of the CP building, with its motor running. The colonel pointed to it and smiled.

"In a tank is the only way that we can get to St. Odilienberg. The road is high and solid and those woods over there are held by the Germans." He was pointing to the northeast to Heide woods. "Those woods over there," pointing to the right, "are held by some of our infantry."

I was wondering how we were all going to get into the tank; it was not that big. We all began to climb onto the deck of the tank and into the turret when the Limey said, "Captain, there is no room for you inside."

"What?" I said.

"No," he said. "You ride on the back. Sit on that canvas there." He pointed to a heavy, folded sheet of canvas near the right rear corner of the tank deck. The bad thing was that the dirty bastard meant what he said.

The tank started off, up the road to St. Odilienberg, with me on the back and the turret half buttoned up. One rabbit ear was down, the other one up. All that I could see of the British colonel was the top of his tam now and then. I started watching the northeast where the Germans were and I decided that as soon as I saw a muzzle flash or heard the first shell pass by, that I was coming off the tank and into a ditch and to hell with it. The first shell didn't come, or if we were shot at I didn't know it.

The British colonel took us on a tour of their observation post. It was a once fine three-story house on the west bank of the Roer River with an extensive kitchen garden in the rear of the house. It looked like a graveyard, as there were several graves scattered around and about. I asked the colonel why so many graves were there and what had happened to those fellows.

"This place gets a lot of artillery fire," he said. "It's pretty hot here at times. That's what happened to them."

He led us up to the attic of the house where we could look to the east and he pointed northeast toward the village of Malik, occupied by the German forces, and indicated where he thought their artillery positions were. There were earthworks, anti-tank ditches, communication trenches, and strong points on the ground. Obviously, there was a lot of stuff between St. Odilienberg, Holland, and Malik, Germany. I did not see any Germans walking around, of course, but in some areas smoke was coming out of pipes in the ground, so there was infantry dug in with a fire going.

Their artillery positions, he thought, were in the western edge of a large forest some distance beyond Malik. I could not see any guns, but I was sure that they were there because they couldn't have been any place else. The ground between Malik and the woods was open. If there were guns in between, we could have seen them.

He also pointed out some likely places where we might get across the Roer. We returned to Montfort the same way we came, with me "sitting on that canvas there," and the Limey colonel's head sticking out of the turret now and then. Again the Germans did not fire.

We arrived in Montfort about noon and Colonel Lilly and I went to have a look at the British battery positions. They used twenty-five pounders, a gun as opposed to a howitzer. It fired a smaller shell weighing twenty-five pounds, with a flatter trajectory and a higher muzzle velocity than our 105mm howitzers. Our 105mms fired a thirty-four-pound shell and were more effective.

The British were old hands at fighting; however, they seemed lax to us. None wore steel helmets, some wore tams and suspenders, and many of the uniforms were different. They seemed to mill about a lot in the battery positions and spent some time drinking tea, usually at 3:00 P.M. sharp. At that time the officers would get together for gin. As we were relieving them, two of our battery commanders joined them for a gin in the afternoon. One got drunk and the other had to have him transported back to his battery. I wondered, as I saw the way that they were dressed and laid around, what would happen if they were in Third Army and General Patton showed up. It would have been something to see.

While we were visiting the British, the Germans put several rounds of 105mm fire in the B Battery position. One of the half-tracks was backing up and the driver was leaning out of the open door, looking back. A shell hit nearby and a fragment struck him in the back of the head, killing him instantly. He was Tech. 5th Grade John F. McCall, Jr., our first casualty.

The next day, we completed the relief and took over all of the British positions. My job then was to go to St. Odilienberg, organize an observation team, register the battalion's guns, and get ready to do some shooting.

Like the British colonel, I decided to go in a tank, but I would not treat my people like that bastard treated me. I assured myself that there was ample room inside the tank; if not, then I would use two tanks. Lt. Sam Blatman, Sgt. Arnold Erpelding and I with the tank crew went on the first trip. We made it up the dangerous road to St. Odilienberg without being shot at. I decided to take over the British OP in the attic of the three-story house on the west bank of the Roer. I then returned to Montfort.

Colonel Lilly said that we would use wire communication instead of radio as the British had. He ordered Lieutenant Weldon to lay wire from the fire direction center in Montfort to the new OP. Wire is much more secure than radio. The Germans probably were tuned in to the British radio net and heard everything that they said. Weldon had the job of laying a line up the road under German observation, not too nice a job. A wire truck stringing wire moves slowly and can be easily picked off. Weldon and his wire crew rigged their spools of wire on the deck of one of our tanks, and off they went, trailing wire behind them. The Sherman moved up the road, flanked by our troops and the Germans, and arrived at the OP in St. Odilienberg at 1:00 P.M. I knew that the wire was in when the telephone rang. Colonel Lilly then told me to go to the OP and register Battery B, the center battery. Things were going to start happening. I headed to the OP in a tank, wondering as always when the Germans would shoot.

When I arrived at the OP I found a British captain, about thirty-five years old and a veteran of the North African campaign, calmly eyeing the Germans with a spotting scope as if he were watching the races.

Observing through a hole in the tile roof of the attic, I selected the corner of the raised brick-paved churchyard as my registration point (base point). While working out the coordinates I noticed a group of German soldiers standing in front of a house across the street from the church. This was even better and, because I could pinpoint the house on my map, I was able to get the exact coordinates of the structure. I called the information in to fire direction and asked Major Oliver, the operations officer, for one round.

It hit about fifty yards beyond the Germans and scared them. One man ran across the churchyard and into some trees; the rest ran into the house that I was shooting at. The deflection was good and the only correction to make was to shorten the range to put the howitzer on the target. I gave Major Oliver the adjustment and requested a converged sheath and fire for effect. Soon all six of Battery B's guns fired as one and all of their shells hit the house. Red dust and other debris flew high into the air. By using a converged sheath, all of the shells impacted in a small area as opposed to placing the shells in relation to the howitzer's position on the ground.

Jan van der Steen, a historian from the Netherlands, has written me that the building (house) was the rectory of the church across the street. At that time it was being used as the command post of a parachute infantry company of the Regiment Mueller. He stated in his letter that the house was cut to ground level and completely destroyed.

I was feeling a little smug when the Germans evened the score a bit. They knew where I was, no doubt about it. Their first shell hit the front steps and shook the house. At this point I ordered Blatman and Erpelding to take cover in our tank parked just behind the house. They were down the steps and gone.

Meantime, another shell arrived, barely missing the top of the house and landing in the backyard. It threw mud all over the tank and two large chunks came through the roof, landing near my feet. I was sitting on a tall stool looking through the hole in the tile roof. I came off my perch, crawled under a heavy oak table, and called fire direction.

"We've already gotten two back and another one is coming. I can hear it." The telephone was open when it hit downstairs and fire direction heard it. The house heaved again and I was sure that the next one would come into the attic.

Then I noticed the British captain. He was breaking tiles off of the roof with his rifle butt. When the hole was large enough, he wiggled through until, from the waist up, he was outside. From my sheltered place, I could see him trying to pick up the flashes of the German gun with his field glasses. Feeling like two cents, and with shells still falling, I came from under the table and walked over and apologized.

"Oh, Yank," he said, "when you have been at this as long as I have, it won't bother you."

A tank soon arrived in back of the house and Colonel Lilly joined us. "How did it go, Tex?"

"I have a good registration," I said.

"Tell you what," he said, "call up fire direction and tell them to shoot a battalion concentration on the base point."

I called it in to fire direction and soon Oliver came back. "On the way," he said.

The shells soon arrived. *Whoomp! Whoomp! Whoomp!*

Six black mushrooms of smoke grew out of the base point. Battery B was right on it. Batteries A and C were off to the left and over by about a thousand yards, out in the flooded area.

Colonel Lilly got mad, threw down the pad in his hand, and started cussing like few that I have ever heard.

I called Major Oliver. "Look," I said, "there is a problem. We are off the base point. B is okay, but A and C are a thousand yards over and are together." I ordered one round from the last setting of the base piece of Battery A.

The round came over shortly, arcing its way into the floodwaters of the Roer. It hit a thousand yards over and 500 yards left. In three rounds, I had A on the base point. Then I asked for a round from Battery C's base piece at the same setting of its last round. Same thing, way off to the left and over. I soon brought Battery C to the base point, then called for a one-round battalion concentration on the base point.

They all came in as they were supposed to, blowing the hell out of everything around the house. Each battery position was about 150 yards wide, which meant all of the shells of the eighteen howitzers hit in the same small area, a block about 150 yards wide and 100 yards deep. Mission accomplished.

We were set and registered and ready to fire. If anything came up, we were ready to blast the hell out of it. Colonel Lilly nodded soberly and got in his tank and left. I stayed until Blatman came to take over the OP, then got in a tank and went on back to Montfort.

In Montfort we began to get intelligence summaries from Division G-2. I read them, edited them, and sent out excerpts to the batteries on things that directly concerned them. The following is from the 8th Armored Division G-2 report of February 22:

ARTILLERY: The organic weapons of 183rd Infantry Division ap-

> pear to be concentrated in the south between BLADBACK and LOVENICK. One light battalion of the 176th Division is believed to be in WILDENRATH area with two remaining light battalions of this division and its organic medium battalion occupying Western edge of EMPTER WALD opposite ROERMOND. An additional medium battalion is believed to be in the same area. Heavy and medium pieces of about battalion strength have been located in MEINWEG area. Approximately ten batteries of dual purpose guns are thinly spread in the area behind the organic artillery across the Corps front. One RAILWAY gun has been firing from positions along RR and DALHEIM and WEGBERG and in the north and a second gun is believed to be operating in the south along RR between ERKELENZ and WICKRAY. Reports indicate that rocket type weapons are also operating in the Corps front. (XVI Corps, Pr sixteen.)

The guns in Empter Wald were probably the ones that had been shooting at us.

In combat situation, it's vital to know the units in front of you, whether they are Waffen SS, Volkstrum, Volksgrenadier, or Panzer. As the G-2 reports filtered in, I learned that in the area of St. Odilienberg, we were opposed by elements of four parachute regiments and the 116 Panzer Division. The Regiment Mueller, the First, Second and Third Battalions, had been identified on our front.

There was a rumor that some SS were in front of us. It set our teeth on edge. They were tough fighters and they had the reputation of being brutal and inhumane. The Panzer Lehr Division was north of us. In the beginning, the Panzer Lehr was a training division, like the 8th Armored. Both divisions furnished cadres for new divisions then being formed. The Panzer Lehr Division quit furnishing cadres in early 1942 and the 8th Armored in February 1943. They were in front of us from the time we reached the Roer River until we advanced eastward to the Harz Mountains. The Panzer Lehr and the 116th Panzer Divisions were among our adversaries during most of our fighting. The only survivors of these two divisions were the officers and men on the division staff. Most of the soldiers were killed or captured by our division.

At St. Odilienberg, we sat waiting as the flood waters of the Roer gradually subsided.

Finally, the war started to heat up for us. We were ordered to reduce Heide Woods south of Roermond, Holland, and to prepare for a crossing of the Roer. We looked it over, taking tanks out for a reconnaissance on a bone-chilling morning. Heide Woods was a patch of woodlands of about 320 acres, with snow clustering the tree tops and

Germans clustering down below. Combat Command Reserve (CCR) of our division was going to attack the woods and kill or capture the Germans defending it.

It would have been possible, I thought, to put artillery on the woods and blast the Germans out, but headquarters chose to send infantry in and dig them out. It took two or three days and some hard fighting, and we suffered some casualties. The German paratroopers put up a ferocious defense. With regard to shelling the Germans out of the woods, there were some fourteen artillery battalions available for this task.

After CCR had taken the woods, we were ready to go. Suddenly, everything changed. We were told that the Ninth Army was to attack across the Roer and advance northeast to Wesel and force a crossing of the Rhine. We were ordered to cross the Roer on a bridge at Hilfarth, and from there we were to drive northeast abreast and east of Combat Command A (CCA) to Lintfort, Rhineberg, and Wesel. Our orders arrived by messenger at 10:30 A.M. on February 27.

CCA of the 8th Armored Division was to pass through the 35th Infantry Division that night and attack to the northeast; CCB and CCR were to follow. CCA was alerted and soon afterward CCB then a little later CCR were ordered to move out. Soon all three combat commands were on the roads, in approach march formations, leading out of the Montfort, Holland, area.

An approach march formation was used when contact with the enemy was expected. It consisted of a point, the support, then the main body of the command. The point was usually no larger than a squad of infantry or an armored car; the support was usually a platoon of infantry or a platoon of tanks. The artillery marched at the head of the main body followed by the tanks and infantry. The term "marching" does not mean that all the soldiers were walking down the road. In an armored division everyone rode in one kind of vehicle or another — tanks, half-tracks, M-7s, jeeps, and trucks. The artillery marched at the head of the main body of the command so it could get off the road and into firing position quickly, if needed, and the rest of the command could move up. The artillery would go into any area near the road that was large enough, about ten acres, and free of trees or obstructions in the direction of the enemy. Behind the artillery marched the tank battalion and the infantry battalion, less the point and the support. Sometimes the order of march was reversed and the infantry was directly behind the artillery tanks behind them. If the situation

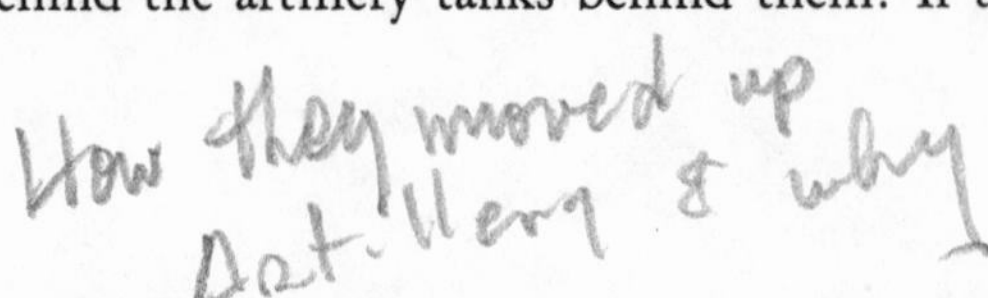

was fluid, the tanks would be forward so that they could get in the rear of the enemy and do more damage and cause more confusion. But, if severe resistance was expected, the infantry went ahead of the tanks so that they could wipe the resistance out.

That was how we were at Montfort, all three combat commands lined up in this order of march, each one over a mile long.

The day was February 27, the weather miserable, with rain and sleet and light snow in the early afternoon. CCA moved up to the Roer at daylight. The river was only twenty yards wide, but it was swift, and the east bank was treacherously slick and with a steep bank. The engineers had constructed a small pontoon bridge across it at the German village of Hilfarth, and CCA moved across it in the morning as we waited in column behind.

In the half-track with me was the driver, Corporal Roth, Sergeant Hale, and three radio operators, Corporals Wakeman, Mahood, and Pottish. As we waited for our turn on the bridge, I saw two bodies lying in water just off the side of the road. They were American soldiers that had been killed while trying to get the bridge across. It bothered me to see them lying there, killed in a little horse-shit German village not worth a damn for anything. The irony of it grated. It was mid-day by the time our column rolled up to the bridge.

A guide waved us on and the first half-track edged onto the swaying, rocking pontoons, then tanks and M-7s followed slowly after. The high, slick bank on the east side of the river was trouble for tanks, but they went, skidding and slipping, engines revving up to full power. It was another cold day and by the time the last of them made it up the incline, it had begun to snow. We moved on to Huckelhoven, just on the other side of the river. The first thing that I saw was the body of a German officer stretched out on the sidewalk. He was shot up and lying in a big pool of blood, his field glasses lying in front of him. He seemed to have been in dress uniform as I noticed that he was wearing dress boots and blouse. Just across the street from him, on the left side, was the body of a German soldier in a sitting position with a stomach wound. An aid man had worked on him but he was dead, sitting there in the doorway.

In Huckelhoven, we didn't know what we were facing. We pulled up and waited for orders. They soon came. We were to move north parallel to the Roer and to attack the next town, Arsbeck. The 36th Tank Battalion started immediately, with half-tracks and M-7s following. Resistance was light and Arsbeck was taken before dark.

About five miles north of town, the column stopped.

Meanwhile, some of the 49th came up on foot, rifles slung, snow on their clothes, boots crunching on the icy road. Their half-tracks were in the column behind us. By that time, the mercury had dropped to about twenty-two degrees. Since there was little traffic on the radio, I thought there might be some kind of problem near the head of the column. I talked to Colonel Lilly and decided to walk on ahead and see what was happening. It took me fifteen minutes to get to the head of the column. Here I found an anti-tank ditch, quite wide and deep. It was 5:30 P.M. and dark.

A platoon of the 53rd engineers was working under lights to build a bridge over the anti-tank ditch so we could cross. Three tanks were in position, near the bridging operation, to defend the engineers. Every time the Germans in some heavy woods some 400 yards away fired at the engineers, the tanks would blast the woods.

It was 6:30 P.M. when I started back to my half-track. I was cold and hungry and had the blues. A short distance from the ditch, I came to a fire with twenty soldiers around it. I asked one of the men what they were doing.

"Just trying to keep warm, Captain."

I asked him what they were burning.

"Furniture," he said, jerking his head toward some German houses nearby. "We got it out of them houses over there." I was cold, too, and I couldn't care less if they burned some German's furniture. I stayed there about an hour, sharing a K-ration with a corporal, before heading back to my half-track to take a nap. I had hardly dropped off to sleep before Sergeant Hale woke me up and said that the colonel wanted to know what they were doing up ahead now. I climbed out of my half-track and hiked off again to the anti-tank ditch; the bridging was nearly finished.

When I passed the fire again at about 2:00 A.M., all the furniture had gone up in smoke. The GIs were now burning the houses one at a time. It took about forty-five minutes per house. By the time the bridge was finished, six houses had been burned.

The tanks started to move again at 3:00 A.M., raking the woods with machine gun and cannon fire as they passed by. As we passed, still in the dark, the woods were quiet, the Germans in them having either been killed or driven away.

A little after daylight, after we had moved several miles, a German 40mm, double-barreled anti-aircraft gun opened up on some vehicles ahead of us from a hidden position near some houses. They were shooting at some trucks and jeeps near the rear of the 36th Tank Battalion column. They apparently thought that all of the tanks had moved on. One was nearby and the commander of the tank could see the muzzle flashes of the guns. The Sherman's turret swung around and he shot the German gunners with his 76mm with two accurate shots. We could barely see the flashes as they hit. The column moved on, and as we passed I noticed that the gun, now tilting crazily on its carriage, had eight rings painted on one of its barrels, indicating it had brought down eight airplanes. Their war was over. The crew was dead, their bodies scattered around the gun.

The war was over, too, for the Germans holding Wachtendonk, another town on our line of march. The town was cleared by midmorning, March 4, sending lines of gray-clad German infantry marching toward the rear under a guard of MPs. We kept moving, heading for Aldekerk cross-country over sandy ground. The going was slow through the sand and it was 10:00 A.M. the following day, a Sunday, before Aldekerk was cleared. We settled into some houses soon after we arrived. I slung my carbine and walked to the center of town.

The central plaza was a block square and paved with cobblestones, and in the center of the plaza stood a large bulletin board eight feet high and twenty feet long, with glass doors mounted three feet above the ground. It was made of varnished hardwood and the hinges and fastening were of polished brass. This was the bulletin board of the Hitler Youth organization with the orders, propaganda, and bullshit still on it. Aldekerk must have had a large Hitler Youth group. I wondered where they were now.

The battalion was billeted in some houses in the southeast part of town. Nearby was a company of the 49th Infantry. I just returned to battalion headquarters when a soldier came in, saying excitedly that there was trouble up the street. I asked him what was wrong.

He said, "A woman there says that two soldiers raped her and killed a girl."

He had been walking along the street when the woman rushed hysterically out of a house. He spoke a little German and had asked her what the problem was.

He led me to the house where she and another woman lived. The women, in their mid to late forties, were still tearful and distraught. They said that they had been raped. I sent the soldier to get an interpreter and an aid man.

When the interpreter arrived, he learned from the women that each of them had been raped by two men. They gave me detailed descriptions of the two soldiers and said that they had taken a fifteen-year-old Polish girl with them. The women thought the men had raped or killed her, or both.

I asked the calmer of the two, "Where did they take her?"

When she answered, her voice was firm. "I do not know. Perhaps the barn over there."

We went to the barn and found the Polish girl. She was alive, and had been badly beaten. One of the men had hit her so hard in the back of the head with his M-1 rifle the stock was broken. The girl had put up a terrific fight, but she was in a bad way. I sent the aid man on the run for Captain Zierler, our surgeon, and when he arrived, they got the girl on a stretcher. She was unconscious. He could not tell whether or not she was going to live.

Zierler found a German doctor in a hospital and the girl was admitted. This was a brutal and senseless act. It made me mad. I had not been close to anything like that before, and it bothered me more than anything that I had seen in Germany. I was determined to find and prefer charges against the two soldiers.

I already knew who one of them was. The description the two women had given us was enough. I found him in a nearby company of the 49th Infantry. From some of the men in the 49th that I talked to, we found who the other man was. He was a Counter Intelligence Corps sergeant. I was trying to sort things out when we were alerted. I promised myself that I would get them the next time we stopped and I had time to spare. Now, though, a runner arrived with the information that I was needed in the CP as we had received orders to move to the Rhine.

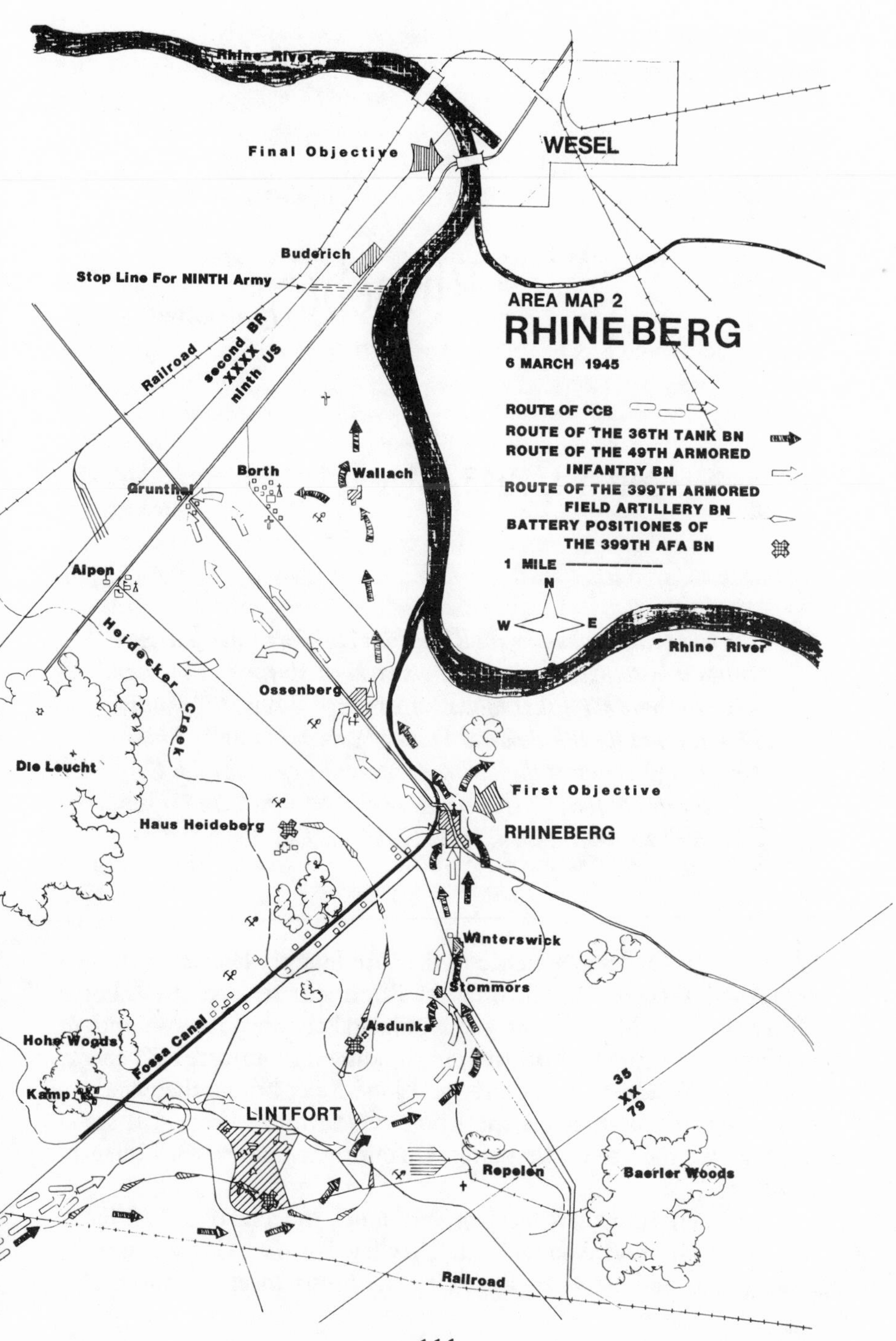
AREA MAP 2
RHINEBERG
6 MARCH 1945
ROUTE OF CCB
ROUTE OF THE 36TH TANK BN
ROUTE OF THE 49TH ARMORED INFANTRY BN
ROUTE OF THE 399TH ARMORED FIELD ARTILLERY BN
BATTERY POSITIONES OF THE 399TH AFA BN
1 MILE
N
W
E
Rhine River
Rhine River
WESEL
Final Objective
Buderich
Stop Line For NINTH Army
Railroad
second BR
XXXX
ninth US
Borth
Wallach
Grunthal
Alpen
Heidecker Creek
Ossenberg
Die Leucht
Haus Heideberg
First Objective
RHINEBERG
Winterswick
Stommors
Asdunks
Hohe Woods
Fossa Canal
Kamp
LINTFORT
35
XX
79
Repelen
Baerler Woods
Railroad

10 Rhineberg

March 4, 1945–March 12, 1945

The four bridges spanning the Rhine from Duisburg north had been destroyed by the Germans when dawn broke on March 5. The great structures were but a twisted mass of wreckage. The 35th Infantry Division and the 8th Armored Division gathered to strike Rhineberg, two miles west of the Rhine. Resistance was stiffening as German paratroops threw a ring of steel in front of Wesel, the only escape outlet for what was left of the German army.

On March 5, CCB was attached to the 35th Infantry Division and then combined with the 137th Infantry Regiment to form Task Force Murry, Colonel Murry being the regimental commander. We moved northeast from Aldekerk at daylight, heading for Lintfort, Rhineberg, and Wesel. We were to capture the Rhine River bridge there and establish a bridgehead across the Rhine. One Rhine bridge still stood and that was the one we were after. On our right was the 83rd Infantry Division.

We were told there was not very much in front of us. As far as G-2 knew, there were no tanks and very few 88s. But G-2 was wrong, as we would find out later. Expecting light resistance, we moved out.

It was March 5, a misty, cloudy day with the temperature in the low forties. We were glad to leave Aldekerk. It had been a trouble spot. Besides the rapes, some men found a lot of wine in the houses and had gotten drunk. One group began to drink five gallons of green schnapps, bottled in 1944, cloudy and super potent. When we got our orders to move out, some of the men in one of the batteries looked like boiled owls.

We were alerted during the night and the battalion moved across country soon afterward in a modified-approach march formation. The support force was the 49th Infantry. We were next, followed by the 36th Tank Battalion. The land was sandy and fairly flat. We came to a road that went north and then made a half turn to the right and headed for Lintfort.

To our left, about 600 yards away, was some high, wooded country, rising 300 to 500 feet for several miles. The hills reached in from the north and cut back toward the east and gradually flattened out before reaching Lintfort. North of us and west of Lintfort was the little town of Kamp. Immediately in front of us, about 400 yards away, was a crossroad with three buildings clustered around it.

After passing through Lintfort, the 49th Infantry hit a hornet's nest of Germans, the main body of the force defending Rhineberg and the Wesel Bridge.

Colonel Kimbell, commanding Combat Command B, ordered us off the road and sent the 36th Tank rushing through us to the aid of the 49th Infantry. We were to follow the tanks.

While we were stopped, a soldier came to the head of the column and told me something had happened in one of the firing batteries. He had heard that a corporal had been killed by a non-com that morning. Then Captain Zierler, the surgeon, came up and said he needed to talk to me. He looked upset. "What's the matter?" I asked.

"A man was killed this morning."

"Who killed him?"

"His first sergeant," Zierler said.

The corporal had gotten too much raw schnapps, he said, and passed out. When we were alerted to move, the first sergeant had roused the man and sent him outside, but the corporal came back in and jumped the first sergeant. The corporal was a big man, six-feet-two and weighing 240 pounds, and the sergeant was a small man. In defending himself, the sergeant had hit the corporal on the side of the head with the butt of his carbine and killed him.

The battery commander was forward and didn't know anything about it. Zierler shrugged and went back to his medical detachment at the rear of service battery. I sat there thinking it was a stupid way to get killed when the Germans were trying their best to kill us anyway. The sergeant was relieved, put under arrest, and sent back to the division rear for trial. We never heard from him again.

Around 11:00 we moved up to the crossroads and stopped on some high ground. To the west of me, I heard machine guns firing and could see men running and falling. Then the Germans, on the hill to our left, started shelling our column, the rounds falling very close. We were bracketed once and Corporal Roth moved our half-track up the road where it couldn't be seen so easily by the German artillery observers.

While stopped, three ambulances and two litter jeeps came by and the Germans put hot fire around them. They had two guns firing at once and the rounds exploded simultaneously on either side of the first ambulance, each of the shells hitting about sixty feet away. They missed and the ambulances and the two litter jeeps cleared the area with heavy feet on the gas. Meantime, I got a radio call from CCB wanting Colonel Lilly. They couldn't get him, so they talked to me. They wanted our surgeon and aid men in Lintfort. There were a lot of casualties and they needed help. I called Zierler at the medical detachment. He gave me a quick answer. "No."

Zierler said his responsibility was not with the infantry and the tankers, but with the 399th. If we got into it and had casualties, there would be no one to take care of them.

We started to move again and reached Lintfort at 4:00 in the afternoon. The days were getting longer and we still had several hours of daylight. Moving along an eight-foot stucco wall on our left, which separated some mines from the road, we went a short distance before pulling into the front yard of a three-story building, occupied by a miners' union headquarters. I ran the people there out and we set up our fire direction center.

An hour had gone by before we were set up and had established communications with the firing batteries. We hadn't heard from Colonel Lilly since noon, and with Major Collins on detached service at division artillery, the only officers left in the command post were Maj. Matt Oliver and me.

I told Oliver I would try to find Colonel Lilly and get a handle on the situation. For a start, I'd heard that CCB had a forward command post nearby. I would try that first. I slung my carbine on my shoulder and started walking.

A few hundred yards down the street, I ran into a couple of infantrymen with M-1s and hand grenades slung on their packstraps. While we were talking, two German soldiers, their hands clasped on their steel helmets, ran out of a house and surrendered. The two infantrymen warned me not to walk in the street by myself. "There are Germans behind you," he said.

I said, "It looks like you two are out here in this street by yourselves."

One of the men wagged his head, making the grenades on his packstraps jiggle.

"Nope, we're not," he said. "Our whole platoon is here, there and yonder."

To show they were not alone, they pointed out the rest of the platoon's positions. I went back and got a jeep with a machine gun, then started out again.

Though it was nearly 8:00, it was still daylight. I picked my way carefully through the streets of Lintfort, and somewhere south of town I ran into the commanding officer of the 88th Cavalry Reconnaissance Squadron. He didn't know much more about what was going on than I did. He said his command had been split up. One troop was with CCA, another with CCB, and a third with CCR. The one with CCB was scattered all over the place and he had lost communication. He told me that normally he stayed with the attacking combat command, but this time he was up trying to find his people. I asked him which way the units had gone. He shrugged and shook his head.

We knew they had gone northeast toward Rhineberg, but there were several ways to approach the town and we didn't know which one to take. He drove off one way, I the other.

Before long, I came to the medical clearing station of the 49th Infantry, a one-story stucco house surrounded by a lawn with the road running in front of it. Some of the battalion's wounded were lying on the lawn in front, the dead off to the left. Three medics were working on the wounded. I counted thirty-eight wounded men. The aid men were cleaning and treating wounds and the surgeon was operating. I scouted the area and didn't see any of our people, so I got back in the jeep and headed back to the battalion.

It was dark by the time I got there and Major Oliver still hadn't heard anything, so I thought I would try another direction. I started off on foot. I'd walked about 500 yards and I was approaching a cross-road when I heard voices and the sound of marching feet. I stepped back into the dark doorway of a house.

Suddenly, German soldiers were going past me. Four hundred at least. But they were prisoners now, dejected men shuffling along. A few guards were with them, infantry from the 49th with M-1s cradled in their arms, an officer from the 49th in charge. I stopped him. He was wearing a steel helmet and a couple of days' growth of beard. I asked him what was going on but he didn't know either. He pointed back down the road the prisoners had just come down and told me his outfit was down there, pinned down since 10:00 that morning. They had lost one or two company commanders, he said. He had no idea where anything was or what was going on.

I asked him where the 36th Tank Battalion was and he gave me a long, glassy look. "I don't know," he said. Then he turned and swung off down the road after the column of gray-clad, shuffling POWs. I was getting nowhere. I turned around and headed back to the CP.

Colonel Lilly arrived soon after I did, and he'd had a bad day. He dropped his gear on the floor, poured a cup of coffee, and told us about it. He left us, he said, before the column was stopped short of the crossroad to let the tanks pass through and had gone to find Colonel Kimbell, commanding officer of CCB. In Lintfort, he left his jeep beside one of the big houses when a German soldier came running out of a basement at him. Colonel Lilly drew his .45 and fatally shot him in the chest. The German went down as if he'd been hit in the head with an ax.

Colonel Lilly was looking down at the German soldier lying crumpled on his back when Captain Salisbury drove up in his jeep. Traveling together, they took a road northeast. They were soon stopped by a storm of machine gun fire from some nearby houses. There was no way they could drive away from it so they scrambled out of their jeeps and dove for the ditch. They were pinned down for more than an hour when Colonel Lilly's driver, Corporal Fisher, was badly hit. About the same time, Lieutenant Verlinder, who arrived with Captain Salisbury, saw a German soldier about thirty yards away struggling to get a machine gun loaded. It looked like the belt on his gun had jammed. It was the pause Verlinder had been waiting for. He opened up on the gunner with his carbine and the others soon joined in. The German gunner went down before he could get his gun firing again.

They took advantage of that respite to evacuate Corporal Fischer. Colonel Lilly came back to the battalion CP, still in the dark about the battle situation. It was a part of the war that would soon become familiar: confusion.

Next morning, orders came for us to move. Headquarters and the batteries packed up and rolled out of Lintfort toward a farmstead compound named Asdunks.

Rhineberg, hub of a railroad, canal and roads, was about two miles west of the Rhine River, where it makes a bend and goes north to Wesel. The only way we could get from Lintfort to Wesel and the bridge we were after was to go through Rhineberg. The country is low; there are estuaries off the Rhine and many canals without bridges. We had to take Rhineberg to get the roads before we could go north to Wesel.

On the map, Asdunks was shown as a small black square, but it was actually a farmer's house, two stories high and very old with a square enclosing a paved courtyard. The front, facing east, was where the living quarters were. Along the north side were rooms for various supplies. The other two sides were used as barns and stables.

The owner was a stocky, brown-haired man of about thirty-eight, his wife a typical German farm woman with dark blonde hair, a solid physique, and three cute kids. He must have been a good Nazi at one time, judging by the pictures of him we found in the house, but now he was subdued and quiet. I told him to stay in his quarters with his wife and children and to keep the doors locked and not try to leave.

"Ja vohl, mein capitan," he said, nodding vigorously. His wife nodded, too. They backed off and we continued searching the place.

In one of the rooms, we found two foreign girls, Russian. They told me that at first they had been with the German army for about six months in a traveling whorehouse, one of the field brothels the German army operated. Then they had been sent to Asdunks for a year to work. They said once they'd gotten to Asdunks, they had been treated well.

We established headquarters in the farmhouse and put the guns in positions close enough to cover Rhineberg, Ossenberg, and Wesel and to shoot across the Rhine River.

On March 7 the sky cleared, and with the sun warming us, the day was fine. By early morning, we had telephone communications with two observation posts in Rhineberg and one north of the town. The wire section under Lieutenant Weldon had begun at dawn and laid wires along a north-south road from Asdunks to Rhineberg. The lines were in, tested, and working by 7:30 in the morning. Around 9:00 the lines went dead.

Weldon thought the lines had been cut by artillery fire. The lines had been laid in a ditch along the road, and the road was being shelled constantly by guns about a thousand yards across the Rhine, mostly 150mm howitzers with a few 105s mixed in. The Germans had been keeping a steady fire on the road, the shells hitting the road, ditches and a few adjacent houses. Weldon said he guessed they had probably clipped his wires. While laying the wire, the crew had to hit the ditches several times and the wire truck was hit by small fragments a time or two.

Groaning, he turned out his wire crew and headed back down the road from Asdunks to Rhineberg, trouble shooting. They would go about a quarter of a mile down the line and splice a telephone to the line, and ring it. If the fire direction center answered, that meant the break was further down the line. They soon found the break about halfway to Rhineberg near a house on the same side of the road as the line. It was a two-story structure with several outbuildings, and there was another house about fifty yards from the break in the line. Weldon guessed that the Germans had been trying to hit the houses and one of their shells had cut the wire. The crew found the break and fixed it, then pushed on into Rhineberg to look into some telephone problems there.

By the time they reached Rhineberg and set up their gear, the line was dead again. The first break had been repaired at 9:00 in the morning. The line went dead again at 10:30. Weldon turned his jeep around and started off down the road to Asdunks again. They found the break in almost the same place as before. It had been cut, but not by a shell fragment, which cuts it cleanly. This time it wasn't a clean cut.

With artillery rounds landing uncomfortably close to them, they fixed the wire again, but Cpl. Thomas Palmer, who was in charge of one of the wire details, decided to find out what was causing the break in the wire. Weldon told him to go ahead, and Palmer unlimbered a .30-caliber machine gun from his jeep and mounted it behind some debris and rocks about 100 yards from the break in the wire. The wire truck moved out of sight and Palmer sat down to wait, observing the wire through his field glasses.

He didn't have to wait long. About half an hour later, Palmer saw a German civilian crawl from the basement window of the house near the break. He inched over to the wire, picked it up, and looked at it. Then he put it on a rock, took a hammer out of his coat, and began beating the wire.

Palmer calmly laid down his glasses and put a two-second burst into the man. It hit him eight times and shot him all to pieces. Palmer went back to the break, stepped over the dead saboteur, and fixed the wire one more time. We had no more trouble with the lines that day.

Sam Blatman was killed in Rhineberg. He had gone in as a forward observer for Company A of the 49th Infantry. The town had been almost cleared, but there was still intermittent mortar fire from the Germans. He was standing in front of a window when a mortar shell burst outside and a fragment cut his throat. His radio operator, Pfc. Alan Shefner, was slightly wounded at the same time.

We also got word that another observer had been wounded in the knee and evacuated, and 1st Lt. Jack Wier hadn't been heard from since the day before. Next morning, Captains George Salisbury and Marvin Sather went into Rhineberg to look around.

They climbed to near the top of the steeple of the only church in town and an incoming shell hit the steeple, wounding them both. Salisbury took a fragment in the stomach, Sather was hit in the leg. Soldiers of the 49th Infantry rigged up litters and brought them down from the steeple. They laid them outside the church, cut off their tank suits, and gave them morphine. Then Salisbury and Sather were evacuated.

They were lucky to get out alive. The battle was in its second day and the church had not been shelled. Apparently, German civilians had seen them go into the church and telephoned the information across the Rhine.

Salisbury and Sather were hit late in the morning when everything seemed to be happening at once. We were firing hard. When we heard about the casualties, Lt. Roy Bostic took over Battery C and Lt. Frank Gillespie took Battery B. By early afternoon, the toll was mounting. Blatman, Salisbury, Sather and several others were wounded or missing. The enemy artillery was firing hard, too.

In the middle of the afternoon, Lt. Bun Baldwin, motor officer of Headquarters Battery, was rumbling out of Rhineberg in his Sherman when a round from a German 88 scored a hit on its right side. Bun was standing in the turret and the round almost took his leg off, then it went on in and killed the loader, Cpl. George A. Kupczak of Chicago.

Pvt. John M. S. Irving received a broken leg and was evacuated with Bun, Cpl. Clare Lefever received a fragment in an arm, and T/4 Ralph Hutchins got some nicks in his back and chest. Hutchins was not evacuated.

Lieutenant Weldon was a few hundred yards behind the tank when it was hit. By the time he got there, Baldwin was sitting at the side of the road, a big man about six-foot-four, wearing a new pair of boots. He'd used a binocular strap to rig a tourniquet above his bloody knee. He sat on the ground and calmly cut off his own leg with a straight razor. When he was done, he tossed his foot, boot, and lower leg into the ditch.

Moose Weldon watched in astonishment, looking first at Baldwin, then at the leg in the ditch. Weldon was a big man, too, maybe an inch taller than Bun. Baldwin looked at him.

"Well, Moose," he said, "do you want my boots? They're not going to do me any good now."

Bun took off his left boot and handed it to him. Weldon couldn't say a word.

"My other boot's over there in the ditch," said Baldwin. "My foot's in it."

Weldon walked over to the ditch and got the foot and lower leg. He didn't know what to say. Years later, Bun said that Lieutenant Weldon (Moose) couldn't talk and that tears were running down his cheeks.

Weldon found that George Kupczak was dead and quickly got Bun evacuated. Meantime, one of our batteries had hit the 88 that got Baldwin. They found the crew dead. It had been a horse-drawn gun. We were surprised much later to find out how much of the German army had been horse-drawn as late as 1945.

By mid-afternoon, we had lost all of our observers. I talked to Colonel Lilly about it and we put in a request to division artillery for two lieutenants to come up as forward observers. They reported the next morning: Lt. Herman Zittel from the 405th Armored Field Artillery Battalion and Lieutenant Myers from the 398th Armored Field Artillery Battalion.

Meanwhile, our aircraft were strafing the Germans across the Rhine, flights of eight P-47s with rockets slung under their wings. They came howling in low across the silvery river and fired their rockets first, striking the German positions in white bursts of smoke. After they made their rocket passes, the planes climbed steeply and wheeled around and dove again, working over the Germans with their .50-caliber machine guns.

The Germans across the river were shooting at us with artillery, self-propelled guns and mortars, arching intense fire onto the streets and houses of Rhineberg. Late in the afternoon, on their last flight, a P-47 was making a strafing pass on the Germans. He climbed and rolled over and black smoke started pouring out of the engine. As he turned west, still smoking but not burning, he waggled his wings, maybe to tell us he was all right. I had a feeling he was going to make it.

The Rhineberg phase of the battle, which had started March 5, was just about over, but the price had been high — not just for the 399th, but for the combat command as a whole. The 36th Tank Battalion, for example, virtually ceased to exist. Sixteen of Company D's seventeen light tanks had been knocked out. The medium tank companies — A, B and C — had lost thirty-eight of their tanks. Several scout cars, half-tracks, and jeeps had been destroyed, most of them in one afternoon by Panzerfausts and 88s that G-2 had told us were nowhere around.

By dark, I'd had it. I had not slept for two days and two nights. I felt as low as I ever had. I went up to the attic where I was sleeping and lay down on my cot. In the near distance, I could hear a lot of firing going on, the heavy rattle of machine guns and the *whoom-whoomp* of mortars. Our fire direction center was still working, but we were not firing much. Most of the artillery going overhead was from Corps Artillery behind us, firing at targets across the Rhine.

With all the drumfire around us, I lay wide awake, thinking. I heard somebody climbing the attic steps, and in a minute John Collins sat down on the cot.

"Tex, how you doing?"

I said, "Hell, John, you know how it is."

"Yeah," he said, "I know."

I asked him if he'd heard anything about Salisbury and Sather. He said he had gotten a report that Salisbury was hit in the stomach but his intestines weren't torn up. He would be back in a month. Sather had a mean wound in the leg, but he would be okay. There was no news of Lieutenant Weir, who was still missing.

Baldwin's leg had been shot off, and he would be evacuated to Paris.

"We'll miss Sam," I said.

He nodded.

"I don't see any end to it," I said. "I don't think it will end until we kill or capture them all. What do you think?"

"I give it another month or six weeks," he said. "We'll get them pinned between us and the Russians and just blow them to bits."

He foresaw a giant battle with the Russians on the east and the Americans on the west and the Germans in between. I wasn't so sure of that. I felt that the war would go on a long time and there was still a lot of killing to do.

But I felt better. John went on downstairs and, in a minute, I drifted off to sleep despite the din outside. When I woke up, it was early and the day sounded like a repeat of the day before. All our batteries were shooting, keeping the gun barrels hot, firing one mission after another. I decided to check with our observers in Rhineberg and started out in a jeep with Corporal Kupsa driving.

The asphalt road was cratered by shellfire and the trees on either side all shot up. We hadn't gotten far when we saw four knocked-out medium tanks, one on the left, two on the right, and one in the road itself. They were black from burning, neat three-inch holes made by armor-piercing rounds.

Near the middle of the road ahead of us lay the body of an American soldier. He had obviously been one of the crew of the nearest tank. He was blond, about nineteen. His hair was long and wavy, and it was blowing in the wind. Last night, he might have wondered when the war would be over, too. I nudged Kupsa to keep going and he let out the clutch.

We hadn't gone more than 300 yards when a German 88 across the Rhine took us under fire. Kupsa hit the brakes and jumped out of the jeep, scrambling for the ditch at the side of the road. He seemed to do it all in one move, leaving me still sitting in the jeep. It flashed through my mind that if a professional boxer moved as he did, he could win all his fights in the first three seconds. I jumped out and went after him and started yelling.

"Goddamnit! Get back in that jeep!"

I ran back and got in. He followed and we roared on into Rhineberg.

It was all shot up, debris everywhere, huge piles of bricks in the streets, half-collapsed houses, exposed plumbing, everywhere the sharp smell of cordite mixed with the ever-present coal smoke.

With a good idea of the situation in Rhineberg, we headed back down the road to our CP at Asdunks. There I found out that the battle had moved further north. We had taken Ossenberg and were fighting from Ossenberg to Wesel over a built-up area. We were moving from one small town to another and the Germans were making a fight for every one of them. In the afternoon, Colonel Lilly ordered a displacement forward and the battalion picked up and moved northeast to the main road from Rhineberg to Wesel and went into position near Haus Heideberg, which was little more than a big farm compound.

We ran the owner and the others out of the buildings and took over the main building for our command post. The firing batteries went into position to shoot north. Directly north of us was a huge slag pile, 200 feet high, several hundred feet long. By this time, the routine of setting up the CP and the fire direction center was as natural as breathing. We soon had the telephone lines in and the observers briefed, and I had a little time to relax.

It was Sunday. I wondered what they were doing at home today. I was worried about Don. She had a new job at the Col-Tex Refinery in Colorado City. She was an inspector of aviation gasoline and as such it was necessary for her to climb on the top of the tank trucks to take a sample and then to seal the tank.

Some of the nights were snowing and the tanks were covered with ice. There was a fair amount of danger in this in bad weather. Our mail hadn't caught up to us for the past two weeks. Then I heard the deep roar of diving airplanes overhead. When I looked up, I saw two Focke-Wulf 190s. As I was watching them, two P-47s swooped down from above and jumped the German planes. One of the 190s kept his altitude and flew north. The P-47s chased the other one, but they were evidently too far away to shoot, and soon they were out of sight. I turned to walk inside, but they were back over me skimming the ground at an altitude of less than 400 feet, the two P-47s chasing one Focke-Wulf with all guns firing, eight on each plane.

Almost above me, the Focke-Wulf broke into pieces, parts of it flying off as it hurtled toward the ground, trailing smoke behind it. When it hit the ground about a quarter of a mile away, it exploded. The P-47s waggled their wings a little and flew almost straight up, really pouring it on.

A minute later, they were back, this time a little further off. By now, I had my field glasses so I could still see the action. They had found the other German airplane and were working it over with their machine guns.

Suddenly, I realized the P-47s were chasing a P-47. Through the glasses, I could just make out German crosses on the wings. Evidently, the P-47 had been forced down and the Germans had fixed it up. The two relentless P-47s on its tail shot it all to pieces and it hit the ground about a mile or so away.

Until that morning, the bridge at Wesel was still standing. We had been fighting northeast, trying to get it. With the Canadians moving in from the west and the Americans from the south, the Germans blew the bridge just as a few tanks from the 36th approached the ramps leading to it.

The battle of Rhineberg was finally over for us and we had suffered serious losses. We had probably lost more tanks in a shorter time than any other unit up until then on the western front. Our losses and tactics were severely criticized by some in higher headquarters. An article in *The Last Offensive* reported:

"The employment of the tank elements could have been improved through the provision of closer infantry support, and undoubtedly such support would have materially decreased the tank losses of the Combat Command."

That was the CCB of the 8th Armored Division.

The article further stated: "The fight for Rhineberg had all but annihilated CCB's armor: of fifty-four tanks, thirty-nine were lost."

Some men who fought there said that the losses occurred because there was not nearly enough artillery support. But proving that is something else. Actually, the attack on Rhineberg was based on false information. G-2 issued a bulletin the day before the attack saying that very few German troops were in the Rhineberg-Wesel area. Actually, there were more than 50,000, including the elite of the German army, remnants of two or three parachute divisions, as well as some Waffen SS.

Looking back, we know what should have been done. When the 49th first hit the Germans and a heavy fight was indicated, the CCB commander should have brought the 399th AFA up as far as possible and ordered us into firing position. Then he should have ordered a coordinated attack of the 36th Tank Battalion supported by the 49th Infantry and the 399th AFA. He could have called for Corps support, too, because a dozen or more field artillery battalions were available in that area.

But in war, nothing is ideal. Colonel Kimbell, CCB commander, had been trapped in a house by the Germans since before noon and wasn't able to communicate with anyone until dark, when he was finally able to get free. But the damage had been done. Colonel Lilly was up front and pinned down in a ditch for a long time, so the fighting was left to two lieutenant colonels in command of two battalions who were isolated from one another.

Nevertheless, our men had fought valiantly. We hadn't run and, in fact, we had defeated a much larger German force inflicting terrible casualties on them. When it was all over, we were in Rhineberg and most of the Germans were dead.

Rhineberg had been a critical objective, the key to Wesel and the bridge we needed. It was a compact medieval town sitting on an important junction of roads, canals, and railroads. We couldn't outflank it because on either side the ground was low and cut up by canals and rivers. We had to go through it. The Germans realized its strategic importance and defended it with everything they could muster: paratroopers, tanks, and anti-aircraft guns. Almost every soldier seemed to have a Panzerfaust.

Soon after that, we got new orders. Combat Command B was detached from the 35th Division and sent back to the 8th Armored. We were going to Venlo, Holland, for rest and refitting. We packed up and the column rolled out of Rhineberg southeast to Venlo.

On March 10, Division Artillery ordered our S-2 section, which was mine, to move up to the Rhine to observe the far bank for enemy activity. On March 12, I took the section up to a town called Baerl.

11 Fighting in the Western Ruhr

March 13, 1945–March 31, 1945

That an assault crossing of the Rhine was about to happen was evident to all of us in Ninth Army as well as the Germans east of the river. Ninth Army consisted of three corps: the XVI on the north, the XIII in the center, and the XIX adjacent to U.S. First Army on the south. North of Ninth Army were the Second British and the First Canadian Armies. The 8th Armored Division was part of the XVI Corps along with the 35th and the 79th Infantry Divisions. First Army was across the Rhine at Remagan south of us, and Third Army south of them was also crossing as the Ninth Army artillery preparation began.

We weren't concerned about security in Baerl, a small town of two or three thousand people on the west bank of the Rhine, because an infantry company of the 79th Division occupied the town and had outposts near our OP.

For an observation post, Sergeant Hale and I chose an old farmhouse about 200 yards from the Rhine. I detailed him to set up an OP in the attic and built another in a house on some higher ground near the town. We equipped the two OPs with telephones and had them sandbagged against shellfire.

Then we found a place to bunk, a three-story stucco house with a full basement. A dentist's office was on the first floor, and in the living room was a player piano. It was good duty away from the brass and we played the piano nightly until the battalion arrived.

Though Baerl was relatively quiet, on the third day Corporal Myers, Sergeant Hale, and some others were outside the OP near the Rhine when they came under mortar fire from the Germans across the river. The third shell was close. It hit near a cow and killed her. A fragment knocked the carbine out of Myers' hand and slightly wounded him. From then on, we stayed in the OP and kept away from open ground between the building and the Rhine. The Germans shot only a few times that day at infantrymen south of the area.

In the Baerl observation post, I did most of the observing, though Sergeant Hale came up and took over for an hour or two. The locals were almost certainly in touch with the German army, using the telephone, radio, or both. I noticed a middle-aged German nosing around our half-track, looking at the bumper markings. My half-track was named "Don" and on the left side of the front bumper it was marked "8A 399A FA BN." On the right side was marked "HQ-3." I told Sergeant Hale to tell the German that if I ever saw him again, he would be like some that were lying around dead. It would have been prudent to evacuate these German civilians, but we didn't.

While we were in Baerl, I had some free time. Lieutenant Weldon and his crew came up one day and put in telephone lines linking the OP on the Rhine with the one in Baerl and our quarters. He stayed a couple of days and we talked about our tank lost at Rhineberg, where Baldwin's leg was shot off.

I had seen several of the 36th Tank Battalion's Shermans knocked out by Panzerfausts, a hollow-charged projectile launched from a tube. It looked like a bazooka but was shorter and the projectile itself was much bigger. When it struck, the force of the explosive focused on a point and burned a hole about the size of a pencil through the armor plate. Fire and molten metal then poured through the hole, burning the crew and usually exploding the ammunition.

I had an idea about installing a shield. If we put a sheet of armor about four inches away from the main armor of the tank, then if a Panzerfaust projectile hit it, the force of the projectile would be spent going through the shield. It wouldn't penetrate the main armor and might save the tank's crew.

The more I thought about it, the more I liked the idea. I talked to Colonel Lilly on the radio about it, and he said to look for a disabled tank so that I could remove the outside armor and attach it to the sides of one of our other tanks. We would place it four inches out from the tank sides and fill the space in between with sand.

Lieutenant Weldon and I found Bun's tank in a large fenced compound south of Rhineberg. The hole in it, on the right side under the turret, had been made by an 88mm. We found that the tank would run, but the gun wouldn't fire because the breech had been damaged. We also found Corporal Kupczak's foot.

Back at the battalion, we presented the facts to Colonel Lilly. He was interested, but the battalion motor officer said over the telephone that the suspension system of the tank wouldn't carry the extra armor. Maybe he was right. We never got a chance to find out. I wanted to talk to him some more about it, but he was with division rear echelon and I did not see him until the war was over.

We were in 21st Army Group, commanded by Field Marshal Montgomery, who was getting ready to cross the Rhine. I went back to Baerl and Lieutenant Weldon joined the battalion in Venlo. The next day, I needed to go to division headquarters for some maps of the area just east of the Rhine and, making a day of it, returned by a different route north of Venlo. I was amazed by the activity along the roads, and by the large number of navy assault boats and pontoons stacked in the fields. There were tens of thousands of artillery shells standing base down along both sides of the roads. The shells were 155mms and larger, and were in rows sometimes twenty feet wide and a mile long. Two days later, the battalion arrived to support the Rhine crossing. The 8th Armored Division was relieved from attachment to XVI Corps and assigned to XIX Corps.

We had been on our own in Baerl for almost two weeks, Sergeant Hale, five enlisted men, and I. It was sunny and reasonably warm, but with a little snow still in the shadows and beginning to melt. A few of the apple and pear trees were already blooming white in the green of the orchards. It was pleasant without a lot of people around. But all that changed when the battalion arrived.

Battalion hedquarters was set up in the house we had been living in, and Batteries A, B and C took positions generally southwest of town. The day the battalion rolled into Baerl, I was in the observation post overlooking the Rhine across from Duisberg. Through my glasses, I picked out some Germans going in and out of a large metal factory building, apparently part of the Krupp works. Late that morning, I received permission to shoot, and Battery B fired a dozen or so shells into the roof of the building. I couldn't see the explosions or smoke and I stopped firing. The Germans didn't shoot back and the area was generally quiet. Most of the activity seemed to be four miles to the north, where there were engineer troops, navy landing craft, and anti-aircraft battalions. The next day, a survey was executed tying all of the guns of the divisions to the corps and army artillery nets. Things were nearly ready for the Rhine crossing.

We opened fire at 3:00 A.M. on March 24, the massed artillery shooting at targets across the Rhine. From the roof of the house in Baerl, I could see the gun flashes for miles up and down the west side of the river. They fired in stages; the guns further back, 240mm howitzers, started to fire first. Then came the 8-inch howitzers, followed by the 155mms and 105mms, and finally the tank guns, all of this timed so that the shells hit at once. The din was tremendous, the shells bursting in terrific flashes over the river about 600 yards from my location. Most of it went on the rest of the night.

Meantime, the engineers were pushing a pontoon bridge across the Rhine, a small, narrow bridge, just wide enough to move a tank across. Before daylight, the first troops of the Canadian XXV Corps were inching across the gently rocking bridge onto the east side of the river. Montgomery was pushing the Canadians across first, though we had taken most of the ground and built the bridges they were crossing on.

I was glad I wasn't going across first. "Hell," I thought, "let them go first. If they want to go over there and test the Germans and get shot up, let them go. We can go later."

Minutes after dawn, the sky east of the river blossomed with parachutes. Paratroopers of the 17th Airborne Division jumped from their C-46s and C-47s over a drop zone about three miles northeast of us. With my glasses, I saw they were hardly out of their harnesses when two flights of A-26s, light bombers, came in low to strike Wesel, making a hairpin turn after their attack to return low over us.

Later that evening, in the basement of the building, I found Colonel Lilly, Major Collins, and Lieutenant Gillespie, who was commanding B Battery while Captain Sather was in the hospital. Gillespie told me a corporal in his battery was an artist and was making sketches. He asked if I would like one. Cpl. Ralph E. Carlson sketched Colonel Lilly, then turned his attention to me. I was posing for him, sitting and looking straight ahead, when I heard a terrible din outside. With my picture half drawn, I left the artist-corporal and ran upstairs.

Three German ME-262 jets, the first I'd seen, were trying to get at the pontoon bridge north of us. Long columns of vehicles were moving across the bridge and it was a crucial time for them to attack. The jets, with three bombs each, came whistling down the river like flying pipes, aiming bombs at the bridge. The last rays of the sun glinted on their fuselages. The bridge was heavily ringed with anti-aircraft guns, but our gunners hadn't been trained to fire at jets. They were too fast to hit. The fire was hot enough to drive them off, though, and they dropped their bombs wide of the bridge. I went back to the basement so the corporal could finish my portrait, which turned out very well.

Early the next morning Colonel Lilly returned from CCB with orders to cross the Rhine that night, beginning after midnight. We reeled in our telephone wires, packed up, and moved out from Baerl north through Rhineberg at 11:00 P.M., forming a single column of vehicles. The 36th Tank Battalion led and the 49th Infantry followed behind us. We began crossing at 2:00 A.M., moving across the 700-foot-long pontoon bridge single-file. It was March 27.

The night was inky black and I didn't relish the thought of going across. I was glad that Corporal Roth was driving the half-track and I was not. A guide with a flashlight was at the head of the bridge, and we started out slowly, feeling the bridge sway beneath the weight of the vehicles. I could see almost nothing as we moved across, just the little red dot of the vehicle ahead and blackout cat eyes of the vehicle behind us, which were moving up and down. Our half-track, which weighed twelve tons, moved up and down a good three feet as we crossed from pontoon to pontoon.

On the other side of the river, we moved up a little way and stopped in the dark by the side of the road. Water was in the ditches and the road was wet. We stopped in front of a white house with a picket fence and waited about an hour for first light before moving southward after the 36th Tank Battalion.

At dawn the sky was overcast, the weather chilly again. As we moved forward, I saw some parachutes hanging in the trees like huge handkerchiefs, but no paratroopers. They had moved on.

We moved on, too, continuing south, moving and stopping until mid-afternoon when we stopped at a farmhouse in a small German village. The house, built low to the ground and very old, was on the east side of a north-south road. The owners were gone, but they hadn't been gone long; the house was warm. I hadn't shaved for three days, so I went to the bathroom and borrowed the owner's razor and shaving brush for a quick shave. Then I went back to my half-track to see what was going on.

I had hardly returned when Colonel Lilly walked up from the head of the column and told me there had been a killing in the street two blocks away. An infantry lieutenant had killed an elderly German man, apparently without cause. The man, about sixty-five years old, was riding a bicycle down the street and passed the lieutenant. Nothing was said. The lieutenant picked up his M-1 and shot the man off the bicycle at a range of fifty yards. The shot blew the man's whole chest out. The lieutenant was arrested by his battalion commander and sent to the rear to be held for trial. He might have had an ulterior motive for the killing, but we never knew what it was.

From the farmhouse on the road south of Wesel, we moved southeast during the night, and by noon the next day reached an assembly area near Hunxe. The 8th Armored Division was the first armored division in Ninth Army to cross the Rhine. By this time, the 35th, 79th and 83rd Infantry Divisions were also across and we were beginning to move. We pressed on east and northeast, skirting the north side of the Ruhr toward Dortmund, Hamm, and Soest.

After the division closed up in Hunxe, I was called to Division Artillery Headquarters by Colonel Holt, division artillery officer. When I walked in the room, he was looking over some maps and talking to Lieutenant Colonel Lynn, division artillery executive officer. Colonel Lynn had replaced Colonel Burba, who had become division G-3.

Colonel Lynn looked over his shoulder and waved me toward a chair. Colonel Holt ran his finger along the map and said, "Here's where we are." He stabbed at a place on the map with his finger. "We are generally moving east. Now notice this, the road here paralleling the Lipp Canal on the north. See it? Good. The road runs due east above the Ruhr." He looked up from the map and settled on me.

"What do you think of the possibility of a light task force going down this road and taking the bridge at Dorsten?"

I was familiar with the area and had been studying the maps. I took another look at the map. The bridge was twenty-five or thirty miles to the east.

"It looks bad," I said.

"Why?" he responded, rather irritated.

"The area is alive with anti-aircraft guns. They're all over the place. Most of them are dug in, and the smallest are 88mms. If the column got in trouble, it could get wiped out."

"That's all," he said rather abruptly. "Report back to Colonel Lilly."

I slung my carbine on my shoulder and headed for my borrowed jeep, wondering why they'd called me in to ask me that. After a while I thought perhaps Colonel Holt wanted me to take a battery of artillery and a platoon of tanks or infantry and make a run for it. I never found out for sure, but if so it would have been a deadly mission. Later the Canadians fought there for three days and it was finally taken by the CCB of the 8th Armored Division.

Outside, it was cold with drizzle and a little freezing rain. We were soon moving again, rolling and stopping, generally heading northeast. Sometime during the morning, we turned north behind a tank column of CCB. The weather was improving; it had stopped drizzling. We were headed toward Dorsten, gateway to the northern Ruhr. Dorsten was the hub of a network of railroads, highways, canals, and the Ruhr River itself. It was set in uneven terrain that could easily be defended, and we were expecting stiff resistance.

About 2:00 P.M., we heard firing up ahead, the sharp crack of anti-tank guns. The column was being held up by German defensive positions near a small town. The land was full of ravines and creeks that might be a problem for tanks if they had to move off the road.

The swoosh of the incoming fire and the sharp crack of the tanks' return fire went on for a couple of hours. Then Colonel Lilly pulled the battalion off the road and moved it into a compound of farm buildings, a big house, barns and outbuildings — enough room to shelter the whole battalion.

Moving toward the farm buildings, I noticed some tank destroyers beside a bluff that seemed to be hanging back, not trying to engage the German tanks we could sometimes see ahead of us. We passed to the left of them, across a ditch and onto a small road toward the farm building. The bodies of three German officers were lying near the road. One had been run over by a tank, another shot by a tank gun, and the third shot to pieces by a machine gun. We rolled on past them into the compound. It was nearly dark by the time we pulled in and the M-7s had formed a perimeter defense.

With the battalion bivouaced for the night, I took the maps out of my half-track, set them up in a room, and updated them with all the latest information available. As usual, we did not know what was happening in adjacent areas. Communication was through Division Artillery, and since they were west of us, at the forward CP of the division, they were still several miles behind us. Our communication was relatively short-range FM radios to our forward observers and liaison officers. We didn't usually communicate directly with the 36th Tank Battalion and the 49th Infantry. We thought they were north of us, and we knew that some elements of CCB were in our vicinity. Colonel Lilly decided to wait until morning to find out what was going on. We knew the situation was fluid and dangerous.

After chow, I went to the room where I had set up the maps and started to go through some intelligence reports. I turned on my liberated German radio to a German station and began to listen to beautiful classical music. Sergeant Hughes gave the radio to me before we reached Rhineberg. A large radio, it picked up the BBC and many German radio stations.

I was writing a letter to Don by the light of a Coleman lantern:

> "Just thinking of you again and hoping you are okay. Another busy day here. Listening to some classical music. German. It made me think of you. Don't ask me why. But it was beautiful and so are you."

Major Collins came in. "Tex," he said, "the colonel wants to talk to you."

It was 10:30 P.M. I put away the letter to Don, turned off the radio and walked two doors down to Colonel Lilly's room. Collins and Oliver were there, and Colonel Lilly seemed disturbed.

"Tex, we've got a problem. I don't know where the 36th Tank Battalion or the 49th Infantry are. I want you to find them tonight. Be back here by daylight and report to me."

"Yes, sir," I said, and went out looking for somebody to drive me. Somehow I knew that this simple assignment would be one of the most dangerous I would ever be on. I found Sergeant Hughes and told him I needed a jeep and a driver. "Ask for a volunteer," I said. "It's going to be a long night." He came back in ten minutes with the jeep and Sgt. Delmos Duckworth, a Headquarters Battery motor mechanic, from Simms, Indiana. I was glad to have him with me on this job.

We loaded carbines, hand grenades, and a .30-caliber machine gun onto the jeep and took off. I studied the map and decided not to take the northern road to Dorsten. Instead, we went south for several miles. Along the way we saw a burning M-7 of the 398th Armored Field Artillery Battalion. Nearby, the road turned west and we drove on about eight miles to a black-topped, north-south road through a forest.

I was apprehensive about the woods. This area had only been partially cleared late that afternoon. There might be German troops who had been by-passed in there, as well as mines. The night was very dark and we drove slowly through the forest, talking as we went, like whistling in a graveyard.

"How much longer do you think it'll last?" Duckworth wondered aloud.

"Can't go on much longer," I said. "Maybe a month. Maybe more, maybe less."

"They've still got fight in 'em," Duckworth said.

I wondered if there were any of them left in the woods. All we could hear was the hum of the jeep's motor and the crunch of the tires on the pavement. "If we can make it through the next two or three weeks," I thought out loud, "we'll be home free."

"It'd be damned bad," Duckworth said, "to get killed now, wouldn't it, Captain?"

"Yes," I said. "Damned bad."

About midnight we came to an east-west road leading to Dorsten and turned east and soon came to a house on the north side of the road. We knew it had to be some sort of CP; there were lights showing and it was surrounded by vehicles.

Duckworth slowed the jeep and we pulled up into the yard of the house. I went in. An old friend, Lt. Robert Tate of Houston, said this was the rear echelon of the 49th. He said that Company C was in Dorsten along with part of the 36th Tank Battalion. There had been mean fighting all day in Dorsten and the town was hot and still had not been cleared.

If I was going to Dorsten, he said, I had better be damned careful. With that cheerful advice, Duckworth and I headed the jeep toward Dorsten.

We came to its outskirts around 1:00 A.M., picking our way through piles of dark rubble. The night was coal black, but we could make out the jagged outlines of bombed-out houses. It had been shelled for two days by the British before it became our job. A few fires lent an eerie light to the lifeless town. We moved slowly, very slowly, worried about mines and die-hard Germans, often stopping to look and listen. When we finally arrived at the center of town, we saw a building, its windows shuttered, still standing in the middle of the street, the street forking around the building on either side. Here visibility was better because of several fires. Three jeeps and five tanks were parked in front of it, and across the street were some guards. Inside, I found the battalion commander of the 36th, Lieutenant Colonel Van Houten.

Most of his tanks were near Dorsten on a north-south road south of town, he said, on the road leading from Dorsten to Recklinhausen. They were in a defensive position in case anything happened. This north-south road was the one we had been on earlier in the day, but fifteen miles south of Dorsten.

Van Houten also said that Company C of the 49th Infantry was in town, east of where we were. "Don't take the north-south road when you go back," he said. "There's a gap of ten or twelve miles that hasn't been cleared. And the Germans," he said, "were still full of fight when it got dark."

I decided to look for 1st Lt. Harold Ezra of Crawfordsville, Indiana, one of our forward observers with the 49th. I left Sergeant Duckworth and the jeep at the tankers' CP and started on foot, walking east down the center of the street, my footsteps sounding unbelievably loud on the rubble-strewn street.

Once in a while, I could hear a burst of firing off to the south and, occasionally, to the north. I could see no flashes, but I could hear the crackle of small arms and the occasional thump of a mortar or artillery in the British zone to my north. To the east, flashes of lightning made it a horror-movie setting.

On my left were knocked-out buildings, on my right were woods. I had walked about three-quarters of a mile when, to my left, I noticed a thin beam of light shining out of a basement. I walked toward the light and suddenly I was face to face with an American soldier standing in a doorway with a Tommy gun on me.

Neither of us said anything for a moment. Finally, I broke the silence: "What outfit is this?"

"Company C of the 49th."

I asked him where his company commander was. He said, "In the basement." He wasn't a talkative type.

He knocked on the door, put a blanket over it to cover the lights, and I went down. The basement was full of officers and men smoking cigarettes, going over maps and talking about the coming attack. One of them was Lieutenant Ezra. By then, it was 2:00 A.M.

The infantry company commander had a lot of news. He told me the positions of the other two companies of the 49th, the location of battalion headquarters, and the plan of attack for the next day.

It was time to go and I was getting ready to leave when Ezra took me aside. "Listen, Tex," he said, "you're going to have to be damned careful. There's a German machine gun section down at the end of the street about 200 yards from here. He hasn't fired now in some time, so when you go back, stay close to the buildings."

The infantry, not wanting to fool with the Germans at night, planned to take them out first thing in the morning.

With this in mind, I started back toward my jeep, about a mile away. Short of tiptoeing or taking off my boots, I couldn't have walked more softly down the street, expecting any moment to hear the ripping sound of the German machine gun. But I made it back to where Sergeant Duckworth was waiting. We took the same route back, rolling into Battalion Headquarters about dawn, and I reported my findings to Colonel Lilly.

Chow was not ready, so I lay down on my bedroll with my clothes on to get an hour or two of sleep. I was exhausted. Colonel Lilly had received orders from division and called me to his room. Collins was already there. The 8th Armored Division, he said, was going to attack Recklinhausen at 2:00 P.M. Since we had no maps of the area east of Recklinhausen, they were being prepared for us at the division CP at Zweckel near the Rhine. I was to go there to get the maps.

The battalion would be moving out about 11:00 A.M. I checked my watch. It was already 10:45 A.M. and I knew it would take me an hour and a half to drive back to the division CP, an hour to get the maps, and another hour and a half to get back. I would have to meet them someplace. John Collins and I got a road map. "We're going to attack Recklinhausen at 2:00 P.M.," he said, "and we don't expect much of a fight there. I'll have somebody meet you here at 4:00 P.M." He picked up a pencil and marked a crossroad in Recklinhausen west of town. It was a prominent intersection of a conspicuous north-south highway and east-west thoroughfare. He gave me the marked map and then marked one the same for himself.

I said okay, got a jeep and driver, and headed back to the Rhine to get the maps, which were supposed to be rolled up and ready for us. We were running late.

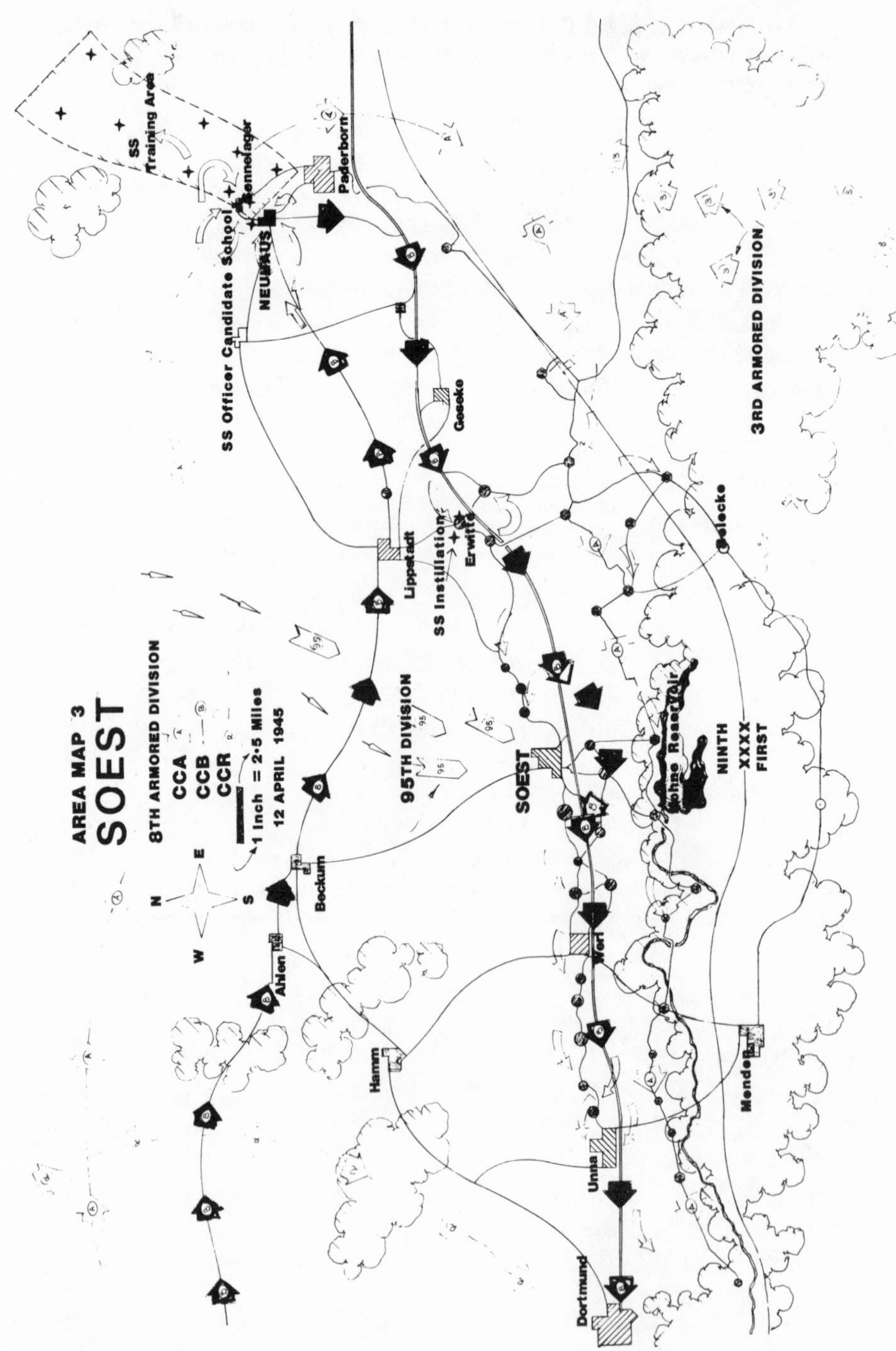
AREA MAP 3
SOEST
8TH ARMORED DIVISION
CCA
CCB
CCR
1 Inch = 2·5 Miles
12 APRIL 1945
N
E
S
W
95TH DIVISION
SS Training Area
Sennelager
Paderborn
SS Officer Candidate School
NEUHAUS
Geseke
Lippstadt
SS Installation
Erwitte
Belecke
3RD ARMORED DIVISION
Mohne Reservoir
NINTH
XXXX
FIRST
SOEST
Beckum
Ahlen
Hamm
Werl
Unna
Menden
Dortmund

12 Reduction of the Ruhr Pocket

April 1, 1945–April 12, 1945

The 8th Armored Division crossed the Rhine at Wesel and advanced eastward to the Paderborn area. On April 2, it was ordered to reverse direction and attack to the west. Soest was the first objective, and fighting in the town was severe. But with a holding attack by the 95th Infantry Division and the main effort from the south by the 8th Armored Division, the German defending forces were caught off balance and the town was cleared.

Division headquarters at Zweckel was in a fine three-story house. The scene there reminded me of a late evening crow roast, noisy and busy. Staff officers and enlisted men were rushing around in all directions. The maps weren't ready. G-2 section said there was still work to do sorting them.

G-2 was on the second floor and maps were scattered all over the floors of three of its rooms, but in less than an hour a sergeant got my maps together and I was ready to go. I tucked the maps under one arm and with the other reached for my carbine. But it was gone. I'd left it leaning against a door when I came in. Somebody had gotten it.

This was a hell of a note, I thought, not being able to leave a carbine around without some bastard stealing it. I beckoned the sergeant over and told him I wanted my carbine and I wanted it quick!

He said if I'd sit down for a minute he'd either get my carbine back or get another one. "No," I told him. "I want *my* carbine, not another one. My carbine has been shot in. I can put a two-inch group at fifty yards. I don't want another carbine, Sergeant. I want mine."

Five minutes later, he came back with my carbine. I asked him where he found it and he said a private had taken it. I picked up the maps and headed back toward Recklinhausen. By then, it was 2:30 P.M. I would have to rush to be at the meeting place by 4:00 P.M., but I wasn't concerned about it. John had said they would attack at 2:00 P.M. and would be well beyond that point by 4:00 P.M. We took off down the road to Recklinhausen, feeling pretty good.

The rain had stopped, the sky was clear, and it was beginning to warm up. The countryside was beautiful. The grass was greening up and a few fruit trees were blooming along the macadam road leading east. Occasionally, there were open fields of sugar beets and signs that gardens were being planted. In the distance, I could see the wheel houses of coal mines.

As we moved east, though, there was evidence of bombing everywhere: craters in the ground, sides of blackened bombed-out houses reaching jaggedly toward the sky. By about 3:30 P.M., we began to pass a company of the 49th Infantry on the south side of the road and in a nearby forest. Not long after that, I saw some of the 36th Tank Battalion assembled that way, too, but it didn't occur to me that the plan of attack might have been changed. I figured those were the reserve of one company of the 36th and one company of the 49th, and that the attack had jumped off and progress had been made.

At about 4:00 P.M. I found the point where I was supposed to meet someone from the battalion. The big, open four-lane crossroad had street signs with arrows pointing to the center of town. There were houses and a factory and office buildings around it. I was in the right place, but nobody was there. The city was quiet. I had a funny feeling because in an attack, there are always supply people and reserve troops, and corps artillery behind the assault troops. Where were they?

I was already scared and it had begun to eat on me. The jeep driver was also scared. He said, "Captain, I don't like this."

Down the street to the east about a quarter of a mile, I saw a vehicle burning. Beyond it, another was on fire. With nothing more to do, I told the jeep driver to drive us down and see what they were.

The first one was a German half-track, which was bigger than ours and capable of carrying twelve to fifteen men and pulling an anti-tank gun or an artillery piece. This one had run its front wheels up on the esplanade against a tree. The back of it was still smoking, flames flickering around the front tires. Around it were the bodies of eight German soldiers, burned and shot to pieces. The second vehicle was a command car, flames licking at its sides and everybody in it dead. Aside from the crackle of the flames, it was quiet.

Then I realized that I had seen no American troops for the past seven miles. I started to get uneasy. When the tanks had come through, they must have really worked these people over. But I didn't see any evidence of tank fire. Tank fire would have made neat round holes or, if they were firing high explosives, they would have blown up the vehicle. Looking more closely, I saw that machine gun bullets from above had penetrated these vehicles and set them afire. The Germans had been chopped up likes pieces of beef. This was .50-caliber stuff from strafing airplanes. I wondered where the tanks and infantry were.

I was still mulling that over when we started back to our liaison point. Suddenly, on both sides of the street were hundreds of men in civilian clothes milling around, both German and foreign workers. They had come up to the surface from the mines that formed a huge honey-comb beneath the streets of the town. The mine shafts and entrances were not prominent and not necessarily visible. I hadn't noticed any of them while driving up the street. Now, suddenly, the street and sidewalks were full of miners with lights on their caps carrying lunch pails and tools. They were walking east on the broad sidewalks past the half-tracks with the German bodies lying around them without paying much attention. Many of them had drifted into the street ahead of us. I stood up in the jeep and motioned them out of the street with my carbine.

I began to realize that my driver and I were alone with the miners, and I didn't like it. We drove back to where the battalion representative was supposed to meet us. Still nobody there! But off to the west, I saw a vehicle approaching. I got out my field glasses. A jeep, really moving fast.

It was Lieutenant Quist, battalion reconnaissance officer. As he reached the intersection, his driver hit the brakes like a ton of lead and turned the wheel. The jeep did a ground loop, 360 degrees. Quist yelled something at me, then back down the road his jeep headed, accelerating as it went.

He got about 400 yards, then stopped and turned around and came back, leaning out the side of the jeep yelling, "Let's go! Let's go! Come on!"

At that point, I wasn't in any hurry. I had been there about twenty minutes and my anxiety had passed.

I yelled back, "What the hell's the matter with you?"

Quist was breathless. "Nothing," he said between gasps. "Except that this town hasn't been attacked yet, it's full of Germans, and we're going to put a three-battalion concentration on it in about ten minutes. I don't want to be here when it hits."

That was enough for me. I jumped in my jeep and we headed off down the road trying to catch him.

About forty-five minutes later, we found the battalion. They hadn't moved more than a mile from where I had left them that morning. It was 5:30 P.M.

The situation was now entirely different. Recklinhausen was going to be attacked, but not by us. The 2nd Armored Division, which was three times as big as the 8th Armored Division, had been given the job. Meantime, we were ordered to move northeast as far and as fast as we could and to try to reach Paderborn. I split up the maps between Colonel Lilly, Major Oliver, and the battery commanders — Brooks, Sather, Salisbury, and Gausman.

We were on the road by 6:00 P.M. that evening, rolling generally north along a secondary road. At a town called Haltran, we saw an Air Corps forward base with tents and a maintenance facility. A flight of P-47s was coming in close behind the combat troops, landing on the hard-packed dirt two and three at a time.

It was getting dark and raining and I started to put the canvas cover over the .50-caliber in the turret when the zipper stuck. I began to pull on it when Corporal Wakeman said, "Hold it, Captain." He then said that "the zipper snap is caught in the ring of a hand grenade pin." I stopped pulling and got down into the half-track and soon saw that if I had pulled hard that the hand grenade would have been detonated. I cut the snap off of the zipper pull. There was silence for quite awhile as we kept on moving. The ground was high and rolling with some woods. After a half hour, the rain stopped, but there were thunderstorms to the southeast, with occasional flashes of lightning. To the southeast, too, we could see the flare of fires. The 2nd Armored was shooting and burning everything they saw. Houses and farm buildings and haystacks were flaming. The 2nd Armored was thorough in its work. I admired the way they went after it.

When daylight finally came, we were still on the road. During the night, we had moved forty-seven miles, meeting only scattered resistance and advancing on a line even with the divisions to our left and right. All of the elements of Combat Command B were together. CCA and CCR were behind us. Soon after daylight, our column stopped and the kitchen section passed out K-rations and we sat in our half-tracks, eating chili and eggs, and glad to get them.

Clouds overhead were broken and it looked like it was going to be a nice day. We moved out, and by 1:00 P.M., time for rest and rations, we had come to a ridge road on top of a hill. I was tearing open some K-rations when I spotted two girls coming down the road.

One of them was a blonde in a green coat and tweed skirt. The other was a dark-haired girl in some kind of rain coat and wearing boots. They were walking down the road to the left of our column. The men were urinating on the right side of the vehicles, out of sight of the girls. The urine had formed little rivulets and it was running across the road. As they passed by, the girls were careful to step over the rivulets. They weren't laughing or carrying on as some did later. They just went on their way, as if an American armored column were as commonplace as a bus. They came from a group of houses about 300 yards ahead of us. There were no houses behind us. No place for them to go. Then why, I asked myself, were they out like this, strolling along as if there were no war? Bizarre, I thought. Women are funny and do strange things.

Soon we started to move again and rolled into Allin, which had taken a beating. Several buildings were ablaze, others smoldering; broken glass and debris were scattered around the streets and on the sidewalks. There had been an air strike, and a company of the 36th had shot up the town. The 49th Infantry was in town with us, and the tankers of the 36th were on the east side of town. We settled down to wait, without knowing what the holdup was. If we were needed, they would soon let us know.

Looking up the street toward the center of town, which was only a block away, I saw three women coming. Two of them had on the habits of nuns. The other was wearing some sort of nurse's garb like a pinstriper in a hospital. They seemed quite gay, laughing and carrying on, paying no attention to the American soldiers, or so it seemed. They were walking on the opposite sidewalk past our column.

My half-track had stopped in front of a large department store whose windows had all been shot out. Somebody had gone in and taken four of the window mannequins, one male and three female, and placed them in an obscene position on the sidewalk. I noticed them, but didn't pay much attention. We were going to be moving out, and I didn't give a damn anyway.

Before long, I heard somebody giggling and I looked around and saw the three German women who had passed by on the other side of the street. They were standing around the mannequins, laughing among themselves and making gestures. One of them moved the mannequins to a little better position. For some reason, it made me mad.

I came out of my half-track and told them they had five minutes to get off the street or get shot. They stopped laughing and started running. I got back in the half-track. The mannequins kept doing what they were doing without criticism. In a few minutes, the column moved on.

In the afternoon, it clouded up and a light rain began to fall. Not long before dark, we were coming over the crest of a hill and into a valley. The road ran down a long decline into the valley, stayed level for a short distance, then went up to the left and into a small village. To the right, on the hill across the valley, lay some dense woods.

At the bottom of the valley, I saw shell bursts about half a mile away, light stuff, 76mms or 57mms. Most of them were hitting on the left side of the road, and I thought they were coming from our right front. I couldn't see the muzzle flash, but I thought it was either a tank or an anti-tank gun.

The tanks were going through the area buttoned up. I thought it would be just my luck to get down there at the bottom of the valley where the rounds were coming in and get stopped. Then if the bastard ever hit one of us and we began to burn, he would get several vehicles.

When we got to the area under shellfire, we stopped. Ahead of me were two men in a jeep. A shell came in and exploded in a field on the left side of the road about forty feet from them. They bailed out into the roadside ditch.

Another round came whistling in on the right side of the road and exploded sixty feet from me. The next one hit just short of the road, about twenty feet from the abandoned jeep and forty feet from me.

I could sympathize with a shooting gallery duck. I sat there and wondered why we hadn't been hit. Maybe the gunner or whoever was firing the weapon, whatever it was, had bad visibility, or else he was having trouble depressing the muzzle, because almost all of the shells went over the road. I saw only two that burst on the right side. Probably range dispersion was working for us. Finally, without a hit, the two soldiers got out of the ditch and into their jeep and the column moved.

Soon afterward, Battery A came under fire briefly. About the same time, Colonel Lilly radioed from his position with CCB that we were going to hole up in the next town for the night. He told Major Collins to put the firing batteries in defensive positions and get the fire direction center organized. We rolled into town, a poor farming village about 100 feet higher than the ground around it. There were about twelve compound-type buildings. We ran the family out of the largest structure and got into position for the night. I was tired and so was everybody else.

The next morning, April 1, was Easter Sunday. We moved out early, dressed as usual, and headed for Lippstadt. Our orders were to move due east to Paderborn. We arrived on the edge of Lippstadt at 10:00 A.M. The town was in chaos. There had been some fighting in town earlier, about 8:00 A.M., and we could hear small-arms fire in some parts of town. Many of the warehouses and apartment houses on the west side of town were burning. Houses and shops were being looted by foreign workers, mainly Poles and Russians, many of them wearing vertically striped clothes made where they worked.

In the center of Lippstadt was a large church where hundreds of Germans were attending services, mainly older men, women, and children. Well-dressed and well-fed, they were calmly walking to church on the south side of the street, while on the other side, buildings were burning and stores were being looted.

The column was moving down the middle of the street toward the east. We didn't acknowledge the Germans and they didn't acknowledge us. We made no attempt to stop the looting, partly because we had to keep going, partly because we didn't care.

The column rolled on, and by 1:00 P.M. we were in the village of Esbeck. We were told to settle in for the rest of the day. While we were in Esbeck, I heard a story about an old friend of mine and one of my former battery officers.

1st Lt. Dale W. Starry of Shippenberg, Pennsylvania, had been battalion communications officer during the 1943–44 maneuvers. Later, he was sent on detached service to Combat Command Reserve. Starry was with CCR as it moved through Westphalia, north of the Ruhr and just north of and parallel to our route. He was in a half-track approaching the town of Elsen. The half-track stopped, and as Starry finished writing a message, he looked up and saw that he was in front of a bank that had been hit by shellfire and an airstrike. The front of it was blown out and the vault door was open. German money was lying all over the street.

Starry didn't realize the money was negotiable, and neither did any of his crew, but he took a musette bag and stuffed it full of marks. He forgot about it as his column moved out, but it would come in handy later on.

In Esbeck the next morning, we got a call from CCB. They wanted a billeting party for a non-combat effort to go forward and arrange quarters for the battalion near Paderborn. Larry Quist, two non-coms, and five privates left to report to Maj. Hiram Walker of CCB. Walker was to lead the group to the east. They left at 7:00 A.M., before we moved out. The billeting party started out with Troop B of the 88th Reconnaissance Squadron, but soon became separated and were on their own.

As they moved east, the billeting party of twelve jeeps and forty men captured a couple of towns and took a few prisoners. The major was elated. He got up on the hood of his jeep and told the men that this was going to be the first time that a billeting party had taken a large town. They would all be in *Stars and Stripes* when they captured Neuhaus.

Then he jumped in his jeep and yelled, "Let's go!" and down the road they went.

Outside Neuhaus, they got shot to pieces.

By the time our column arrived west of town around 2:00 P.M., there was action between the remnants of the billeting party, now reinforced by the 49th Infantry, the 36th Tank Battalion and some of the 88th Recon people, with some Waffen SS. It was pretty hot from the sound of it.

We pulled off the highway at a farmhouse, a big six-room building on the north side of the road, and the firing batteries went into position. East of the farmhouse was a meadow of about 250 acres, longer than it was wide, and beyond that was the town of Neuhaus itself. Off to the northeast was heavy forest and a road leading to Sennelager.

As we pulled into this area and set up, I noticed a jeep parked behind the house near the highway with a body in it. I didn't have time to look then, but that afternoon things quieted down and I went out to look at the jeep. The dead man in the jeep, the back of his head gone, had been a member of the billeting party that had gone from Lippstadt that morning. He was one of those I thought had been involved in the rape of the girl in Aldekirk. The war had exacted a justice of its own.

Several others had been killed in that fight. We had lost Pvt. James B. Keegan, the private who had started the news sheet on the ship coming over. He hadn't liked officers and he had lost his life, ironically, because of a stupid error in judgment one of them made. Major Walker foolishly led Keegan and twelve jeep-loads of men — men armed only with pistols and carbines — into an SS training school area heavily defended by several SS units.

We stayed in Neuhaus for two days and throughout that time there was an on-going fight. 2nd Lt. Don Sears was walking around a building in Neuhaus when a big SS lieutenant came charging at him bare-handed. Sears shot him twice with his pistol, literally knocking the man back with the impact. Shortly after that, Sears was trying to smoke some Germans out of the basement of an adjacent house. He kept yelling at them to surrender, but they wouldn't. Finally, he had his tank fire into the basement and they were all killed.

We found out later that we were fighting the staff and students of an SS officer candidate school in Sennelager. They were well equipped with Tiger and Panther tanks, assault guns, machine guns, mortars, and artillery. They put up a hard fight.

At 3:00 A.M., the SS mounted a counterattack down the road from Neuhaus toward our artillery positions. We fired all of the artillery shells we had. Then the infantry cannon platoon of the 49th, which fired the same kind of ammunition, brought us what they had. When the attack was finally beaten back, we were down to three rounds per gun.

We were firing close to the infantry's front, using proximity fuse. This was developed by the navy for shooting at airplanes. The fuse was a radio transmitter, and when the waves hit anything ten or twenty yards away, they bounced back and made the shell explode. It was particularly effective to sweep bridges with because it killed people on the bridge without damaging the bridge itself.

Before the fight was over that night, several hundred SS troopers had been killed and it was nearly daylight before the 49th was relieved.

As the GIs passed Battery A on the way to the rear, they left the road and climbed up on the M-7s to shake hands with the cannoneers. The ground was littered with the black-clad bodies of SS troops; I saw no prisoners. Not until mid-morning did we get more ammunition.

I learned later that on the first afternoon of the action, Colonel Kimbell had put in a call for assistance to General Devine, who deployed Combat Command A to our north. It hit the SS that were left at Sennelager and wiped them out. Meantime, we had dealt with the ones in front of us. The 3rd Armored Division came up from the south, out of First Army, and met the 2nd Armored in Paderborn, just a few miles east of us. That sealed the Ruhr pocket and trapped 400,000 German soldiers, more than the Russians got at Stalingrad.

New orders crackled over the battalion radio. We were to move east to the Elbe River. We packed up and rolled. That night, we got as far as Bad Lippspringe, bivouacking in fields near the road and going into defensive positions for the night. The 36th Tank Battalion was off to our right, the 49th Infantry behind us.

During the night, several tank battalions of the 116th Panzer Division tried to slip out of the Ruhr pocket and head east. One tank battalion came through our area just before daylight. Battery C was bivouacked in a little clearing off the main road between Paderborn and Hamlin. Near dawn, they heard the low growl of Tiger tank engines and saw the dim shapes of the Tigers themselves not more than fifty yards away. Battery C wisely let the Tigers rumble on.

Our surgeon, Capt. Ken Zierler, always traveled at the rear of the battalion column with his ambulance and aid men. He rode in his jeep behind the ambulance and just ahead of the battalion's tank recovery vehicle. Zierler worried that the recovery vehicle would run over him while we were moving at night under blackout conditions. That night, he was asleep in his jeep, parked just ahead of the "wrecker."

He woke up at 3:00 A.M., aware that vehicles were passing by. As they went by his jeep less than four feet away, Zierler, who speaks German fluently, came wide awake when a tank stopped next to him for a couple of minutes and he heard one of the crew saying: "*Ja,* Herr Hauptmann."

From then on, Zierler parked his jeep well off the road when the battalion was bivouacked.

When dawn came, no Germans were in sight. They had moved up the road and were into a fight with the 5th Armored Division between Hamlin and Hanover.

On Thursday, we were ordered to turn around and head west into the Ruhr. Our first stop as we moved west was Geseke. We arrived there on the second Sunday in April, finding a few troops from the 1st Division, and the town itself virtually untouched. There was no resistance from the Germans and the 1st Division had little fighting to do. We stayed in Geseke for a day. It was a very old town surrounded by a moat and a wall, a Catholic church at its center. Nearby was a hospital full of wounded German and American soldiers.

We received word from CCB to remain in Geseke until further orders and were advised that we would be there overnight. I selected a large house near the center of town as our command post and staff officers' quarters. I went to the front door and knocked. An attractive woman of about forty opened the door and asked me in fluent English what I wanted. I told her that we would be using her house for a day or two. "You have thirty minutes to get your personal things and get out," I said.

She began to cry and became quite abusive and finally, fed up with it, I told her to shut up and get going. With that, I turned and went back to my half-track parked in front of her house.

I took advantage of the slack time to get my maps in order. I went out into a storeroom in the rear of the house and found seven four-by-eight quarter-inch sheets of plywood. I took four of the sheets to mount my maps on. When Sergeant Hale and I removed the sheets from the storehouse, the woman I had ejected from the house saw me from an upstairs window of the house next door, which I later learned belonged to her brother, and came over again, entering the patio through a gate between the two houses. The patio was quite nice. Bulbs were blooming and so were a few rhododendron. Sergeant Hale was busy mounting the maps and sawing the plywood to the right size when the woman started up again. She said that she was not a Nazi and neither was any of her family. "How are you going to pay for that plywood?" she demanded.

I gave her a long look, then said, "I don't give a good goddamn whether you like me using your plywood or not, and as for paying you for it, you are crazy."

"But I am not only not a Nazi," the woman pleaded, "I am anti-Nazi. Always have been. And it doesn't seem right you taking my plywood. You're no better than the Nazis."

That got to me.

"I know what you mean. We have been in Germany for several months now and we have yet to meet a Nazi. Nobody is a Nazi. They were never Nazis. They're like kangaroos in Texas. And all those funny, thin, round-headed people dressed in striped clothes, I suppose they were just visiting relatives in Germany. As you and I both know, madam, there was no such thing as the SS, the Gestapo, concentration camps and slave laborers." I could feel the blood throbbing in my temples. "Now shut up and get the hell out of here. And don't come back!"

She left like she was spring loaded.

Late the next afternoon, we rolled out westward toward Soest. It was soon getting dark and we were out of contact with the 36th Tank and 49th Infantry battalions. For the night, we took over a farm compound on the north side of the road, some eight miles west of Geseke. The batteries went into defensive position around the farm and we settled down in some houses and barns, with headquarters in the main farm building.

The family was cooking dinner when we moved in and they had just sat down to eat. There was an older man, bent and tired, in his early sixties; his wife was a tall, slim woman; and they had two attractive daughters, about sixteen and eighteen. I ordered them out and they quietly picked up their pots and pans and left. I sent them into a back room and told them to stay there.

Colonel Lilly decided the next morning he would go forward to find CCB. He took his jeep and started off before the column moved out. About ten minutes later, he radioed back that there were two Regal mines on the road ahead of us. He told Major Collins to send me up to either remove the mines or explode them.

I was familiar with Regal mines. They were the largest and most powerful of the German anti-tank mines. Another German mine, the Teller mine, was smaller and made of steel. It could be picked up by a mine detector. But the Regal mine, which was in a wooden box with a plastic charge and plastic detonators, couldn't be picked up with a metal detector.

The Germans had put the mines on the side of the road, thinking they would stop us or at least slow us down. Stopping that night instead of moving on had saved one or two vehicles and their crews.

I knew that they couldn't be disarmed or moved. Once they were placed and set, nothing could be done but destroy them in place. The mines were laid on the left of the road, one near the center line and the other on the left shoulder. The road was straight for a mile or so each way and the ground was nearly flat. This area, with the mines, went through a shallow cut with a bank on the right side about twelve feet higher than the roadway. I went over close to the mine and examined it. Something that looked like a wire was on the edge of one of them. And if so, that would indicate it was sitting on a plunger. So I decided to try to explode it by shooting it with my carbine. I climbed to the top of the cut, about fifty feet from the mine, and began shooting at it. I exploded one of them, but couldn't get the other.

I shot at the mine from the side and the bullets were going through it, but the mine wouldn't explode. Several displaced persons, huddled in the ditch beyond the mine, thought I was shooting at them. They jumped out of the ditch and scrambled to the top of the embankment, waving their arms. I didn't shoot in their direction anymore.

Lieutenant Verlinder, who had been with me in the church steeple in Kirchhoven, arrived and said he thought he could blow it up. He went to my half-track and got a concussion hand grenade, walked up to the mine, and armed the grenade by pulling the pin. Then he put the grenade on top of the mine and ran as fast as he could back toward the half-track.

Whoomp! The grenade went off and blew up the mine, and when it blew, a piece of pavement as big as a washtub flew past Verlinder's head and hit a jeep, shattering the windshield and wrecking its frame. It also blew a crater in the pavement three feet wide and three feet deep.

The battalion went forward: tanks, half-tracks, and jeeps swerved around the holes blown by the mines. Colonel Lilly had found the 49th Infantry with his radio. They had detailed Company B to move southeast to establish contact with us until we could get further west, where the bulk of the 49th was.

Communication between ourselves and the rest of Combat Command B were not good, and during the move from Geseke we lost touch with the infantry and the tankers. They had moved out a day ahead of us and we were behind them. When Colonel Lilly made contact, we were about ten miles behind the leading vehicles of the 36th and the 49th.

Shortly after we joined them, they pulled off the main east-west road and attacked Schallern, a small town where resistance was light. The tankers of the 36th took it easily and kept moving down the road a mile and a half to take Lohn, another village.

At this point, we learned the attack on Soest had been assigned to the 95th Infantry Division, so our combat command pulled south of

Soest, an important manufacturing city and canal and railroad junction in the Ruhr. The XIX Corps had assigned us to the 95th Division, figuring the 95th would have problems clearing Soest. We made a swinging move to the south and attacked Soest from that direction.

During this movement, Captain Sather of Battery B left his battery position and was heading forward to find his next position. He pulled in behind a half-track of the 53rd Armored Engineer Battalion, which was heading out of a wooded area. As the half-track emerged from the woods, it was hit by several shells from one of four German Mark IV tanks some 500 yards away near a small village. The half-track was destroyed and six men were killed.

Sather had been about ten feet behind the half-track, and when it was hit, his jeep struck the back of it. Both vehicles started to burn, the flames quickly spreading from the penetrated fuel tank of the half-track. Sather and his driver, Corporal Humphrey, jumped out of the jeep and ran for a ditch.

Sather had not been back on duty long since his wounding in Rhineberg and was still weak. He ran about sixty feet and fell with such a crash that he stunned himself. When he finally looked up, he saw German tanks moving toward him. While he was trying to think what to do, two American tanks, Shermans, came rumbling up, saw the Germans, and started firing.

Sather lay there as close to the ground as possible, watching the tank battle. The Americans got all four of the Germans. Corporal Humphrey extinguished the jeep fire and they went on their way.

Sather wasn't through with trouble for the day, though. He and Humphrey drove on about three miles toward a small village. Sather saw a side road leading to a large field with several large trees in it. He thought it would make a good position for his battery and told Humphrey to make a left onto the side road. They had gone about 200 yards when the road looped around three trees. In the trees, not fifty feet away, sat a German machine gun crew.

One soldier was standing up looking at them. Another was lying down alongside the gun and had it pointed directly at them. Humphrey saw them the same time Sather did.

"What do we do now?" he asked.

"Turn around and drive back down the road," Sather said.

Humphrey swung the jeep into a U-turn and floorboarded it. The Germans held their fire.

Ampen was taken after we put three concentrations on it, and the 36th made a short fight out of it. CCB moved on west to attack the town of Ost Onnen. We went into position and fired on the town for fifteen minutes. Then we went on in with very little trouble. While we were there, Colonel Kimbell sent a scout, a corporal and driver in a jeep to West Onnen, a neighboring town. They drove around without seeing anything and had just turned around to come back when a sniper shot the corporal in the back. When the driver got back, the corporal was lying on the windshield, dead. The round had made a small hole in his back, but his chest was gaping open.

Colonel Kimbell yelled, "Where's that air-corps boy?" That was his name for the young-looking lieutenant who was the air control officer.

The lieutenant stepped forward. "Yes, sir," he said. "Here I am."

I was standing next to the colonel when he said, "Tell those airplanes up there to bomb the hell out of that town."

The air control officer got on the radio and called down an air strike.

The colonel also ordered Colonel Lilly to put three battalion concentrations on the town. Then he got on the radio and ordered the 36th Tank Battalion and the 49th Infantry to attack the town and kill every son of a bitch in it. The airplanes struck the town, we fired concentrations on it, and the tankers and infantry attacked. As far as I know, they killed every son of a bitch in it.

West Onnen was a good-sized place but compact, as all German towns were. They built their houses very near each other. We were on the eastern edge of the town. Across a field about 200 yards, we saw a large farmhouse, and one of our men went over to it.

It was a torture place, he reported. He showed me a whip, a piece of wood about a foot long with a hole in it, and out of the hole came three narrow leather strips about twelve inches long, with three knots near the ends of each strip.

It was said that the Germans used these whips on their laborers. They evidently manufactured the whips there. The whip made me mad. I went over and found out that slave laborers had been making the whips. They were hiding in the building to stay out of the gunfire. Through an interpreter, they told me they had been reasonably well treated and that the whips had not been used on them. If the whips had been used on them, I would have burned the place to the ground. I was still thinking about it, and was about ready to set it afire anyway, when artillery shells began falling in front and on both sides of Battery C. I was standing not a hundred feet from them when the first round came in, hitting next to an M-7. They picked up in a hurry and moved to their alternate position, happy there were no casualties.

Battery B, about 500 yards north of Battery C, was getting some fire from the west. The gunner on one of the anti-aircraft quadruple 50s had seen something suspicious, a man carrying a box into a shed. The gunner thought the man might have a radio set and perhaps was directing the artillery fire that was hitting nearby. He swiveled the four 50s toward the shed and fired a tremendous volume into it. Timber and debris flew. When the 50s stopped firing, the artillery stopped with them.

Later, one of Battery B's non-coms had a look inside the shot-up shed and found pieces of a radio as well as pieces of a German officer.

That night, we took over a German house. As usual, I found there was no room to sleep in the basement; it was full. Those of us in the CP had to sleep wherever we could find a place. It was raining and getting cold, and to warm things up, I tried to build a fire in a stove in the CP room but couldn't get the damned thing lit. I poured a little gasoline in it and went off and forgot about it. When I came back twenty minutes later and threw a match on the stove, it blew up. I was disgusted and went to bed.

About daylight, Capt. William A. (Rigor) Morris got up to urinate. He opened the door and stood in the doorway urinating on the steps and possibly his feet. At that moment, a shell landed in the garden about twenty feet away and exploded with a terrific blast. Morris grabbed his stomach and started hollering.

"Medic! Medic! I'm hit!"

He'd been hit, all right. When we scrambled out of our sleeping bags and took a good look at him, we found out what the projectile was.

A big piece of mud had hit him right in the stomach. All he got was a bruise. It took him a long time to live that one down. This was another example of telephoning ahead by German civilians, I'm sure. One of them probably phoned the next town west and gave the German forces our street address, which was No. 6, Adolph Hitler Strassa.

We wasted little time getting into action that day, starting to fire early in the morning on the next town to the west. We took it during the morning with few problems and prepared to go on west to assault a town called Werl. Each town seemed like the one we had just taken.

They were about a mile and a half apart and the procedure was always the same. We would shell one from the other, call down an air strike, and the infantry and tanks would go in to run the Germans out into the open, where they could be killed or captured. Then we moved the artillery up and made rubble out of the next one.

We took Werl early in the morning. By 2:00 P.M. we moved out, heading west to Unna, about ten miles away. To the east, I saw a column of men approaching, moving on each side of the road, deployed and ready.

They were part of the 17th Airborne Division, paratroopers who had dropped into Wesel a few days earlier. The colonel leading them was a big man, six-foot-four, and armed to the teeth. He was decorated like a Christmas tree, with a submachine gun in his hand, a pistol on his right side, a rifle slung on his back, and grenades hung all over him.

His men were armed the same way — a rough and ready looking bunch. He stopped and asked to see my maps. I showed them to him, we chatted a moment, then he led his men off the road toward a forest a couple of miles southwest.

That's where they captured Franz von Papen, the notorious German diplomat. Von Papen had been prominent in government affairs for many years. He had headed the German government briefly before Hitler took power. In the Nazi regime, he had been ambassador to Turkey.

While the paratroopers were bagging Von Papen, we moved west toward West Hammerle. Battery A was asked to put a concentration of violet smoke on a hilltop where there were several German tanks. A flight of P-47s was waiting above, ready to bomb the tanks when the violet smoke marked the location.

As Battery A was getting ready to fire the smoke shells, one of them began to leak violet smoke in the battery area. That caused a lot of anxiety because as soon as violet smoke was put on a target, an air strike would quickly follow. Captain Brooks contacted the air-control officer who called off the P-47s. The flight finally hit its target, though, knocking out six German tanks.

Late that afternoon, the 36th and 49th captured Unna and we moved in with them. It was a large industrial town in a hilly area, the hub of many roads, two canals, and railroads. Prowling around the town, some of our men found a warehouse full of swords, daggers, and other Nazi regalia. Everybody in the battalion who wanted a sword or dagger got one.

With Unna taken, we got orders to bed down for the night, and the firing batteries started searching the nearby houses for billets. Battery A was in an open field near a large residential area close to the center of town when the order reached Captain Brooks. He told his executive officer, 1st Lt. Frank Gillespie, to leave the M-7s in position and look for lodging for the men in the nearby houses. Then he went off to a meeting at battalion headquarters, which had been established in a small downtown hotel.

When Brooks got back to the battery, he couldn't find anybody except the guards on the M-7s and the other battery vehicles. He asked a sergeant where the men were.

The sergeant grinned and pointed. "They're in that house over there," he said. The house he pointed at was a fine, three-story residence.

When Hank Brooks got to the house, he was greeted by the sounds of music, laughter and gaiety. One of the billets the sergeants had picked was a working bordello, fully staffed.

It was still working when Hank left a few minutes later.

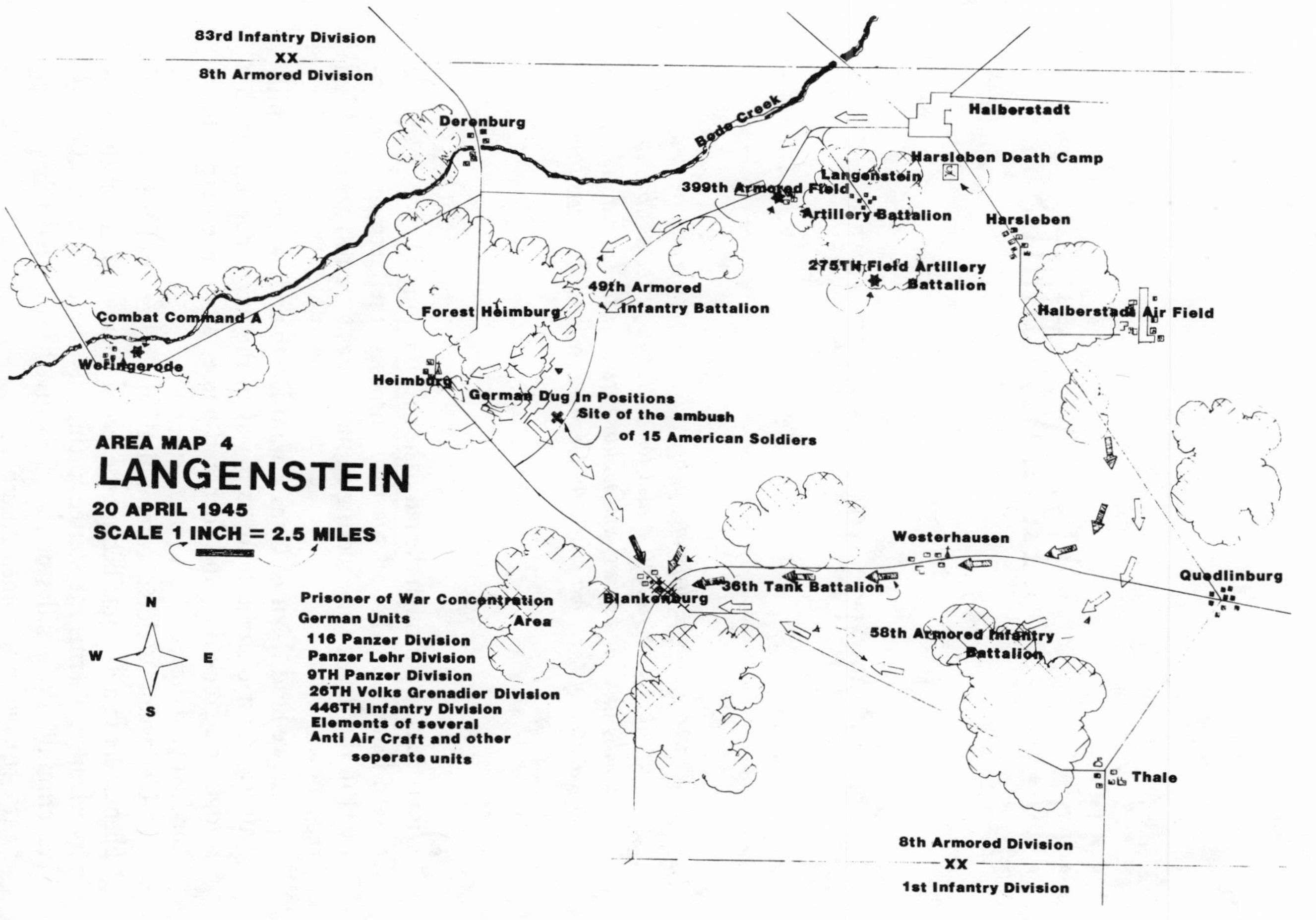
83rd Infantry Division
XX
8th Armored Division
Derenburg
Bode Creek
Halberstadt
Harsleben Death Camp
Langenstein
399th Armored Field
Artillery Battalion
Harsleben
275TH Field Artillery
Battalion
49th Armored
Infantry Battalion
Forest Heimburg
Combat Command A
Wernigerode
Halberstadt Air Field
Heimburg
German Dug In Positions
Site of the ambush
of 15 American Soldiers
AREA MAP 4
LANGENSTEIN
20 APRIL 1945
SCALE 1 INCH = 2.5 MILES
Westerhausen
Quedlinburg
36th Tank Battalion
Blankenburg
Prisoner of War Concentration
Area
German Units
116 Panzer Division
Panzer Lehr Division
9TH Panzer Division
26TH Volks Grenadier Division
446TH Infantry Division
Elements of several
Anti Air Craft and other
seperate units
N
W
E
S
58th Armored Infantry
Battalion
Thale
8th Armored Division
XX
1st Infantry Division

13 Harz Mountains

April 13, 1945–April 23, 1945

We were facing a desperate, dangerous enemy, an enemy trapped, with all the ingredients needed for a struggle to the death: dense woods, caves and mines, and winding roads easily blocked. There was some of that, but mostly the Germans realized that their cause was lost.

Orders crackled through the radio the next morning and we moved out toward Dortmund. For all practical purposes, the Germans were finished in the Ruhr, surrendering in most cases as fast as we could run them down.

As we headed out of Unna toward Dortmund, we got into hilly country, most of it built up as it was in the western Ruhr, with a bridge or a creek now and then and houses along the road about a hundred yards apart.

Lieutenant Weldon, communications officer, and Sergeant Stephens were in a jeep just behind the leading platoon of the 49th Infantry when small-arms fire started hitting all around them. Soldiers advancing along the sides of the roads dived into the ditches. Then mortar fire began to come in nearby.

Lieutenant Weldon and Sgt. Lynn Stephens were moving down the road very slowly when a mortar shell exploded on the pavement about thirty feet ahead of the jeep.

Sergeant Stephens yelled, "I'm hit! I'm hit! Get a medic! They've shot off my balls!"

Weldon jumped out of the jeep and ran around to the other side and pulled Stephens into the cover of the ditch, with the mortar rounds still coming in with frightening frequency. They hadn't been in the ditch more than a couple of minutes when two medics came running up, disregarding the mortar fire on the road.

They cut away Stephens' pants to get to the wound and found quite a lot of blood around his privates. One of the aid men looked at the other.

"My God!" said one of the medics. "This man ain't got no hair. He's got feathers!"

There was blood inside his pants and feathers were stuck to it like glue. He looked like some kind of strange bird.

Sergeant Stephens had been riding for a couple of days on a feather pillow he had liberated. A fragment from the mortar shell ripped through the front of the jeep beneath the light, knocked off the carburetor, went through the fire wall, and hit the feather pillow just in front of Sergeant Stephens' leg. It cut a five-inch gash on the back of his leg and clipped the bottom of his scrotum, ripped his pants, and tore the pillow, filling his underwear with feathers. After that, it went through the seat of the jeep and out the back.

Sergeant Stephens' injury was minor, but in this fight the infantry started to take some real casualties. One of our forward observers, Lieutenant Bill Hawley, was walking down the road with the commanding officer of Company B of the 49th when the captain and Hawley's radio operator were wounded. Since there were no infantry officers left in the company, the captain ordered Hawley to command the company, telling him to keep the attack going. The company was attacking toward Haultom, a town some distance away. Hawley had the good sense to know that the infantry sergeants knew more about what they were doing than he did. He got with them and kept the company moving. Deploying in the ditches and fields, they moved about five miles down the road. Along the way, they knocked out a mortar, two half-tracks, and several machine gun positions. For this, Hawley was later awarded the Bronze Star.

That night, the 49th sent a first lieutenant to take over the company and three second lieutenants to take over the platoons that had no officers. The Germans were still active and shooting, mainly firing from Haultom to the east. The infantry was dug in nearby.

Hawley, who had had a hard day, needed to get some sleep. So he made an overlay of a map and designated some concentrations on areas he felt the Germans would occupy should they attack during the night. Then he called these in to our fire direction center and gave a copy and explained the details to the new infantry company commander. If the Germans attacked during the night, the infantry commander would have a map that showed pre-figured concentrations of artillery fire that could be put on these points right away.

Hawley got some chow and, after dark, he and Sergeant Green went off to a big barn to the north, slightly ahead of the infantry positions. It was full of hay and looked like a good place to sack out for the night. They went up into the loft and buried themselves in the hay.

They hadn't been asleep much more than an hour when a racket woke them up. They heard the guttural sound of German being spoken. Hawley dug his way through the hay to the edge of the loft and saw lights beneath him in the barn.

It was full of German soldiers.

Hawley and Sergeant Green lay still, wondering what to do. But not for long.

The infantry lieutenant had called the fire direction center and ordered fire on three of the concentrations. Two of them were near the barn, but not on it. Hawley would have been a fool to select a target for a concentration, then sleep in it.

The fire came. *Blam!* It landed near the barn, spooking the Germans on the ground floor, who took off. The artillery fire broke up the attack.

Meanwhile, we had been ordered to advance on Dortmund, a large city west of us in the Ruhr complex, and occupy the eastern edge. Moving west, we found mostly built-up areas with little patches of green and occasionally canals. By 1:00 P.M., we were on the outskirts of Dortmund.

We pulled into the city's east side and took some high ground. Colonel Lilly positioned the batteries around the area and ordered me to look for a good place for a battalion command post and battalion staff officers' quarters. I found a likely looking three-story stucco house that hadn't been bombed. Most of the multi-story houses nearby were in ruins and the people were living on the first floors or in the basements.

I knocked on the door and a woman about thirty-five years old opened it. Speaking perfect English, she asked me what I wanted. I told her I wanted to look at her house; I was looking for a place for battalion officers' quarters.

"The house is occupied," she said. "There is no room for the officers."

I told her I wanted to look anyway and walked in the door, shoving her out of the way. She got mad and started to raise hell. I listened to that for a minute, then told her to shut up.

The house was adequate with lots of nice things in it. I told her to gather up everything she didn't want to lose and take it with her. She could have the third floor, as could her father, her mother, and whoever else was there.

She started crying and wailing. They were not Nazis, she said, and they didn't even know any Nazis and they were all sick and she couldn't move them. I listened to her a minute and then told her again that anything she wanted she better take out because I wouldn't be responsible for any of it. We weren't thieves or robbers, but whatever she had of value, she'd better take upstairs. "You have thirty minutes," I told her.

When I left, she was on the floor, crying and wailing.

Half an hour later, we moved in and took over the bottom two floors, establishing the CP on the first, the officers' quarters on the second. We had been told we would be in reserve for two or three days, so we settled in and started making plans to search that end of town for Nazis and soldiers and see what was going to happen.

Nothing happened in Dortmund, except that a sergeant in Battery C shot himself in the stomach while cleaning a submachine gun. We marked time until orders came through to assemble in the vicinity of Wolfenbuttle, 180 miles to the east and fifty west of the Elbe River. We moved out in fighting formation, with orders to vigorously engage any enemy forces we met on the way to Wolfenbuttle. We were under observation from the hills to the south from the time that we left Geseke until we reached Dortmund. Often we were under observed fire from these hills and were glad to leave the area. (See Appendix II.)

The situation, we knew, was fluid. First Army was coming up from the south and was well behind us. Ninth Army believed that everything up to Wolfenbuttle had been fought over, but that was not true. A lot of small villages had been bypassed. We didn't know what we were going to run into.

We formed our column and headed east. Fruit trees were blooming, fields were greening up, and I felt the war was nearly over. This was a Saturday morning and I recalled when I was a school boy in West Texas, the day I finished my seventh-grade final exams. I knew I had done well and was looking forward to a good summer, and high school in the fall. I didn't expect the battalion to have any more battle casualties. If we did have casualties, it would be because of unexpected problems or accidents. All of us were in high spirits as we left Dortmund.

The kitchen sections issued two days of K-rations for each man. We would be on the road for a couple of days and there would be no chance for hot food. The column moved off toward some areas we had already fought over, through Paderborn, northeast to Hamlin, east to Hildesheim, then east toward Wolfenbuttle.

It was dark when we got to Paderborn, a light rain falling. We took a macadam road northeast to Hamlin, where the legendary Pied Piper led the children away. We were moving under blackout conditions, the only lights being the small cat eyes in the front of the vehicles and the dim red dots behind. The villages we passed through were dark and we saw no one but the guides from the 88th Cavalry Reconnaissance Squadron.

I was napping off and on most of the night, curled up on the floor in the front of the half-track. When I was asleep, Sergeant Hale stayed awake, along with Corporal Wakeman or Corporal Pottish, two of the radio operators in the back. It must have been nearly morning when the convoy stopped. I woke up and asked Sergeant Hale where we were.

"Hildesheim," he said. I had read about it somewhere, an old German city with several fine museums. We were stopped on an east-west street and it was chilly. It had been raining since about 8:30 the night before. I got out and walked around a little to warm up. Then I started up toward the head of the column.

"Just a minute," said Corporal Wakeman in the half-track. "Something's coming in on the radio net."

My half-track was the battalion communications vehicle and this message was coming through in code. He wrote it down and handed it to me. I scanned it in the dim light.

It said President Roosevelt had died.

I was surprised and sorry. I had had a lot of confidence in President Roosevelt.

I went forward and found Colonel Lilly and John Collins and told them the news.

We talked about it and what would happen next. Nobody knew much about Truman, except that he came from Kansas City. The consensus was that he was mighty small for the job and he would have some big shoes to fill.

We moved on toward Wolfenbuttle, arriving at 9:00 A.M. on Sunday. The town was dead. No activity. Nobody around. We pulled up to the first big house we saw. The German family was at home. I told them to go upstairs or get out. We set up our headquarters and got in touch with the firing batteries, which were scattered about to the north side of town. Once we were established, I went out to see what was going on in Wolfenbuttle and found the 49th Infantry in the center of town.

They had taken over a couple of beer joints and were drinking it up. Strangely, there were no officers around. A few of the men were getting drunk and raising hell, yelling and singing boisterously. That bothered me, but it was none of my business. I went on scouting around.

I soon ran into barbed wire, a huge prisoner of war compound the 5th Armored Division had established the day before. They strung three rows of concertino wire in a square of thirteen or fourteen acres, each corner guarded by a half-track with a machine gun. A couple of light tanks were parked nearby. On the other side of the wire were about 5,000 German prisoners, a sea of gray, most of them sitting and talking, a few smoking. They were in winter uniforms with long overcoats and gloves, a really desolate bunch.

Directly across the wire were three boys in their early teens. I talked to them in a mixture of English and German phrases I was picking up. I asked the youngest of the three how old he was.

"Dreizehn," he said in a voice that hadn't quite changed yet. He held up all ten fingers, then another three. He was thirteen. The other two said in finger code that they were fourteen.

I gathered that they were badly shaken, but glad to be alive. Waving, I headed back to battalion headquarters to get busy on my maps, which needed updating.

While I was working, a couple of men from the battalion brought in a German captain in full uniform, with three rows of ribbons on his chest. He had been shot up in Russia, he told me through an interpreter, and had been sent home to convalesce. Our men had found him in bed, ordered him to dress, and brought him to me. He could hardly walk. I sent him back to bed.

A few minutes later, orders came relieving Colonel Lilly as battalion commander. Colonel Kimbell had been relieved and Lt. Col. Edwin Burba was to command Combat Command B. Colonel Lilly would be his executive officer. He designated Major Collins as battalion commander and packed up.

I hated to see Colonel Lilly go, but I had unlimited confidence in Major Collins and felt that for us the war was nearly over.

About mid-morning the next day, we were ordered to move to the vicinity of Halberstadt, some thirty miles southeast, to await further orders. The name had a familiar ring to it. I had read about Halberstadt in stories of World War I. The Halberstadter, an observation plane, was built there.

We packed up and moved out again, covering the thirty miles to Halberstadt's outskirts by 2:00 P.M. When we reached our division boundary, Major Collins stopped the column on high ground northwest of the city. The 2nd Armored Division had cut north in front of us and one of their tank battalions had shot up the place going through it. They had also called down an air strike. Two flights of thirteen P-47s were still flying around above. They had bombed the center of Halberstadt and given it a thorough strafing. From our position, we could look down into the town and see burning buildings and tremendous confusion. The tankers from the 2nd Armored had gone on through. There were no American troops in Halberstadt.

I went up to the head of the column to talk to Major Collins. As far as he knew, he said, we could be where we were for two or three hours. We had reached the eastern boundary of our division and XIX Corps had to give us new boundaries, which would take several hours. If we went any further east, we would be in the 2nd Armored Division area, and this was dangerous because of the possibility of being mistaken for Germans. We didn't need a shoot-out with the 2nd Armored. I told him I was going to go into town to have a look.

Intelligence was my job, but I had something else in mind. The war was almost over and I didn't have many guns. I had picked up a few, but I wanted more pistols, shotguns, and rifles. This was a chance to get them. There were no American troops in town and the Germans were confused and demoralized. I hunted up my friend, Lloyd Weldon.

"Moose," I said, "let's go into Halberstadt and hi-jack the police department."

Moose grinned. "Sounds like a good idea," he said.

He took a carbine and I had a Tommy gun, and in the jeep we had a couple of barracks bags. Into Halberstadt we went. We knew that if we didn't get the guns first, the follow-up troops in the military government would confiscate them and sell them to the rear-echelon troops.

The town was burning, with a few bodies lying around. We saw a few German soldiers at a distance, but when they saw us, they took off.

The police station wasn't hard to find. By this time, we had been in many German cities and most of the police stations were substantial buildings with big Nazi flags flying over them. We asked a German woman for the *Polizei* and she pointed down the street toward a dingy gray stone building four stories high with steps leading up to an imposing entrance.

We walked through the front door as if we were the chiefs of police. In a big room toward the front of the building, about thirty policemen were standing around, not seeming to know what to do.

Moose looked them over and hollered *"Achtung!"* at the top of his voice.

They all jumped to attention with a clicking of heels.

I walked in behind Moose and said, "At ease."

They seemed to know what I meant.

"Now, put your guns on the table," I told them, holding the submachine gun on them in a way they couldn't mistake.

The Halberstadt cops slowly and grudgingly unsnapped their holsters and unlimbered their pistols, placing them on a table in the center of the room. Moose had a duffle bag from the jeep and started stuffing pistols into the bag. When he filled it up, I turned to a man who looked like he might be their chief.

"I want all of your guns," I told him, "every goddamned gun you have in this place."

He looked like he could have shot me, but he and two policemen went off with Weldon into the next room and came out with three boxes of pistols, and thirty rifles and shotguns.

By this time, some of the cops were mumbling among themselves and I could not understand what they were saying. I couldn't watch them all while Moose was gathering the guns, so I decided to take what we had and get back before we got in a shooting scrape that ended up with a lot of dead cops. We had the duffle bags full of pistols; the rifles and shotguns were placed in the back of the jeep by the police. We got in the jeep and drove off.

When we got back to the column, we kept quiet about the guns. Moose was going to look after them, so I went on back to my half-track. Not long after that, we moved out to the southwest part of the city near some school buildings and a sports arena. It was dark by the time we got into position, where we were to stay for three days. Fighting was going on northeast of us. The 2nd Armored and the 83rd Infantry Division were crossing the Elbe River near Magdeberg, fifteen miles away. We weren't involved, though.

We found an area southeast of us like one of the mobile home parks in this country today. Tents were full of German families and some singles. I found the man in charge, who spoke good English, and he said there were a lot of German soldiers around. They were changing clothes in the woods, he said, and they came into the park at night to eat. I set up some sentry posts to round them up, but we never caught any of them.

Meanwhile, I was getting worried about our not having maps. We had moved off our maps. I had a road map that showed the airfield south of Halberstadt, and the next day I told Collins I was going to see if I could find any maps. I had heard a rumor about more fighting and we didn't have suitable maps to fire from.

The airfield, six miles away, had not been cleared. In a jeep with Corporal Roth driving, and a Michelin road map as our guide, we went south of town to find the airfield. We were there at 1:00 P.M. The place was alive with displaced persons, some of them drunk or half-drunk, some unruly, mostly Russian or Polish.

As we drove up to the entrance of the airfield, they all began jabbering and pointing, but I waved them aside and we went steaming down the main road about a quarter of a mile before getting into a complex of buildings and barracks.

We swung around a corner to find eighteen German soldiers lined up in the street ahead. We stopped.

They looked at us for a minute and surrendered. For them, the fighting was already over. I called the battalion on the radio and had a detail come out to take them to the POW cage in Halberstadt. Then I went looking for what I had come for — maps.

I tried the headquarters building first, but it had been pretty well ransacked by the DPs. Then I went to the officers' club, built on a ledge 100 feet high overlooking the airfield through a glass wall twelve feet high and sixty feet long. On two other walls were murals of the Luftwaffe. Kitchens of stainless steel and tile were first-class.

I found a lot of maps in the airfield operations office, but they were not much help. They were aviation maps, and not the scale we needed. We drove down and looked at the aircraft below. Some had been shot up, some burned, others looked ready to fly. This was where the Halberstadter observation plane had been built for the German Air Service in 1916–17.

I looked at the scene with a sense that I was part of a great adventure that was winding down. I knew myself better, pretty well knew my limits. I knew fear, but did not run. I knew I had nearly made it through the war and that felt good, but I knew my life would never be the same again. I was sad in a way. Without quite being able to put it into words, I sensed that future relationships and experiences could never equal in intensity what I had seen and experienced these past few months.

Then I snapped out of it and we headed back to the battalion area. There was still "one more river to cross."

While we were going through the hangars, a detail from battalion trucked the German prisoners off to the POW cage. When we returned to the battalion area, I discovered that one of the firing batteries had captured four more Germans. Two of them had already been taken away. I put the other two on the hood of my jeep and started for the POW cage near Halberstadt.

The two Germans were youngsters, about fifteen and scared to death. We were driving down the road to the cage and I saw a couple of rabbits a hundred yards off in a field. Weldon was driving and I told him to stop. I took out the carbine and got off a couple of rounds at the rabbits. The two Germans started trembling. They thought they might be next. So I put away the carbine and we took them on to the cage.

On the way back, we saw a couple of deer and decided to have a shot at them. We pulled off the road to try to get closer to them. I didn't want to shoot them with a rifle, so I got out my pistol. Weldon drove the jeep as close as he could and I shot them with my pistol. I'm not proud of it. I wouldn't do it now. Maybe being in the war had something to do with it. After killing the deer we drove up to them and looked them over. If they'd been in good shape, we would have taken them in to the kitchen and we'd all have had venison that night. But they weren't. Eating these deer would have been about like eating a dog.

Next morning, we were ordered out of Halberstadt to Langenstein. We were to support an attack on Blankenberg within a couple of days. Blankenberg was one of the few towns west of the Elbe that hadn't been cleared. It was on a direct rail line to Berlin and there were rumors that many Nazis running out of Berlin were in Blankenberg, and in caves near the town we heard about Nazi currency, stolen art, and government records. The town was also headquarters of the German Twelfth Army, which was defending Berlin from the west.

Our mission in Langenstein was to go into position, prepare to fire, and scour the area for Germans. Langenstein, a beautiful place, is southwest of Halberstadt, about six miles in the foothills of the Harz Mountains.

When we got there, we took over a building as big as a castle. It was four stories high and 200 feet long, complete with a formal garden, a forecourt, a service court, and outbuildings, all arranged in perfect order by a landscape architect. We moved in late in the afternoon, expecting to be there for a week or ten days.

The building, which probably had fifty rooms, was warm and quite well furnished. I took a room next to the main dining room for an S-2 office. It was the most elegant S-2 office I'd had so far. The table in the room was about ten feet long, four wide, with a number of large, comfortable chairs. The interior walls were lined with mahogany bookshelves full of books, and there was a thick Persian rug on the floor. The south wall, which was half glass and half paneling, looked out onto a formal garden with topiary figures. The ceiling was twelve feet high.

The main dining room to the east contained a twenty-foot table. The walls were of leather and paneling, with about 200 animal heads mounted on them, mostly deer and boar. I wondered who in the world lived here. Somebody told me it had been a German general.

We set up the firing batteries in position around town and sat down in our elegant headquarters to wonder what was coming next. Weldon and I had sorted out all the pistols we had taken in Halberstadt and realized that we couldn't take that many guns home, so we gave one to every enlisted man in Headquarters Battery.

But first we went through them. There was one fine Walther in a presentation case that I took. Moose found one he liked, which was about the same as mine. By then, most of the other officers had a pistol. I kept three shotguns and Moose kept three or four himself. The rest we gave away. The next day I had to go into Halberstadt to a meeting. I left in a hurry, but first hiding the Walther pistol in the library. When I got back, the pistol was gone.

Things began to pick up. We were firing on Blankenberg, about 4,000 yards south of us, and some interdiction fire was being placed on a road junction east of Blankenberg. A fire mission was coming in when MSgt. Gerald Davis came into the CP and told me there was a problem outside.

I went out with him and found twenty or thirty enlisted men of Headquarters Battery surrounding a group of two displaced persons and a German civilian. I had seen the DPs the night before. They were from a nearby death camp which had been liberated by our forces the previous day. Of the 6,000 prisoners brought in, about 500 were alive in the death camp. They were French resistance members, Polish and Russian political prisoners, and Jews. Two Americans had died of malnutrition the month before we got there. One man had been severely beaten about the hips for stealing potato peelings.

These survivors had left the camp and were sleeping in a hedge and eating out of our mess truck or garbage cans. They were emaciated men in the blue-and-white vertical stripes of the concentration camps, about thirty years old. They had short hair, thin necks, and round heads.

They saw a German man riding a bicycle down the road and ran out and stopped him. Somehow, despite his well-fed vigor, they brought him back into the courtyard. They screamed and yelled that he was a guard at the death camp and they wanted someone to kill him. When I got there, the German was down on his knees, scared to death. He grabbed me by the legs and started screaming in German for me to help him.

I wouldn't stand around and watch these DPs kill him, but about the time I was ready to decide what to do with the German, Sergeant Hale ran out and said Major Collins needed me in the CP. We were about to start firing on Blankenberg. I swung around and walked back into the building, leaving the German crying and hollering.

Back in the CP and busy with other things, I put the German out of my mind. About ten minutes later, Sergeant Davis came in, quite disturbed.

I said, "What's the matter?"

He waited a minute, looking sick.

"You hadn't any more than gotten into the building when one of those DPs hit the German in the back of the head with a pipe and knocked his brains out."

Sergeant Davis said it hadn't killed the German, though. He had lain there screaming and hollering, with the DPs and the men all around watching.

"One of the men in Headquarters Battery handed the DP his grease gun. The DP shot him twelve times right there at my feet."

But when I went outside, the thing was over and done. The German was dead and buried in the hedge. The DPs were eating and laughing and everything was back to normal.

It was as if someone had killed a rat.

The next day, Cpl. Morris Pottish of New York City was sitting in the yard near my office when a rifle bullet missed his head by centimeters. Then came another. The firing came from a steep hill about 600 yards from the castle we were living in. Pottish ran inside to get away from the sniper. The hill was almost vertical and we couldn't get up there to hunt out the sniper. He never fired again.

About half an hour later, a sergeant came in and said, "Look at this." He had a knife, a fork, a teaspoon, and a sugar spoon. They looked like they were solid gold.

I said, "Where did this come from?"

He grinned. "We were digging a latrine in the garden and found it."

"Where's the rest?"

"It's in this basket," he said. Then he brought in a bushel basket full of gold service.

We were under strict orders not to take anything belonging to German civilians, so I took the gold service to the caretaker of the building and told him to keep it in a safe place. He said he would. He probably sold it after the war and got rich.

I went back to the S-2 office to work on my maps. After a while, something about the room bothered me. I noticed that it was rather odd-shaped. I checked it out more closely and found a concealed door in a closet. It was locked, but I forced it. It led to a staircase. I went down the stairs to a steel door.

The staircase was dark and the door, which was six feet wide and seven feet high with an oval top, was securely locked. I couldn't budge it. I shot the lock with my pistol but the door still wouldn't open, so I sent for an M-1 rifle and blasted the lock. The door swung open.

Behind the door was an underground corridor about ten feet wide and eighty to one hundred feet long. From this central hallway were a number of rooms, each with round tops like a military ammunition magazine. It was a dungeon.

One of the rooms near the staircase had a steel mesh door. I shot the locks off. The door didn't want to open at first, but I finally blasted it loose and got in. It was a wine cellar.

The room was fourteen feet wide by thirty feet long and full of wine and other spirits, French and German wines, liqueurs, schnapps and vodka. No bourbon or Scotch whiskey, though. A lot of the wine was of 1905 and 1906 vintage and others on up to 1939.

We decided this didn't fall under the orders not to confiscate German property and posted a guard on the cellar to keep anyone from going down and getting drunk and causing problems. Then we took what we wanted and also distributed some to the enlisted men.

I wondered what kind of family could afford such a fine place in this part of the country. The land was poor and cut up by hills. The farms were not big and there was little evidence of livestock. I guessed the owner must be from Berlin, forty miles away. Years later, I learned that the place was owned by Bridger Dahlrus, Swedish industrialist and a friend of Herman Goering. Before the war, he had tried talking the English into surrendering without a fight. He used his Langenstein Castle for entertaining high-level Nazis, serving them elaborate dinners in the elegant dining room that we used as our CP.

The day after we found the wine, we heard we were probably going to have to reduce Blankenberg. The rumor was that high-ranking Nazis had just arrived from Berlin. Ninth Army ordered the 8th Armored Division to go in and clean them out. Blankenberg was three miles south of us over a ridge and surrounded by hills that were 300–500-feet high. From the hills, you could look down into Blankenberg.

Our maps of the area were inaccurate, so I told Major Collins I would get a jeep and go to Darenberg, three miles west of us, and see if there were any maps there. Most German schools taught map reading, and burgomeisters usually had maps.

Sgt. Delmos Duckworth volunteered to drive me to Darenberg and we got a jeep with a machine gun mounted on it. Darenberg, untouched by the war, had a population of about a thousand. But where was everybody? We saw nobody.

All of the stores had iron lattice work in front of the windows and doors, and some had steel sections, like an overhead door that pulled down. We stopped in front of a drug store and I beat on the door. Nobody answered. I was getting aggravated. I started hammering on the door with the butt of my carbine.

A minute later, a window opened above me and a woman stuck her head out. I thought it was strange how women always answered, not the men.

"What do you want?" she said in English.

I told her I wanted to speak to the burgomeister and asked if she could direct me to his house.

"Yes," she said. "He lives in that house."

The house she was pointing to was behind me and about a block away, a rather nice two-story house, somewhat isolated. I thanked her and we got in the jeep and went down to the burgomeister's house.

I knocked on the door but got no answer, so I beat on it and finally the door opened about an inch. A woman about forty asked me, in English, what I wanted. Her hair was dark brown and she wore it shoulder length. She wore bulky clothes because it was cold.

"I want to speak to the burgomeister," I told her.

When she heard that, she tried to shut the door in my face, but I stuck my foot in it and went into the entrance hallway. I repeated that I wanted to speak to the burgomeister.

"My father is the burgomeister," she said, "but he's sick and cannot see anyone."

I told her I didn't give a damn about that, I wanted to talk to him.

She said, "He's sick and he can't see you."

With that she started upstairs. I followed her.

When she reached the top of the stairs, she turned into a sitting room. Through an open doorway, I could see an old man lying in bed.

Once again she said, "My father is sick and cannot see you. What do you want?"

I told her I wanted all his maps. She went in and talked to him for several minutes, then came back out.

"My father has no maps," she said.

"I know damned well he has," I said. "All burgomeisters have maps. I need them and I want them now."

She looked at me coldly.

"We have no maps."

I said, "But, I think you do, and I'm going to burn this goddamn house up with the old man in it if I don't get your maps!"

I left her standing at the head of the stairs and went on down and told Sergeant Duckworth to pour gasoline around the foundation of the house and through the front door. He grabbed a couple of jerrycans off the jeep and started dousing the place with gas, sloshing it all around and into the house.

The woman had come down the stairs to watch. I told her that she had ten minutes to get me the maps or I was going to set fire to the house with her and the old man in it. I told her I didn't give a damn which way it went. If I got the maps, I would leave; if I didn't, there was going to be a big fire.

She went back upstairs and I heard them talking. Seven minutes later, they were still talking. Sergeant Duckworth was standing at the door with a submachine gun. I was standing inside the door with a carbine.

A little before her ten minutes was up, the woman came back down the stairs, and under her arm was a big roll of maps. I took them and we got in the jeep and headed back toward Langenstein.

As we drove off, she stood in the doorway, watching us. The burgomeister's daughter had traded maps for a house. I probably would have torched it, just as I had threatened. There was still a war on.

Back in the S-2 room, I found that the maps were just what we needed. They were maps of Blankenberg and Westerhausen and all of the places in between. There were three copies of each. That was a big plus.

By then, it was 1:00 P.M. An hour later, a two-and-a-half-ton truck from one of the Ninth Army rear echelon units got lost on the road from Darenberg to Blankenberg and came under fire from German soldiers in Forest Heimberg. It was not far from where we had been that morning.

The truck was full of men, fifteen of them, and they were all killed. We heard about it at 3:00 P.M., and it infuriated everyone. Major Collins pulled Battery A out of position and placed it on some high ground outside of Langenstein, east of Forest Heimberg, then he ordered four anti-aircraft half-tracks positioned nearby. He put up one of our liaison planes with an observer and began to rake the woods from one end to the other, shooting the hell out of them for more than two hours. The air observer reported seeing many Germans in the woods. A lot of German aid men were milling about.

Early the next morning, Colonel Burba, CCB commander, launched an attack against the woods and cleaned the Germans out. He did it with two companies of the 49th Infantry and our battalion in support. It turned out to be a mean fight.

We put a storm of fire on the woods, methodically raking the area with high explosives, before the infantry went in. About 300 Germans were in the woods; I didn't see a single one of them get away. If they hadn't attacked the GI truck, we might have bypassed them for more important objectives.

The 49th suffered some casualties in the fight. Our only one was Lt. Arthur Johnson of Battery C, who was hit in the back by a shell fragment. Major Collins almost became a casualty when a mortar fragment knocked his helment off, leaving a deep dent on one side. The German soldiers were in the woods while I was in Darenberg, and a few were probably hidden in the houses. But they didn't challenge me. If they had, we wouldn't have gotten back alive.

The Germans in the woods disposed of, it was time to think of Blankenberg again. Lt. Col. Morgan G. Roseborough, commanding officer of the 49th Infantry, came to our CP to talk to Major Collins about the next day's attack. He was amazed to find that we had several sets of fine maps of the area. He said he needed a set of maps, that it might save him some casualties. I gave him a complete set and Colonel Burba got another set. The reluctant burgomeister's daughter and I had provided the maps for the last attack of the 8th Armored Division.

We were to attack at 11:00 A.M. on April 20. Colonel Burba, determined to suffer as few casualties as possible, requested a P-47 air cover of twenty-six aircraft to circle above Blankenberg.

For a while, it looked like there might not be an attack. Quadlenberg, which was east of Blankenberg, had surrendered without a fight. With the burgomeister of Quadlenberg in his jeep, Colonel Burba had arranged to meet the burgomeister of Blankenberg. The burgomeister of Westerhausen was also there to parley.

The two burgomeisters were sent off to Blankenberg to talk the German forces there into surrendering in order to save both German and American lives. It didn't work. The Blankenbergers had pride, or they were out of touch with reality, or they were afraid of their superiors, or all three.

They stalled, saying that if there were a big enough show of force, they would probably surrender. To them, a show of force was some airplanes overhead and fifty to seventy-five tanks around. Colonel Burba told the air control officer to dispatch the twenty-six P-47s over the town, then ordered the 36th Tank Battalion into position on the edge of Blankenberg.

Nothing happened. It was becoming apparent that it would take more than a show of force to accomplish the surrender of the town. Colonel Burba gave new orders. Our battalion and the 275th Armored Field Artillery Battalion put a TOT on the center of town — two battalion concentrations of artillery fire that impacted within one minute in the middle of Blankenberg. When the P-47s overhead saw that, they dived in to bomb and strafe hell out of the center of town. That was all it took. Blankenberg surrendered.

They should have surrendered earlier. The town was a mess. Buildings were burning, people were running everywhere, and there were some bodies lying about. The infantry went through the town and on to the hills on its west side. The tankers stayed east of town. There were no American casualties but the Germans suffered heavily, for no good reason.

I still didn't feel that I had enough German rifles and pistols. Weldon and I decided we would hit the police station in Blankenberg as we had the one in Halberstadt a few days earlier.

In a jeep, we rolled into town with the infantry, which was moving east to west. We saw nobody but the dead lying around in the streets and on the sidewalks. Many buildings were on fire and a lot of others were rubble. We went to the police station and found fifteen German policemen, mad and grumbling. We stood them up and disarmed them. I cussed them out and told them what sorry dumb bastards they were. We took all of their guns and I ordered them delivered to our jeep parked in front.

This was not "looting." Looting is going through German homes and taking personal items like jewelry, furs, and valuable pictures. We were taking arms from an agency of the German government, which is quite different. Some looting went on. The infantry did it more than the artillery, and the rear-echelon soldiers seemed to do it more than those in the front line. Some of the worst recorded cases of looting in history occurred in Fredricksberg, Virginia, after the Civil War battle there. Union soldiers looted and pillaged like barbarians, throwing fine pianos, organs, stoves, and portraits out into the street and running over them with their horses. Russian troops pillaged and raped German women as a matter of course. German troops in the occupation of France conducted themselves in a proper way, but the Gestapo made up for it, taking hostages and killing or torturing them, or both.

With the guns collected, we went off in the jeep to see what we could find, picking our way through the rubble. Out in a residential section, we came across a new German army one-and-a-half-ton truck, with an air-cooled engine. That was just about what we needed to carry our stuff.

By this time, Moose and I had a lot of rifles, machine guns, shotguns and other items, and I had a fine radio. I had so much stuff, I couldn't carry it in my half-track.

We checked the German truck carefully. As far as we could tell, it was not booby-trapped and it had practically no miles on it. We jeeped on back to Langenstein and Weldon got a mechanic from the Headquarters Battery motor section and went back to Blankenberg to get the truck. It had a short cab; the back was covered with a tarpaulin painted in desert colors; and it was painted olive drab like a U.S. Army truck, with the familiar big white star on each side. We stuck our guns inside, then turned it over to Sergeant Patrick and Sergeant Stephens. They were glad to have it, and they, in turn, looked after our stuff.

The war still wasn't quite over. A lot of attacks were made on lone American soldiers by German soldiers and civilians. Usually, the Germans would do it in bunches. Six or eight of them would jump one or two Americans. Eight American soldiers were killed in our area this way within three days. One soldier, walking down the street of a small village, was chopped to death by a German soldier with a hatchet. We heard all kinds of rumors. We all carried one or two weapons and were in a dangerous frame of mind.

The Russians were crossing the Elbe, Hitler was still alive in Berlin, and we heard strange stories about werewolves, whatever they were. Then we were ordered to move from Langenstein west again, to the vicinity of Gottingen, Hann-Munden, Hede-Munden, and other villages in Lower Saxony. When we got there, we were to organize patrols and search the area for German soldiers.

That was it, we realized. The German army was finished. The war was over. There was nothing left but mopping up.

For the first time in many months, I began to give serious thought to my future. Since I had entered the army out of college, I had no job to return to, nor did I have a family business waiting for me in Texas. I liked the atmosphere of army life and Don did too. I was leaning toward a career in the regular army. I somewhat enjoyed the excitement of war, and I was pleased that I had known fear but had not run. My mind occupied with thoughts along this line, we moved east toward Wernigerode and I began to think of other things.

From a letter to my mother:

> Looks like the war is over, all but a few die-hards in the hills.
>
> Keep my chair at the table warm, cause I'll be home before you know it.

By this time, I hated the Germans intensely. As we moved across the country, my contact with German civilians, mostly women and older men, had been as brief as I could make it. It was a task to be civil to them. During our advance eastward, I had seen many sights that were utterly insane: death camps with bodies scattered about like wood cut for the winter and not yet stacked; slave laborers everywhere. All this, combined with the supreme "innocence" of the German population and the loss of some of my friends, served as a reminder of the Nazi degeneracy.

14 Occupation — Hann-Munden

April 24, 1945–June 4, 1945

The war was over and soon most of us would be civilians again. With much on our minds, we began to carry out our duties in the occupation and governing of assigned areas. The 8th Armored was assigned to VII Corp and given a beautiful area in Lower Saxony to establish order. It was a time to wait and to live a little.

Colonel Lilly returned as battalion commander by the time the battalion left the Harz Mountains. We moved on April 24, heading west through a fairyland, a country with high, tree-covered hills laced with creeks and speckled with ancient, picturesque villages that had inspired tales of witches and goblins in German folklore. Our route took us through Wernigerode, Bad Harzburg, Goslar, and Osterode, the road leading us along high mountain ridges.

As we approached Bad Harzburg, it began to snow, flakes as big as popcorn falling straight as there was no wind. Mount Brocken, which is often mentioned in German lore, towered over us.

Moving slowly through the falling, silent snow, we needed several hours to get to Hann-Munden in Lower Saxony. An exceptionally beautiful town untouched by the war, Hann-Munden had been taken by the 1st Division without a fight two weeks earlier. The town sits in the hollow where the Werra and Fulda rivers join to form the Weser. It was one of the original German city-states established before the year 1000, and has been recognized as one of the seven most beautiful cities of the world. Hiding there were many Nazis, and it was our duty to find them and lock them up. We had a list.

Though the shooting war was over in all but name, there was a Dodge City atmosphere in the battalion. Officers and men all had two or three guns apiece and plenty of ammunition. They tended to be trigger-happy, too. That was the biggest danger now, I thought. That and the possibility of vehicle accidents.

We had strict orders from VII Corps against fraternizing with German civilians. Our job was to take charge of the place, ferret out all German soldiers who were hiding, and set up a collection station for displaced persons. Another order from Division Headquarters spelled out the way we should handle German civilians, pointing out that most German men were in POW camps or were dead. It was emphatically stated that there would be *no* social contact with German women. Such contact would be grounds for court-martial.

A small billeting party preceded us to Hann-Munden and had taken over the Jung Hotel for the enlisted men of Headquarters Battery. Near the Jung was a handsome three-story residence, Gruss Aus, which was going to be home for the battalion officers. The Germans who lived there were moved out and we moved in. Colonel Lilly took a room on the northwest corner of the second floor. My room was opposite his, on the northeast corner.

Downstairs was a large drawing room and a dining room. Capt. William A. Morris of North Canton, Ohio, Headquarters Battery commander, was responsible for the staff officers' mess. He employed a German chef and his staff. He then arranged for fresh produce, meat, and other items by placing a levy on the burgomeisters of the surrounding villages. The chef was moved into the basement of our quarters, and the mess was established in a large room on the first floor. We started to eat very well. Every evening we dressed in blouse and ties and gathered in the drawing room and had a drink or two. A string ensemble played during dinner.

We were responsible for governing the area, and also for feeding and providing medical care for the displaced persons. Helping me was Capt. Ken Zierler, battalion surgeon. To assist in this, we had a British military government team of three majors (two British, one Canadian), which was there when we arrived. The Canadian major, a hospital administrator in civilian life, proved to be a source of friction right away. He acted as if he had authority over the health care of the DPs. Zierler disliked him and made no attempt to hide his feelings. The Canadian major spoke fluent German, and was brutal and overbearing in his interrogation of Germans.

A German military post, the Kur Hessen Kaserne, was perched on higher ground in West Hann-Munden and had quartered German engineer soldiers for a hundred years or so. We started filling it up with displaced persons, Poles, Russians, Yugoslavs, Romanians, Czechs, Bulgarians, Belgians, French, Dutch, Hungarians, and some Italians. They had been dragged out of their homelands for forced labor by the Germans, and now found themselves in a strange and unfriendly environment. The caserne was big, several hundred acres, but it was hardly big enough for all these nationalities, many of whom were hostile to each other. There were several varieties of Russians, for example: Georgians, Ukrainians, and White Russians.

Each night the men fought among themselves, mostly because of women, though the women I had observed among the DPs hardly seemed worth fighting for. The men had time on their hands and were eating regularly, so with lots of energy and nothing else to do they were horny all the time. Most of the women with children tried to take care of them, but they got little or no help from the children's fathers, if they knew who they were. The men spent their time drinking, gambling, and lying around.

We disarmed them as best we could, taking all the guns and daggers we could find, and began to separate them according to nationality. Then we broke them down by marital status. I thought I had the place under control and went off to another job.

A couple of days later, I went back and found them exactly the way I had found them in the first place, drinking and gambling and fighting. Four old men were playing a card game near the entrance of one barracks building, and behind them, about twenty feet, three couples were having sexual intercourse, nobody paying attention to anyone else. I watched in amazement. Two of the women were ugly and fat, and the other one was as hairy as a bear. I decided we would feed them and let them take care of themselves, unless they got too violent, which they often did.

Three days later, two of the Russians decided to get married, a bit late, I thought, since they already had two children. During the celebration, a Russian killed another Russian and we arrested him. But right away we had a problem. We didn't know what to do with him.

He was a sorry specimen, about six-feet-one and slightly built, with ragged clothes, short hair, and whiskers all over his face. He had long arms, a low forehead, a neanderthal mouth, and a flat nose. He looked like a Slav, and not a very intelligent one.

There were no laws in the DP camp. German law didn't apply and neither did U.S. law. We couldn't shoot him outright and perhaps the other man had needed killing.

I got him outside and, through an interpreter, told him he had fifteen minutes to get out of the area, and if he ever came back to Hann-Munden, he would be shot. He looked me in the eye for what must have been a minute and decided I was serious. He ambled off down the street, occasionally glancing back over his shoulder to see if I was watching. Soon he came by on a bicycle heading up the road to Gottingen. That was the last we ever saw of him.

The DPs continued to be a problem. A couple of nights later, I was sitting in my quarters listening to the radio and writing a letter to my wife when a lieutenant came running in, yelling that there was trouble in the DP camp.

"Damn!" I said. "What's the matter now?"

"Hell, I don't know," the lieutenant said, "but if you look out there to the west you can see it."

I went over to the window. The sky was full of flares, one after another — red, green, white, and yellow, like the Fourth of July.

This was dangerous. The flares could set the buildings or something else on fire. I yelled for the officer of the day. The OD and the sergeant of the guard rounded up four or five men and a half-track and a jeep and we roared up to the caserne as fast as we could get there.

It wasn't hard to find the DPs. Most of them were sitting on a hillside facing Hann-Munden, roaring drunk, and having a hell of a time. It looked to me like they all had flare pistols and were firing them at Hann-Munden. I realized that somebody was orchestrating the whole flare show. From some distance away, I could see somebody near the front of the mob, exhorting the others and working them into a frenzy. I worked my way down to where all this was going on.

It was a woman! The one doing the haranguing was a woman in her late twenties. And what a woman! She was about six feet tall and good looking, with a magnificent body and very little to conceal it, nothing but brief shorts and a halter. I don't think I've ever seen a woman who was better built than this wild Russian. She must have been forty-two in the bust with a twenty-six-inch waist and about forty in the hips, and she couldn't have weighed more than 140 pounds.

She had big, beautiful breasts, and full, wide, rounded thighs like women depicted on space-age calendars. I thought about having her arrested so I could get a better look at her in the daylight. She strode around haranguing the people, men following her around like dogs after a bitch in heat, and like dogs they were doing everything but barking and smelling.

Through an interpreter, I told her to cut it out. There would be no more shooting that night. She glared at me for a minute, breathing hard, with an angry glitter in her eyes. Then she relaxed, talked quietly to the people around her and everybody settled down. Then, glancing at me over her shoulder, she walked away, shaking her ass.

I stood there for a minute watching her in the subdued light, wondering what kind of a scene she would cause if she had walked down Main Street in Colorado City on a Saturday night in cotton-picking season. The town would never have been the same again.

The guards collected all of the flare pistols and threw them in the river, and I went back to Hann-Munden to finish my letter.

Hann-Munden was a pleasant medieval town, many of whose buildings dated back to the fourteenth century. In the older sections, many of the buildings were three and four stories high, and each higher story was closer to the center of the street than the one beneath it, forming an arch over the street. They were made of wood, brick, and plaster and many of them were dated. One or two were from the 1500s, perfectly preserved.

To govern the town, Colonel Lilly installed 1st Lt. Francis E. Gillespie, executive officer of Battery A, as municipal judge. Gillespie had been a New York City cop in civilian life, so he was qualified to be a judge as far as Colonel Lilly was concerned. He put on his number one uniform and went up to the Rathaus, or municipal building, to assume his duties.

There was a strict curfew, and anyone caught out after curfew had to answer to Judge Gillespie. At one time or another, I brought in several curfew violators, one of them an old woman who absolutely refused to obey anybody. She went down to the lock-up screaming and carrying on all the way. Her daughter told me afterward that her mother needed a lesson. Anyway, after a night in jail, she didn't go out after curfew anymore.

Life was good in Hann-Munden, for the most part, but I was getting tired of riding around in jeeps and half-tracks. I told Colonel Lilly I wanted a car.

"Go get one," he said. So I put the word out that I wanted a car.

Next day, Sergeant Hughes brought me a brand new Hanimag, which is like a Volkswagen. I didn't know where he got it, but later I heard he had taken it out of a German civilian's garage.

I drove the Hanimag around town a few days before I realized that Colonel Lilly didn't have a car. We decided to get him one.

1st Lt. John W. Ray saw a German army doctor going east on the autobahn and ran him down. He was in a Dellahey, a sixteen-cylinder French-made convertible with front bucket seats, a small bench seat behind, and an electric shift. Ray kicked the doctor and his French woman out on the side of the autobahn, and brought the car to Colonel Lilly, who had it painted olive drab with white army stars on the side.

Meantime, I decided my Hanimag wasn't big enough. I wrote myself a requisition, which I had no authority to do, and went to Gottingen to the impounded automobile storage yard. The requisition authorized me to get any car I wanted. In Gottingen there were about 3,000 cars to choose from, and I walked around the yard until I found a beautiful four-door Mercedes built just before the war. I also picked up an Alder, a fine Czechoslovakian car, for Major Collins.

With a Dellahey, a Mercedes, and an Alder around, Colonel Lilly issued a stop order, saying we didn't need any more civilian cars in the battalion. But Marvin Sather didn't hear about the order. One day, he arrived at Battalion Headquarters in a 1930 four-door Buick touring car, a really beautiful automobile with the spare tires in the front fender wells. It came complete with chauffeur. Colonel Lilly let him keep it. Sather rode in the back seat of his Buick until we left Hann-Munden later for Czechoslovakia.

There was a lot of mopping up to do in the Hann-Munden area. We had to comb the countryside to bring it truly under U.S. Army control. Weldon and I spent a lot of time doing that. One day, we found a glider school in a high meadow southwest of Hann-Munden. About 600 acres had been cleared out of the carefully planted woodland, and it had been planted just as one would plant corn. The school had a hangar, repair shops, and several classrooms. We found pieces of gliders, the fuselage of one, a wing of another lying around the hangar.

A lot of Luftwaffe pilots had begun their training on gliders.

We also ran across the body of a 1st Division soldier who had been wounded and left leaning against a tree. He had been tagged by a medic, which indicated where the man had been hit and what the aid man had done for him. No one had come back to pick him up. We figured that must have happened about three weeks earlier.

In the woods we found many hideouts where German officers had moved in, changed clothes and left, melting into the general populace. The hideouts were littered with German army uniforms.

On our second Sunday in Hann-Munden, Colonel Lilly had the battery commanders and the battalion staff officers to lunch. The chaplain showed up early and held services out in the street in front of the Jung Hotel. The open-air service on this crisp cool morning was well attended by the men of the battalion.

By lunch time, some of us had been drinking (there was plenty of wine, scotch and vodka) and we were about half shot. We were nearly through lunch when one of the guards outside the quarters came in and said two Dutch DPs were outside and they were very agitated. I was asked to go out and talk to them.

When I got outside, I found them jumping around and speaking Dutch.

I asked, "What's wrong now?"

They replied through an interpreter. "German SS officers," one of them said. "Eight of them."

The men held up eight fingers in case the interpreter didn't get it right.

The Germans were holed up in a nearby village, they said, and they would lead us to them if we would go in and get them.

"Okay," I said. "That's fine with me. Let's go get them."

I went inside to Colonel Lilly's lunch and asked who else wanted to go. Salisbury, Sather, Weldon, and three of the others all volunteered.

Armed with carbines, pistols, and submachine guns, we piled into my Mercedes and two jeeps. The two DPs led us to the little village of Vedherhausen, on the Weser River twelve miles north of Hann-Munden. We had gone no more than four miles toward Vedherhausen when we spotted a big open-pit mine on top of a hill southeast of us. The mine, surrounded by a few buildings, had an aerial tramway going down from it to a village at the foot of the hill. We got to the top of the hill and found that the mine produced a fine white powder. Soft white ore was excavated from the top of the hill and put into clamshell-shaped buckets on a cableway. Then the material was transported downhill to the edge of town, about a mile away.

As we looked down the cableway from the top of the hill, we could see that many people were walking around in their Sunday clothes, talking and visiting. Church was out and it was a bright sunny day. The Germans were feeling good. The war was nearly over and they were alive.

We were about half full of spirits, and not necessarily friendly spirits. Just for the hell of it, we decided to get their attention by sending one of the six clamshells full of ore down the cable to the mill. The German civilians were walking some distance from where the cableway hit the level ground and made a left turn.

We loosened the brake of the clamshell, removed the stops from the arresting cable, and pushed it about fifteen feet. Down it went, swinging and sliding on the big shiny cable. It went faster and faster, bouncing up and down as the cable flexed, and the clamshell bucket, going about ninety miles an hour, was spilling out the powdery white ore and making quite a scene, sparks flying as it leaned out almost horizontal to make its left turn. Then it jumped the cable and tumbled end over end about 100 feet in the air, cartwheeling toward the Germans. They broke and ran, scattering like a covey of quail in every direction. None of them got hit, though, and it was such a spectacle that we decided to let the other five clamshell cars down the cableway, too. We did, but the Germans were well under cover by then.

That taken care of, we loaded back into the car and jeeps and went looking for the SS officers. We scoured the village, ransacking four or five houses and interrogating the Germans, then went through the adjacent woods, but didn't find them. I was starting to sober up and was mad and decided to arrest the DPs. I told them I was going to throw them in jail for sending us on a wild goose chase. We piled back into the cars and drove off to Hann-Munden. I don't think there were any SS officers in the village. All the Dutch DPs talked about on the way to the village was how easy the German women were. When we got back to Hann-Munden, I kicked their asses into Gillespie's jail and forgot about them.

Monday morning, Lt. William Hawley got word from his father, Maj. Gen. William Hawley, that he was sending him some whiskey in a DC-3. General Hawley was surgeon general of the European Theater of Operations. He said the plane would land in Gottingen and for him to have a truck there to pick up the whiskey.

The airplane came in on schedule, and the truck was waiting. General Hawley had found the booze in a warehouse near Reims and impounded it for medical supplies. He had had a heated controversy with a rear-echelon quartermaster general who wanted the whiskey for his yard birds to drink, or sell, but General Hawley held fast, sending the bulk of it to his son.

It included cognac, armagnac, scotch, vodka, and various wines. Hawley distributed it throughout the battalion and we put our part aside and used it with care. Nobody got drunk and went on a binge, at least no more than usual.

The next day, Weldon and I went out looking for stray German soldiers or anyone who looked subersive that might still be on the loose. We usually went in twos or threes, though I went out alone a few times. We were in the hilly area northwest of Hann-Munden and found a small building that somebody had used as a hideout. It was several years old and had been used for a long time. Inside we found the uniforms of three or four high-ranking German officers, one a greatcoat with a general's insignia and the label of a Berlin tailor. I kept the coat and brought it home.

About a mile from the hideout was a village down in a deep valley. Near it, the Germans were building a powerline, which they had apparently been working on for some time. Its steel support posts were huge, some of them as high as eighty feet, much like those seen around nuclear plants today. The war had apparently interrupted their work.

On the right-of-way, we found an empty, gigantic wooden drum which had a four-foot center spool and ten-foot wooden wheels supporting it. Here was a drum four feet wide and ten feet high, a tremendous thing, sitting on a cleared right-of-way, and at the foot of the hill about three-quarters of a mile away was a German village. By twisting and turning it a bit, we lined the drum up on the village street.

I drove the Mercedes up behind the drum and gave it a nudge. Down the hill it went, running arrow-straight and picking up speed. Soon it was coming off the ground, spinning in the air, and coming back down again eighty to ninety feet away, a gigantic long jump. It hit the ground and kept on going.

In the village, some Germans out in the street saw it coming and cleared out. The drum went down the main street of the village at about eighty miles an hour. The main street turned left but the drum kept going, over a creek and up the side of a hill on the other side for about 200 yards. The Germans must have been terrified.

That it was an irresponsible thing to do, I realize now, but then it didn't matter. The Germans had killed millions of people, including some of my friends, and I didn't give a damn about them or anything I did to them. I felt that with a clear conscience I could do anything to them as long as it didn't include stealing, murder, or rape. I didn't feel bad about it then and I still don't.

That afternoon, some DPs told us about a parachute factory in a nearby village, so we went over to see it. It turned out to be an elaborate layout, with thousands of bolts of material, most of it silk with all kinds and colors. I picked up eight or ten bolts, took them back to headquarters, and gave some of them to whoever wanted them.

That same afternoon, the battalion got its own patrol boat. We were driving down by the Weser, a river 200 yards wide and fairly deep, and I noticed there were no boats on it. I found an elderly German and asked him if there were ever any boats on the river.

"Ja," he said, "many, many boats."

I asked him where they were and he said he didn't know but there had been a government boat that used to work the river. It was downstream about thirty kilometers, he said.

We got in my car and started off along the river road. About twenty-five miles down the road, we saw a big house some distance from the river and I thought I could see a boat shed. I got up on top of the car with my field glasses. Yes, it was indeed a boat shed. Where there was a boat shed there was probably a boat, I figured, so we checked it out. We found a forty-foot boat and three Air Corps captains. They had spotted it from the air in their P-47s. But the boat wouldn't run. It had no carburetor. We left them tinkering with it, headed back to Hann-Munden, and got John Collins, who outranked the Air Corps captains. We would bring him, a mechanic, and whatever we could find in the way of carburetors — one off a jeep, a half-track, or a GI truck — and see if we couldn't get the boat running.

When we got back, the three Air Corps officers were still messing with the boat. Collins told them to get the hell off the boat, that we were governing this part of Germany and it was our territory. They gave us dirty looks and took off. Sergeant Duckworth worked on the boat and soon had one of the carburetors fitted. He hit the starter and the big inboard engine started to purr. The battalion had its own navy.

We took the boat upriver to Hann-Munden and moored it in the locks where the Werra and the Fulda rivers joined to form the Weser. We had no idea what we were going to do with the boat. It was just one more thing to play with.

By the time I got back to my quarters in Hann-Munden, it was almost dark. I remembered the bolt of silk and decided to make myself some silk sheets. The silk on the bolt was wide enough to be tucked on either side of the bed, so with my pocket knife I cut a length off to make a top sheet and another for a bottom. After months in a sleeping bag, I was going to spend the night between silk sheets.

It felt funny at first. It was so slick, I kept sliding off. But after a day or two, I got to like it, though I thought it was a hell of a note sleeping on silk sheets alone. I wondered how long I would be able to stay on the sheets if I were not alone. My friends soon found out about the silk sheets and I had enough silk, so pretty soon we were all sleeping on them. When they needed washing, we just threw them away and cut some new ones.

Meanwhile, Colonel Lilly received word that V-E Day (Victory in Europe) was expected in two or three days. He told us he wanted us to renew our efforts to find "Werewolves," a reported group of underground Hitler Youth, and to keep the DP camp under close control. We kept checking the countryside.

The next day I left headquarters about 9:00 A.M. and was driving along the autobahn when I met a westbound German military convoy of ambulances, trucks, and several other vehicles. I stopped them. It was a German medical battalion with a lieutenant colonel in charge. He said he was moving his medical battalion into the Ruhr and he had a First Army pass, signed by the adjutant of First Army, that gave him clearance to go. We were in Ninth Army. I didn't give a damn about First Army and I didn't give a damn about him, either.

I didn't like the idea of these Germans driving cross-country in a medical convoy, using our gasoline, when I didn't know whether they were medics or not. I didn't like them anyway. I wanted to check them out. There was a big German hospital in town. I got on the radio and got a couple of sergeants out in jeeps to escort the whole bunch up to the German hospital, where they were kept until a week after V-E Day.

With the German medics turned around, we headed on down the autobahn, scouting around. A few minutes later, I saw some people under a tree about one hundred fifty yards off the road and drove over to them. There were three German soldiers and three women. I stood them up and made sure they were not armed. The women in uniform were all blondes, medium in height, and very pretty. I don't know who these women were, but they were not nurses, nor were they in the medical corps.

I looked at them with mixed emotions. It was probably better, I thought, for these three girls to be traveling with these three men than to be going cross-country by themselves. They were trying to get home. They should have been handed to a POW cage or interned, but I let them go on their way.

Late in the afternoon, some DPs came in and said that an airplane had landed outside town with three Germans in it. One of them had been hurt and the other two had carried the injured one with them into a nearby village. It was about 9:15 P.M., still not dark, and I took one of the DPs and Captain Zierler, battalion surgeon, and we went to look for the airplane.

We soon found where the plane had gone down. It was a small, open cockpit biplane with the German cross on the fuselage. Inside, it was bloody. Somebody had been hurt. In the cockpit, I found some maps of the Munich area and an aviation first-aid kit. Whoever had been hurt must have gone into the nearby village. We went to the village and asked around, but nobody would tell us anything and I didn't feel like searching. I didn't care that much, so we went back to Hann-Munden.

The next day, Weldon and I were driving down along the Werra River when we saw a number of barrels about the size of beer kegs at the water's edge and one or two floating out in the river. We went down to see what was in them, thinking they might be full of beer.

We found one at the edge of the water and opened it up. Inside was some sort of caustic liquid. We took out the bung, which was on the side instead of the top, and pushed the barrel back into the water. Smoke squirted out of the bung hole with tremendous pressure, shooting a good forty feet in the air, and the barrel started spinning like a top. It was some spectacle, and so much fun we set off some more. We opened up another one and it started to spin like the first, drifting off down the river as it spun.

On the twelfth barrel, though, I don't know what happened, but the caustic stuff inside squirted out and got all over my boots and pants. The lower part of my pants disintegrated and my boots started getting soft. I couldn't get them off. I had a feeling this stuff was going to eat right through them.

A group of people inside a house across the road were watching us, and we went over and asked them for a bathtub of water. They provided one. I cut off my boots, got into the tub with what was left of my clothes still on, and washed myself off. I could not get in the river because the banks were vertical to allow barges to be pulled alongside the river and also to be moored there. We never found out what the chemical was, but it smoked up the valley for fifteen miles. When we came out of the house, we saw that the barrels were drifting northward toward Hann-Munden. The liquid in the barrels lasted a long time. The barrels drifted about five miles before they emptied. The wind was a zephyr from the south, and some of the smoke reached Hann-Munden.

When we returned, I went to the supply room and got some new pants and boots. In my office, I found a German man about thirty-five years old with his daughter, about nine. The man had been at the office several times trying to find his truck. The MPs had confiscated his truck, he said, and he needed it to make a living for his family.

The man spoke good English and so did his little girl, who was as pretty as any child I had ever seen. I told him that if he found his truck, he should tell me where it was, and I would get it back for him. I didn't think he would ever find it.

He did, though. He came to tell me he had found his truck in Fulda, about forty miles away on the Fulda River. He said the truck was an Opel and he described it and gave me the license number. I told him that I would get his truck for him the next morning. With Sergeant Patrick of Headquarters Battery we took a little sports car and drove to Fulda. We went to the military police compound where the man said the truck was and I presented the MP in charge with some documents I had prepared. They took me to the truck, a ragged-looking little thing, about a half-ton.

But it meant a lot to the man. It was all he had, and he needed it to carry farm goods to market and try to keep his family fed. I got the truck and started back toward Hann-Munden. The man was waiting with his daughter when we got back. He was tickled to death and started to cry, thanking me profusely. I was glad I had helped him. I gave him the truck and never saw him again. Had it not been for his little girl, I know that I wouldn't have bothered.

The next morning, I got up at 6:30 A.M. It had rained during the night and the day was cool enough for a field jacket. We had slept under a blanket and silk sheets lifted from the parachute factory. The sky was clear when I headed for battalion headquarters, buttoning my jacket against the early morning chill. A few apple trees were still in bloom and the first light of the sun turned them a brilliant white against the rolling green of the fields. To the north, the heather had brushed the hills of Lower Saxony with random patches of purple.

Hann-Munden was quiet. It had met the dawn like this since the Middle Ages. I glanced up at the old gray caserne towering on a nearby ridge. It had been the home of German engineer regiments for more than a century. Some of the forces in the Ardennes offensive had been staged there. Now it was full of displaced persons, ragged, confused, and hard to manage. I shivered and hurried to Headquarters Battery mess, hoping the coffee was hot.

We had been in Hann-Munden ten days. Headquarters Battery was in the Jung Hotel, four stories high and painted gray. The firing batteries were spread out among smaller towns nearby. Sergeant Reed poured scalding black coffee into a cup and I took my time with it. Later, I would check on the DPs at the caserne. There was no hurry, though. What was left of the German army was a long way off. We heard it was on the Elbe between our 12th Group and the Russians. It was finished. I had known that since we left Blankenberg. If I didn't have an accident or do something stupid, I would have made it through the war.

Around noon, a column of about forty olive drab GI trucks, mud spattering the white stars on their doors, raced through town nearly bumper to bumper. They were crammed to the cab with gray-clad German soldiers, standing because they were packed in too tight to sit down. When the trucks came through, the people of Hann-Munden lined up at the sides of the street to watch. Occasionally somebody waved, and sometimes one of the soldiers waved back. Most of the time, though, they were silent. Just the whine of the truck engines and the noise of the tires on cobblestones were the only sounds.

We quit early that day and headed back to our quarters, a big, comfortable old house with a lot of heavy furniture. We showered and had a good dinner, with wine and a vegetable salad. After dinner, I was cleaning a Luger taken from a German captain in Unna. I had it in pieces on a little round table. Colonel Lilly was writing a letter, and John Collins and Bill Morris were drinking scotch, and we were shooting the bull. About 9:00 P.M., the phone rang. It was division headquarters for Colonel Lilly. He went in and talked awhile. I wasn't paying any attention.

When he returned, he looked at me and said, "Let's drink to the end of the war. The war's over at midnight."

Somebody got a bottle and poured the glasses full and we drank it down. We sat around for a while, drinking and talking about how great it was. Colonel Lilly said we ought to celebrate this night. We should do something we (and the Germans) would never forget.

Nobody said anything for a moment, then finally I said, "Colonel, I think we ought to get an M-7 in here and wake these German sons of bitches up."

"That's a good idea," he said. "Tex, go call Hank."

Hank Brooks had the firing battery closest to Hann-Munden. I got him on the phone, told him what Colonel Lilly wanted to do, and he ran in the first section of his battery. An M-7 came roaring into town, a snub-nosed 105mm howitzer on a tank chassis, and a lot of men in jeeps following behind it. He put it in the middle of town with the front end of it up on timbers. If you want to shoot high angle, you've got to elevate the front.

The wire section ran a phone line from battalion headquarters down to the gun. Colonel Lilly had them elevate the tube so the round would go nearly straight up and cut the fuse at the minimum setting to make it explode harmlessly in the air. We left the crew in the middle of Hann-Munden with the howitzer pointing up. Three rounds were prepared and the gun was ready to fire. We went back to headquarters to drink and wait, Colonel Lilly keeping an eye on his watch, and by midnight we were pretty lit up. Colonel Lilly picked up the phone and got the battery.

"FIRE!"

The first round exploded with the familiar sharp *crack!* we'd come to know so well. Then two more cracks. They went off at about the height of the surrounding hills and made a hell of a racket. When they exploded, they shook up one of our gunners sitting behind a machine gun somewhere. We had .50-caliber machine guns covering all the roads with regular fire plans in case of trouble. When the shells exploded, the gunner got nervous and started shooting his .50, then one by one, the rest of them joined in. Machine guns were going off all around the town, tracers flying everywhere. We could see criss-crossing trails of fire in the dark. When the guns ran out of ammunition, we went back to our quarters.

This symbolic end of the war made me start thinking of the friends we lost: Sam Blatman and Baldwin and the leg he'd lost and thrown away, and all the rest. I thought of the soldier whose body was leaning up against a tree — dead. The medic had worked on him, and left him tagged, but no one came to pick him up. He died alone leaning up against a tree, 2,000 miles from home. A blonde young soldier, lying dead on a German highway, with the wind whipping at his hair. I thought of all the guys who'd gotten killed in little chicken-shit German places. The war was over, but that didn't mean the world was going to be a better place. There was no need to think that far ahead. Looking around at my friends, warm and secure, I realized we were the lucky ones. We had made it. I didn't know it then, but more than a hundred of my A&M classmates had been killed.

The end of the war made little real difference, however. We went on patrolling and exploring the area.

For some time now, I had noticed the castle high on a hill outside Hede-Munden, a town near Hann-Munden on the road to Gottingen. The hill was higher than any of the surrounding hills and the castle stood at its very top. I had made a mental note that when things slowed down, I would go up and see who lived there and what they were doing. Perhaps we could take it over as a retreat for either officers or enlisted men. Early in the afternoon one fine spring day, Lt. Harold H. Ezra of Crawfordsville, Indiana, and I went up to look at the castle.

Working our way up to the entrance wasn't easy. The road didn't go around the hill, but doubled back with hairpin turns. When we finally got to the structure itself, it looked huge.

We pulled up in front of the entrance, a gateway of two massive wooden doors, each of them twelve feet high and six feet wide with an oval top. They had no visible hinges, locks, or handles. I beat on the door.

Nothing happened. I honked the horn of the Mercedes two or three times, but still nothing happened. Then I honked the horn again, one long loud blast, and waited. There was some activity on the other side of the gate and a panel in one of the doors slowly opened.

An old man looked out through the panel. He couldn't speak

English, but I was able to tell him I wanted to look around. He said he would get the countess.

In a few minutes, he came back with a woman about forty-five years old, rather tired-looking, but still very attractive. She spoke perfect English and introduced herself as the Countess Henschel.

The name struck a chord. I knew the name Henschel. There were Henschel trucks and a lot of other things in Germany had been made by Henschel.

The countess asked what I wanted. I told her I wanted to look around.

"Why?" she asked. She seemed gracious, not resentful.

I said, "Well, for several reasons. I want to know who's here, for one thing. I want to know if there are any men here of military age." I told her, too, that we might want to use the castle from time to time.

"It's full," she said. "It's full of people. Every room is occupied, but you are free to look. If you will follow me into the drawing room, I'll get my son and he will show you what you want to see."

She led us through many rooms to a very big one much like the formal dining room in Langenstein. It had a massive table, animal heads on the walls, and at one end a case of trophies. On either side of the case was a full suit of armor and opposite the trophy case were some flags or banners crossed on ten-foot staffs. It was a magnificent room.

A moment later, a man slightly older than I came in and introduced himself. He once was a captain in the German army, a field artillery officer, he said, and had been at home convalescing after receiving a wound at the Russian front. He was discharged from the army, and had been at home about seven months. He had been hit in the right side and his right arm was still bound. He was a frail, pleasant-looking fellow who spoke fine English.

"What would you like to see?" he asked.

"I don't want to see the living quarters. I would like to see your kitchens and the keep."

He said, "Let's look at the keep first."

He led us to the base of the tower and through a door on the same level as the banquet room. It was arched at the top and made of heavy timbers. The keep was fifteen feet in diameter and seventy feet high. Inside was a circular stone staircase along the wall which had no railing to keep you from falling off to the inside, but there was a leather-covered rope to hold onto about three feet off of the step and fastened to the inside wall.

Keeping close to the wall, we went up the staircase to a trap door, which opened onto the roof. It was apparent that the staircase had seldom been used and that no one had been there for a long, long time.

The keep was classic, a perfect circle, with battlements, slots for archers to shoot from. There was even a staff holder so you could hoist a banner if you wanted to. We went through the trap door in the roof and stood up. The top of the revetment was head high; two-foot firing slots, all around the keep, were up to the chest. I had seen castles in England and others in France and Belgium, but not like this one. This one was a storybook castle, with everything but knights and their ladies, troubadours, and gallant war horses.

Instead, when I looked down I saw formal gardens and eight or ten young ladies in bathing suits. I raised an eyebrow at Henschel.

He shrugged. "Some of them are my sisters," he said, "and some are my cousins. We lived in Kassel, but the bombing drove us away. A lot of my relatives are here with us, my mother, some of my father's people, some aunts and uncles and their children." He shrugged again. "There are 140 people living here."

The sleeping quarters, he said, were scattered mainly on the second and third floors, some on the fourth. The first floor held dining rooms, banquet rooms, and drawing rooms.

The south and east walls formed the outside wall of the building, and above twenty feet there were a few windows, but the rest of the windows faced the interior court. The north and west interior walls faced open areas, stables, a kitchen garden, a parking area, and the formal gardens on the south.

I asked Henschel what his family did and how they could afford such an establishment. He said they owned a locomotive factory in Kassel. The family had always had lots of money. I knew that they also built Tiger tanks, but I didn't say anything about that, nor did he.

I looked below to the south, where there had been a skirmish between an American unit and the Germans. Two German half-tracks had been knocked out and burned on one of the slopes of the hill below the castle. Henschel said there had been fighting nearby, but nobody had come near the castle. He said he thought it had been the American 5th Armored Division, which had come through two weeks before.

While we were talking, I heard some airplanes very close to us and looked up to see them.

"Down there," Henschel said, pointing.

I looked down to the west and saw two P-38s flying off southward several hundred feet lower than we were.

I asked Henschel about his experiences in Russia and he said he was glad he had done his service there, and hadn't had to stand up to the American artillery. He asked me how long I thought the Americans would be in Germany. I told him they would be there a lifetime. Germany had started two world wars, I said, and neither our government nor the British would allow that to happen again.

"I imagine American troops will be in Germany fifty to sixty years," I said.

He seemed quite surprised, and said he thought they would be gone in a year or two.

He led us back down the circular staircase and we left.

When we got back to Hann-Munden, we found that a German woman had been raped and shot that morning. She was in the big German hospital in town. I got in the Mercedes and drove there immediately to talk to the German doctor. He was a pleasant, middle-aged, white-haired man in rimless glasses, and he spoke good English.

"The woman is going to die," he said simply. The doctor said the woman had told him that a black soldier had caught her that morning, raped, and then shot her. It had happened near the little town of Blume, a mile or two away. I got in my car, drove to Blume, and found the area. On the ground, I found two hulls of 7.65 pistol cartridges. It was getting dark when I returned to Hann-Munden.

A black engineering company was upstream on the Fulda River repairing a bridge, and I figured one of their people had done it. They were the only blacks I had seen in the area. The next morning, I went to the company commander and laid out the problem for him.

I was indignant. There was no sense in this sort of thing, I said. There were too many willing women around for this to happen. I asked the company commander if he could account for all of his men on the previous morning.

"Most of them," he said.

I told him I was acting under the authority of our division commander, Maj. Gen. John Devine. Since the engineering company was in our division area, we had authority and I ordered him to account for all of his men. Anybody he could not absolutely account for, I wanted. He went off with his first sergeant and platoon sergeants and I sat down to wait.

A couple of hours later, they came back and said there were only three men they could not account for during that period.

"Fine," I said, "now, I want those three and I want three more that you can absolutely account for, that you know beyond question were here and working."

The company commander got his company clerk and two corporals that he was sure of, and I took the six men in one of their trucks and went to the hospital in Hann-Munden.

I told the doctor that I had six men who were suspects in the case and that I would like for the woman to take a look at them. He said she was close to death, but he would talk to her. I told him to tell her I would be in the room with her. I would be armed and these men would not be armed. All she had to do was to tell us which one it was. He nodded and left, returning in several minutes to say that the woman had agreed to try.

The doctor stood at the head of the bed and I took a place beside it with two armed sergeants. The men were brought in one at a time.

The first four got no response, but when the fifth entered the room, she screamed weakly. This was the man who had raped her, she told the doctor. The sixth man was sent through and he got no response from the woman.

Then I had the men change jackets and come in again. The fifth one from the previous review came in third, but the woman picked him again.

"Okay," I said, "we'll take it from here." She was crying and I thanked her. I had the soldier put under guard and was getting ready to go when the doctor said, "Just a minute."

I turned back to him.

"She's dead," he said. "She died as soon as you left."

I had seen a lot of killing in the past few months and I thought I was hardened to it, but I was wrong. The woman was about twenty-five and quite attractive. She had two small children, and her husband, who was in the German army, was either dead or a POW somewhere.

The only defense German girls had was to stay inside, and sometimes that was not enough. Some soldiers, particularly rear-echelon troops, seemed to think it was their right and privilege to rape and loot.

The soldier the German woman had picked twice was a short man, lighter than the others. His company commander told me he knew that the man picked by the woman had not been away from the company at the time of the attack. The man was his company clerk. The captain said the clerk had been at headquarters at the time and the first sergeant said the same thing. The woman had evidently made a mistake. I wrote a report and sent it forward. That was the end of it as far as the U.S. Army was concerned.

The day after the woman died, Weldon and I went to check out a section of town on a hill overlooking Hann-Munden. We hadn't been there before. When we started to look around, we noticed a lot of fine two- and three-story houses, well kept but unoccupied. Something didn't look right. We stopped the car and got out, and I walked about twelve feet in front of the car.

I said, "I don't like the looks of this at all. The street may be mined." Weldon agreed and we started back down into town. It was 10:00 A.M.

Around the middle of the afternoon, we heard a terrific *whump!* The explosion occurred where we had been that morning. I looked up and saw smoke and fire.

The next day we learned that a truckload of the black soldiers from the engineering unit had been going through houses there, traveling down the same street that Weldon and I had been on, and had hit a regal mine fifty feet down the street from where we stopped.

The explosion killed twelve of them and burned the truck. I hoped one of the twelve was the man who had raped and killed the young German woman.

Amid all this, normal life went on. An effort was being made by units of Ninth Army to round up all the displaced persons in the area and take them to Hann-Munden. From there they would go to Gottingen to be separated into nationalities in preparation for the trip home by train. Toward the end of this roundup, we found that quite a few French prisoners of war, some of whom had been captured as early as 1940, had established liaisons with Russian, Dutch, Polish, or German girls, and had one to five children by them.

Several hundred of them wanted to get married. Love and the U.S. Army found a way. Lt. James E. Russ, formerly of the 399th but then with Division Artillery, was detailed to marry them.

Jim Russ married them on May 20, 1945. Standing on the hood of a jeep in the town plaza of Gottingen, he married 250 ragtag displaced persons, all dressed in their best clothes, their children in attendance. Afterward, he issued them marriage certificates under his own signature. Russ and two other lieutenants stood around signing certificates on the hood of a jeep until all the newlyweds had one.

That allowed the Polish, German, Dutch, and Russian girls to go home with their French husbands. The mass marriage got widespread publicity, and Russ would later occasionally mention that he had married 250 couples, with a total of 500 children. He could no more legally marry people than I could, but at least it legalized a lot of bastards.

Next day, I had reason to unofficially relax the army's strict nonfraternization order. Sergeant Hughes came into my office early in the morning and told me one of the eighteen replacements had received a letter from his mother in Milwaukee. She said his grandmother and two aunts lived in Hann-Munden and gave him their address. She said if he could find Hann-Munden, he should try to see them as she had heard nothing from them in four years. When the replacement received the letter, he was in Hann-Munden and only a block away from his grandmother. Fraternization was forbidden, but he wanted Sergeant Hughes to get him permission to see his relatives.

The address was near the Jung Hotel. I told Sergeant Hughes to take him to visit them; I would be responsible.

That same day, several DPs walked in from the south and told us a large airplane had landed on the side of a hill near Hede-Munden about daybreak. They said it was full of Germans who had gone to the nearby villages and woods. Collins, Weldon, and I went out to the scene, taking with us an armed detail. There it was on the hillside: a big tri-motored JU-52, which was capable of carrying forty to fifty people. With an engine in its nose and one on each side of the cabin, it looked a little like the old American Ford Trimotor. The plane was still armed with a machine gun in the turret on top. The big Junkers didn't seem to be damaged, and it would have taken considerable skill to put such a big airplane down where it had landed.

We saw no one in the airplane or near it and no indication where they had come from. They simply melted into Germany.

We spent the next few days trying to round up DPs in the outlying areas. We were also looking for former German soldiers. Major Collins and two or three other officers took his Adler and drove to Paris. George Salisbury, of Battery C, was in Gottingen, stationed at the caserne, and had charge of political prisoners, both men and women, including some *gauleiters* (Nazi district political leaders) and various other high-ranking Nazi officials.

They were a troublesome crowd. One killed himself and several of the women tried to bribe Salisbury, he told me, with one thing or another. During this period he learned that during the advance from Selm to Bad Lipsprings, one of his non-commissioned officers had gone into a German bank with a submachine gun and gathered up all the money in sight, the equivalent of several thousand dollars.

Salisbury ordered him to turn it in, but since he couldn't give it back to the bank, he used it to supplement the battery's rations, buying fresh produce, chickens, and beef when there was none around for the taking. The battery ate well for a while, but a new currency was soon issued to the troops. American troops wouldn't be able to use German reichmarks anymore, though the German people could.

With this in mind, George went to a jewelry store in Gottingen and spent it all on 130 pieces of jewelry. The items were numbered and each man drew a number for a piece of jewelry.

Meanwhile, we were getting ready to move. On May 29, the 8th Armored Division was assigned to V Corps of Third Army, which had its headquarters in Pilsen, Czechoslovakia. We were told to move out of Hann-Munden to the vicinity of Pilsen by June 4.

Word was out that the 399th Armored Field Artillery Battalion had several civilian automobiles. The orders said they could not be taken to Czechoslovakia. But I didn't want to lose my car and Colonel Lilly didn't want to lose his, either, so he detailed me to take my car, his car, and Major Collins' car on ahead of the division. With two sergeants and a mechanic, I was to go on ahead to the village of Horsica, twenty-five miles south of Pilsen.

We made a trip out of it, swinging through Leipzig and Nuremberg on the way to Pilsen. This was hilly country and very beautiful, the fruit trees still blooming, fields painted yellow with wildflowers.

Leipzig was in ruins. Nuremberg was a wreck, too, with nothing but the shells of buildings standing. The streets had been bulldozed clear. It was full of rear-echelon troops, quartermaster and service troops, and practically everybody was chasing one German girl or another. In Hann-Munden, we were under strict orders against fraternizing with the German population, and the officers and, as far as I knew, most of the men had obeyed them. In Nuremberg, fraternization was widespread. We found a quartermaster truck company and stayed overnight. In the morning, we resumed our trip to Pilsen.

Heading northeast toward the Czech border, we noticed that the churches began to have onion-shaped tops instead of steeples, especially on the Czech side. Most of the onion tops were painted bright colors. We entered Czechoslovakia at Rozvadov, a small frontier town on the western edge of a belt of fortresses that Czechoslovakia built after World War I. Mountains in this area were steep, with rounded tops. The road went up and down and wound around. We were entering an area known as the Bohemia Wall, which was a formidable defensive belt with a number of powerful forts.

After we passed through a belt of forest, we came to tillable land and I noticed plants growing on tall poles, which were joined together at the top like an Indian tepee. The poles were about twenty-five feet high and the plants were growing around the poles. Later, I learned that these were hops. Beans were growing in the fields, and in one field were about sixty Czech soldiers picking them. They were not gathering the beans in sacks or buckets, but were picking them and eating them raw, going down the rows and cleaning the field.

Fifty miles from the frontier, we came to Pilsen, where the division would have its headquarters. We spent a couple of days on the outskirts of town with a field artillery battalion of the 2nd Division, lying around and talking about home, the war, and what kind of people the Czechs were. Once we went into Pilsen, but there was nothing doing there. On the morning of June 3, we went on to Horsica. The battalion came rolling in that afternoon.

From a letter to Don:

> Here we are in Pilsen, Czechoslovakia, with nothing to do but think of you. And I do. Some day, Don, we must return to this beautiful country. I want to walk through the woods here with you.

Karlovy Vary
RUSSIAN
OCCUPATION ZONE
RED ARMY
XXXXX
U S ARMY
Pilsen
ROKYCANY
N
W
S
Rozvadov
AREA MAP 5
CZECHOSLOVAKIA
JUNE – NOVEMBER 1945
INTERNATIONAL BOUNDRY
SUDETENLAND EAST LIMIT
Scale 1 inch equals 8 Miles
Horsica
Blovice
XXXXX
Domazlice
Klatovy
KLENCI
Horadovice
Furth in Wald
Strakonice
Cham
Susice
To Neuburg au Donau
GERMANY
WINTERBERG
Prachatice
Danube River
Isar River
Passau
Inn River
AUSTRIA

15 Czechoslovakia

June 5, 1945–June 26, 1945

Thousands of Russians were found in German uniforms and were being sent back to Russia. Other nationalities were being rounded up and moved out. The United States Tenth Army cleared Okinawa, and the Luzon Campaign was finished.

Horsica was a strange place. Here, the pavement stopped and the road forked, one branch leading over some hills to the east, the other through a forest to the village of Petrovice. Horsica itself had one public building, which was a dance hall, bar, and town hall all in one. We took some rooms on the upper floor for our headquarters. Near the end of the paved road was a schoolhouse built in the late nineteenth century. It was a rather nice building and we put Headquarters Battery as well as our aid station there.

To the south was the municipal duck pond, an acre of stagnant water in a low area surrounded by trees. Every day, the old ladies of the village gathered the family's geese and headed for the pond. The geese, mostly white, were trained and at about 10:00 A.M., when it was time to go to the water, the old lady would open the gate and the geese would file out in a line.

Sometimes there would be as many as ten, sometimes as few as three. They waddled through the village to the pond in single file, always in the same order, and slid into the water. Meantime, the other old ladies who had geese were headed that way, too. There were columns of geese coming toward the pond from all directions.

Around noon, the old ladies got up and started some kind of jabbering and the geese came out of the water, lined up, and waddled home. This went on every day.

I moved into a stucco house that had been built in the early 1930s. The family that lived there included a man, his wife, her mother, and their two children, a typical peasant family. He was short and stocky. She was shapeless and generally unkempt, wearing no makeup. The women didn't shave their legs or underarms. The woman's mother, though, was a slender, nice-looking, white-haired woman of sixty-five. The little girl was about eight, the boy six. It was the grandmother's room that I moved into, and it was rather comfortable. A few days later, I noticed that the old lady was sick with a swollen jaw. I took her to our aid station. She had an abscess in her jaw. Captain Zierler gave her some sulfa and lanced it and took care of her.

One thing that made Horsica easier to bear was that I still had my car. Colonel Holt, Division Artillery commander, came down one day and raised hell about the civilian cars. He said to turn them in. I asked myself: Turn them in? Where? To whom? I turned mine into myself and kept on driving it. When he left, we forgot about it. We had places to go. In the evening, there wasn't much to do, so I used to get in the car and drive to some of the other Czech towns, some of them fifty miles away. One of them, Pisek, was full of Russian soldiers. I kept exploring the surrounding towns every evening after dinner, since it didn't get dark until 10:00 P.M.

One evening, I drove over to a little town called Blovice. Everybody was in the plaza in native dress and a little band of about four or five pieces, mostly old men, was playing a lively schottische. They seemed to be having a parade. Everybody was walking down the road. The town fire department, a 200-gallon tank on two wheels, was pulled by two men and pushed by two more. Behind them were young men in their teens in traditional dress. The band was walking along behind them, getting a lot of sound out of its trumpets and trombones. Bringing up the rear behind the band were the townspeople, strung out and walking. I wondered what in the hell they were doing.

Then I noticed that one of them was wearing a British uniform.

The British had trained a Czech brigade, so I figured he spoke English. I got out of the car, walked along with him a little way, and tried to get him to tell me what was going on.

They were celebrating the unification of sports, he said. I asked him what that meant, but couldn't get much out of him. The only sport I had seen was men chasing women and vice versa. The people ended up on the top of a hill near a shrine. I wasn't sure what was happening, but it was more interesting than Horsica.

Life was slow in Horsica. The battalion spent the days working on equipment or training. In the evening, the men loaded up on trucks and went into Pilsen to get drunk, get into fights, and visit whores. I spent my time wandering around western Czechoslovakia. Once I was driving near Pilsen when I found a secluded one-room building in some woods accessible only by a narrow wagon-type trail. I very carefully looked it over and, exercising extreme care, was able to enter. It was crammed with various kinds of ammunition. All I wanted was some 9mm pistol shells. I found several boxes and took some for myself and my friends.

From there, I went on to the airport in Pilsen and found hundreds of DPs lined up to be flown to various places in Europe, many of them ultimately to the United States. They were not the kind of DPs we had been accustomed to handling: Poles, Ukrainians, Russians, Bulgarians, French, and Hungarians. These were wealthy people, some of them Jewish, boarding DC-3s and leaving about every five minutes.

One family I noticed particularly, a small man and his wife, two girls about twelve and fourteen, and a little boy. They told me they thought they were being sent to Wisconsin, where they had some relatives. They seemed apprehensive as hell, afraid they would miss their plane, and they didn't say much. I think they had been brought in from Austria. They were not from Germany, I was sure.

The next day, members of the Czech Armored Brigade were investigating the building in the forest that I had discovered the day before. They had tripped a booby trap wire and the building exploded, killing six soldiers. When I was there, I was extremely careful. The place had not looked right to me.

In Horsica, where there was plenty of open country, we spent time shooting with pistols and carbines. I got to know the family I was living with very well and took the children riding with me at night. Our mail caught up with us for the first time in a month, and I got twenty letters from Don.

The division was in limbo. Rumors were going around that the division would be dissolved, broken up. We heard that it would be a carrier for high-point men.

Rank had nothing to do with how soon we were going to be sent back to the United States. A man got one point for each month in the service and an additional point for each month spent overseas. He got five points for each decoration, five for each campaign, and five for each legitimate child. A high-point man had ninety points or more. Generally, we were low-point people because we had not been overseas that long.

But we didn't think we were going to the Pacific. Some of the division had already been picked out and formed into special units to be sent there. The 18th Tank Battalion had been pulled out and sent with Lt. Col. Gwin Goodrich for amphibious training. With nothing much to do, we just sat there in Horsica, waiting, with no idea what was going on.

Around the middle of June, Colonel Lilly called me to his office.

"Let's go to Paris," he said.

My face lit up. Paris sounded a lot better than the Czech towns I'd been visiting every night. "Sounds fine," I said.

Colonel Lilly said he would have the orders cut and we would take a jeep. I was instructed to find a driver, and to try to make the jeep comfortable by getting some decent seats and a rack for baggage. I rounded up some comfortable seats and recruited Tech/5 Roth to drive it. He had driven my half-track halfway across Europe and he was my friend.

We had the mess sergeant pack a big lunch and took off from Horsica early in the morning, heading for Bad Tolz, where Third Army headquarters were. Colonel Lilly wanted to see some friends in Third Army. A couple of days later, we went on toward France, through Munich, Augsburg, Ulm, Stuttgart and on to Mannheim, driving through the Black Forest area along the way. It was hilly country with deep narrow valleys between the hills, with a road on one side and a stream on the other.

In mid-June, little more than a month since V-E Day, we found plenty of reminders of the war. We found where the Air Corps had caught a German horse-drawn regiment and destroyed it. Hundreds of shot-up vehicles had been bulldozed off the road to make it passable and the carcasses of the horses were still lying where they fell, decaying. The stench was horrible — eight miles of it.

In Metz, we found a room in a walk-up fleabag hotel and spent the night. Heading out for Paris at first light, we drove through Verdun, Reims, and Chateau-Thierry. By 2:00 P.M., I saw it, the black needle of the Eiffel Tower reaching up into a blue sky. Paris!

A few minutes later, we were on the Avenue Foch, a few blocks from the Champs-Elysees. The city was busier than a yard full of chickens at feeding time, the streets full of military vehicles and people crossing wherever they liked. There were tables on the sidewalk and people were sitting at them drinking wine. Everybody in Paris was having a good time.

Roth pulled up to a curb near a serviceman's center and the first person I saw when I stepped out of the jeep was a soldier I had shipped out fourteen months before for stealing from other soldiers in Headquarters Battery. He looked fine. He had made corporal in the 17th Airborne Division. He was glad to see me and I was glad to see him. While we were talking, Colonel Lilly got us billets on the third floor of a small hotel off the Champs-Elysees, about two blocks east of the Arc de Triomphe. Paris was waiting.

Colonel Lilly knew what he wanted to see. He had mentioned that he wanted to go to the Louvre, the opera, and the Palace of Versailles. I wanted to go to Versailles and the Folies Bergere. He didn't  seem much interested in the Folies. That night, we went to a cabaret full of fat, ugly dancers who looked as if they had had a rough time during the occupation. Next day, we found the Armed Forces Ticket Center off the Avenue Foch and I got a ticket to the Folies for Wednesday night, the same night Colonel Lilly got a ticket to the opera. We went our separate ways.

I had a map of Paris and thought that I could find the Folies Bergere on the Metro, the subway, and I did. The Metro was crowded and the attendants were actually cramming people into cars during rush hour.

I went in and found a woman in a cage ready to take tickets. Inside, the theater was empty. I was the first one there. A tall old man came and took my stub and led me to a seat. It took him about twenty minutes because it was on the fifth tier, undoubtedly the worst seat in the house. The stage was hardly visible. I left my seat and worked my way back to the main floor and found the usher, who spoke English.

"This seat isn't worth a damn," I told him. "I want another one."

"It is impossible, monsieur," he said. "It is out of the question. The place has been sold out for some time."

I asked where the manager was and he said I couldn't see the manager because he was a very busy man. When I insisted, he led me to the manager's office, which was large and lavishly furnished. The well-fed manager, who spoke perfect English, was immaculately dressed and obviously had had no trouble during the occupation. He asked me what the problem was.

"I'm just an ordinary soldier from Texas," I said. "I've heard about the Folies Bergere all my life and I want to see it." I put the accent on the word "see." The seat I had bought, I told him, was on the fifth floor behind a post, and I could hardly see the stage, much less the performance. Then I showed him my stub.

He made some conciliatory sounds and started talking to the old usher in rapid-fire French. I could understand a little French, but not much of what he was saying. The first thing I knew, the usher picked up a big overstuffed chair, so big he could hardly carry it, and started out the door.

The manager said, "You will follow him. He will take you to where you can see the Folies Bergere with my compliments. I want you to enjoy the show and I'm glad you came in and told me you were unhappy with your seat." He smiled and offered his hand. I shook it and went off after the old man carrying the chair. I had no idea where he was going. I figured he would put me in an aisle someplace.

By then, the theater was three-fourths full. People were pouring in, most of them GIs, officers, nurses and WACs — mainly an army audience. The old man was looking tired with the chair on his back, so I picked up the back of it and we started down the center aisle. It was full of people and he was crowding them out of the way and they were hollering and cussing each other, and I was coming along behind him with the back of the chair.

The old usher pushed through to the front of the theater. There was a barrier between the seats and the orchestra pit, and he handed the chair over the railing to somebody in the pit, chattering to him in French. Then he and two other people took the chair and started rearranging chairs in the center of the orchestra pit. Finally, he stood up and beckoned to me and I crawled over the barrier.

The old man made a sweeping bow, and with his right hand, he made a sweeping motion to the chair. He stood there smiling. I had a damned good seat, the best in the house. I smiled back. I tipped him and sat down, ready for the show.

Soon, people in the audience started to holler at me, and after a minute or two, the whole place was yelling. I stood up in the chair and held my hands over my head like a boxer, hands clasped together, and shook them four times. They cheered the roof off and I sat down to wait for the show.

I didn't have long to wait. The orchestra tuned up and soon they were into the overture. The curtain went up and out came the chorus line, good-looking girls fully dressed, dancing and kicking higher than I had thought a dancer could kick. They were followed by a comedy team, a man and a woman, and the woman had on less than the dancers had. The man was making suggestive remarks and feeling her up.

That went on for a while, with the audience howling and carrying on, before the chorus line came back wearing less than before, but not quite bare, kicking around not quite three feet above me. The angle I was seeing them from was a little bit different from the rest of the audience, and some of them were just damned good-looking.

Next came a comic, a nasty type who was always fooling with his britches and rubbing himself. He looked down, saw me and made some wisecracks, all the time fooling around in his britches and looking at me. It half made me sore, but I didn't feel like getting up and saying anything. Everybody was laughing at him or me, but I didn't know which.

When the chorus came back, kicking at the ceiling as usual, they were down to the G-strings, right up there above me dancing to beat hell. One or two of them really had big tits. I kept watching one of them whose tits were bouncing up and down so much I didn't see how she stood it, but it didn't seem to bother her a bit. The G-strings were small and kept slipping around on the girls, and I was sitting there looking up at all that; it was just about more than I could stand. Some of the musicians were in about the same shape, and it sounded like they weren't all playing the same tune.

When intermission came, everybody got up and went out for some fresh air, but I was reluctant to leave my seat, afraid I'd have to fight for it when I got back. So I sat there for a while. Finally, the man in charge of the orchestra came over and told me that if I wanted to go outside for some air, he would see to it that no one got my chair. Standing outside, I heard some of them talking about the "captain sitting in the orchestra pit."

The rest of the show was a repeat of the first part: gorgeous girls right above me, dancing, kicking, shaking, grinding. One chorus line toward the end of the show was made up of tall girls, all of them over six feet. I've never seen prettier or more well-built girls except once. I don't think they got any of them in West Texas, but they might have found one in a DP camp in Hann-Munden.

I got back to the room about the same time Colonel Lilly did. When I told him what happened he didn't believe it. I wasn't sure I did either.

We decided to spend Saturday on the streets, have dinner at a sidewalk cafe, go to some bistros, and generally see what was happening. It was a beautiful day, crisp and clear — summer in Paris was not like the West Texas summers I remembered. We took in the Louvre museum, the Arc de Triomphe, the Eiffel Tower, and all the tourist sights. Late in the afternoon, we split a bottle of white wine, but it was 9:00 P.M. before we sat down at a sidewalk cafe for dinner. We were well into another bottle of white wine when we saw one of the division staff officers, Col. Philip Malcolm. Colonel Lilly hailed him and he joined us at our little round table.

Malcolm was pretty well plastered. He had a bad case of the red ass, a "howling case of the red ass," as we used to say at Texas A&M. We tried to find out what was eating him and the story spilled out.

He had finished college in 1917 and since there was a war on, he had enlisted in the army. Accepted into Officers' Training School, he had graduated in the late summer of 1917 and had been assigned to the 2nd Division. He came to France as part of the American Expeditionary Force, sailing in January of 1918. They had landed at St. Nazaire and moved on to Chaumont. In July of 1918, he had been in the big fight with the Germans at Chateau-Thierry, which was about forty miles down the road from Paris, and as an infantry officer, he had had a pretty rough time there. He had been scared, but he hadn't been wounded.

In August, he had gotten a fifteen-day leave and came to Paris, without really knowing what he was going to do. Not long after he got there, he had found a very nice bordello on the Avenue Foch and the Champs-Elysees, near where we were. The madam had taken a liking to him and he had liked the girls, and spent his whole fifteen days in the bordello. He hadn't gone out to eat. He ate all of his meals with the girls and had a great time.

He told us that it was probably the most wonderful experience of his life and he'd always wanted to go back and see it. He wanted to see if any of the girls were still around or where they were. He felt that Madam Jacqueline might still be there because she hadn't been much older than he was, and she had owned the place.

He knew that it was close to where we were, but he could not find it. He had been hunting for it since 2:00 P.M. He'd hunt awhile, and drink awhile, and hunt some more, then drink some more. When he got to our table, he was pretty well shot and almost crying with frustration. He described Madam Jacqueline's place quite vividly. One girl he remembered so well that he was crying.

I felt sorry for him. I liked the man even if he was a colonel. All of a sudden, he straightened up and looked alert.

I said, "What's the matter?"

"See that lieutenant over there? I know him."

The lieutenant was some distance away and the light was not that good, but he began to walk toward us, and a shaft of light hit his face. The colonel knocked over a chair jumping up. He called out a name and the lieutenant froze in his tracks. Then he started running toward us and the two of them grabbed each other in a bear hug. A minute later, both of them were crying.

The colonel had found his son, an infantry officer, that he had not seen in three years. He had not heard from him since April and didn't know where he was or whether he was dead or alive. And he'd found him while sitting in a Paris sidewalk cafe reminiscing about a bordello he'd been in so many years ago.

The colonel brought him over and ordered some more wine. We all drank together for a while. Then they went off together, the colonel's arm around his son's waist, the boy's arm around his father's shoulder.

I felt sad and quiet, thinking about my own dad. We had buried him a year before to the day.

Early the next day, we headed for Czechoslovakia, following a route through Chateau-Thierry, Rheims, the Argonne Forest, and Luxembourg, where we spent the night. Soon we were back in Germany, taking the road to Frankfurt. The road was lined with apple trees hung with ripe, red fruit. The trees had straw tassels hung on them to scare off the birds, and they were whitewashed with lime. We stopped and I gathered half a dozen apples from the nearest branches.

Roth headed the jeep toward Frankfurt again and I settled down to munch an apple, first wiping off the whitewash. They were moist and juicy and I ate a couple of them, peel and all. As I was to find out later, it was the wrong thing to do. By the time we rolled into Frankfurt, I was sick.

Later, after a really unpleasant day, I discovered that the whitewash on the apples wasn't whitewash — it was arsenic! We waited a day and then went on to Horsica. I ate no more roadside apples along the way.

On June 24, the rumors were confirmed. The 8th Armored was effectively broken up. Most of the officers with under eighty points were transferred to the 94th and 83rd Infantry Divisions. The enlisted men were shipped to various other units. I was ordered to the 94th, and then assigned to the 301st Field Artillery Battalion, which was stationed in the Czech town of Vimperk, about seventy miles south of Horsica. Brooks and Capt. Willis F. Gausman from our battalion went to the 301st, too. Colonel Lilly went to the 919th Field Artillery Battalion, along with Don Sears and a few others.

I packed my gear and went in to tell the Czech family goodbye. The man asked me for my radio, but I had carried it with me since early in the campaign and I didn't want to part with it. I did leave him my Mercedes, which was hidden behind his house, thinking maybe he could either sell it or get some good out of it. Then I got a jeep and driver and started off for Winterberg (the Czech name was Vimperk) and the 301st Field Artillery Battalion.

Established before the year 1000 A.D., Winterberg was one of the most delightful villages I had ever seen, friendly and interesting, a relatively small place built along a north-south road paralleling Ernstberger Creek, and surrounded by hills about 300 feet high.

A Catholic church there dates from the fourteenth century and some of the houses near the schoolhouse were especially old, though not so old as some I had seen in Hann-Munden. The town had burned in the 1600s, and again in the 1800s. Part of the Sixth Crusade had camped near Winterberg for a while. About all that was standing of the old town were some of the walls and a block house on the corner.

I checked in to the headquarters of the 301st, commanded by Lt. Col. Samuel E. Morrow, and learned that the morale of the battalion was low. The lieutenants were critical of the captains and majors, the captains were critical of the field grade officers, and the field grade officers were critical of everybody, up and down.

I didn't really care. The war was over in Europe and the war with Japan was drawing to a close. The quarters were good. The officers were living in a large apartment house some distance from the command post. The 301st had a fine officers' mess, and duties were almost non-existent. The food was good and there was plenty to drink. The countryside was beautiful, the climate great, with mild afternoons and cool evenings.

The 356th Field Artillery Battalion was also in Winterberg, and as soon as Major Collins got there, he was given command of the battalion. With all this, I thought I could live with it.

Winterberg lay among some low hills and supported four water mills along the creek. The town had three glassworks and two publishing houses. There were some winter sports in the area, too, but it was not a resort town. Mostly, people seemed to trade and live off each other.

Adolf Hitler's ancestors came from the region, most of them from about eighteen miles south near the villages of Waldkirche, Freuungin, and Aigen in Austria.

Shortly after I reported to the 301st, I was appointed battalion intelligence officer, the same job I'd had at the 399th, and in a few days I got some business.

An Air Corps officer from Linz knew a Czech girl in Winterberg and he was shacking up with her every time he could get some time off. One weekend when he came to see her, he left his Air Corps jeep in the street, and a Czech stole it. The same weekend, one of the enlisted men in Headquarters Battery took a weapons carrier and wrapped it around a tree, losing an arm in the accident. Colonel Morrow detailed me as investigating officer for both incidents, and instructed me to write a report with recommendations.

The man in Headquarters Battery was a cook who had been under a strain because things had not gone well in the battery for him. That night he took the weapons carrier with the idea of going to one of the firing batteries and getting something for the kitchen for the next day. It was a dark, rainy night and the roads in the area were treacherous, curving and traversing up and down and right and left. I spent about three days investigating the incident with the cook and two days, or less, with the stolen jeep incident.

It had caused some concern in Headquarters Battery when I was appointed investigating officer in the incident involving the cook because I was a new officer and unknown. The men had no idea what I might do. But some of the enlisted men who had known me in the 399th had come to the 301st along with me and one of them, Cpl. Edmund Carroll of New Albin, Iowa, told them that the man would get a fair shake.

I wrote the report in longhand. It was ten pages long and it had to be typed by Corporal Carroll before I signed it and sent it to Colonel Morrow for his signature. I handed the report to Carroll and went off to get a drink of water. When I turned around, six GIs were circling his desk. When I came back from lunch, there was still a crowd around the desk, wanting to know what I had put in the report.

My findings were that this accident should be declared in the line of duty. Colonel Morrow approved the report. In the matter of the jeep theft, I recommended that our people not be held responsible for the theft of the jeep. The Air Corps officer who had driven it there was negligent and should be held accountable.

A week later, Colonel Morrow called me in and said my reports were organized and written better than any reports he had seen in twenty years of army service. He thought they were professionally done, and he had been proud to submit them to higher headquarters.

At the same time, he told me that his executive officer would soon be transferred and when that happened, he would make me executive officer. That meant my responsibilities would be greater and I would be busier, but I had lots of time.

That afternoon, I was returning to my quarters from the mess when I saw a man in the street yelling up at some windows in a large apartment building. People stuck their heads out of a window now and then, and others were passing him without surprise on either side. He kept yelling at the top of his voice and I thought he must be the village idiot.

Finally, he quieted down and sat on a curb. I walked over to get a better look at him.

"Good afternoon, Captain," he said in good English, so calmly that I knew he wasn't crazy.

I nodded and said, "Why are you yelling like that?"

"I am the town crier," he said.

Yelling was his job. He had been delivering some kind of proclamation to the residents of the apartment building. I saw him now and then after that, and we talked about Texas. Later, when I left Winterberg, he gave me a painting of a cowboy on a horse.

The officers' mess was in a *schloss* owned by the widow of one of the prominent men of Winterberg. It was a large building just north of the center of town. One entered through a covered archway and then a paved courtyard. The entry was about fifteen feet square with a staircase on the right side. The walls were covered with trophies, deer and boar. On the right side were a suit of armor and three mannequins dressed in the uniforms of dragoons. These uniforms had been worn by the men of the family that had lived there.

Her family owned one of the glassworks and she was of the lesser nobility. Most of the men of her family had been army officers of the Austro-Hungarian Empire for generations. They were small people, apparently, since one of the mannequins in uniform reached only up to my shoulders. Judging from all the trophies, though, they had spent quite a bit of time hunting, drinking, and lying around.

The woman had a way of irritating Colonel Morrow. She would steal his cigars every chance she got, and then go off to her own apartment to smoke and drink alone.

Colonel Morrow lived in the southeast corner room upstairs and the mess was in quite a large room downstairs. Upstairs were two bathrooms but I never found out what else because the upstairs were occupied.

Our quarters were in a three-story apartment building some distance away. I moved into a four-bedroom apartment on the second floor occupied by Capt. James Nickerson of Chicago, Capt. Clair Stevens of Horsehead, New York, and Capt. Gardner Cook of Lenunburg, Massachusetts. We became fast friends. Life in Winterberg was pleasant, but we were beginning to have trouble with the Czechs.

This was Czechoslovakia, and the Czechs were in charge. Those in charge were Communists and the Russians were not far away. Occasionally, I saw a Russian officer, usually early in the morning.

The Czech people we had to deal with were after the Sudeten-German population with all the energy and power they could muster, denying them jobs, food, and medical care, harassing them in every way they could think of.

Sometime before I arrived, an arrangement had been made between the American forces and the Germans for some of the German girls to work for us as chambermaids and be paid in food and supplies. The girl assigned to our quarters was Ria Allesch.

16 Winterberg

June 26, 1945–September 26, 1945

"Field Marshal Sir Bernard Law Montgomery last week noted a new form of German sabotage. He said that German women were wearing fewer and fewer clothes, thereby undermining the U.S. and British Armies' non-fraternization policy. German girls in brief shorts and halters systematically sunned themselves in full view of U.S. engineers building a bridge over the Weser River. Sometimes the girls shed the halters. There was no pretending Hiroshima had never happened; no ignoring a source of energy that might spin all the wheels ever cast. Man had been tossed into the vestibule of another millennium. It was wonderful to think of what the Atomic Age might be, if man was strong and honest." — Time, *August 21, 1945*

Ria was nineteen, her hair was brown, shoulder-length, and her eyes were brown. She had a ruddy complexion with a healthy tan, and her figure was full. She was always smiling.

Ria was from a Sudeten-German family and spoke several languages. She was polite and friendly, but she paid no attention, I heard, to the overtures of any of the officers in the building. She didn't join in their banter. She just did her job and went home.

The first week in Winterberg had been busy for me. I had the investigating to do and the reports to compile so I didn't spend much time in my quarters. Ria was gone by the time I got back, and I didn't see her the first week. During the second week, I went back to quarters to pick up something. Ria was just finishing her work, so we sat down to talk for a while. Her English was fair.

I asked her where she had spent the war.

"In Munich," she said. "I had to go there to work in a war factory."

Her childhood boyfriend had been drafted into the German army and had been sent to the Russian front. He had been gone for two years and no one had heard from him. She felt that he was dead and accepted it. It was just something that had happened.

She was concerned about her future and that of her parents because she knew that Czechoslovakia was Communist and that ultimately it would come under the influence of the Russians. Someday, the American troops would leave.

We talked for half an hour before she went home and I went off to have a drink before dinner.

Dinner in Winterberg had become a pleasant ritual. We had a good chef and good food served by four German girls, and a string ensemble playing during the dinner hour. We always dressed for dinner, meaning we put on ties and jackets.

Nobody had much to do. One of the lieutenants who lived nearby would go off every day fly-fishing in the creek near the town, but he seldom caught anything. I thought that kind of fishing was interesting and I tried it once, but I couldn't fish that way.

A couple of days later, an eleven-year-old boy who had been hanging around told me he had caught fish with his hands and he could show me how. I went off with him to a creek some distance from town. We took off our shoes, rolled up our pants, and waded into the little creek about two feet deep and not more than six or seven feet wide, though the water was quite fast.

He told me the way to do it was to reach around and feel the fish, or see them, and then ease up to the fish and grab. He felt around under the rocks and ledges, and to my amazement, he caught three of them, just grabbed them in the water. I watched him for a while and decided I was ready to try.

He showed me where a fish was and I edged up on it, felt around, and grabbed. Got it! That made four. I was determined to get another one. I went a little further up the creek, and under some overhanging shrubs in full leaf I found what I thought was a fish. I rubbed it a bit, and grabbed.

It wasn't a fish. It was a Teller mine. Fortunately for me, it wasn't rigged to blow up when moved. Apparently, it had been thrown off the road into the creek. I lost interest in fishing.

A few days later, I came by the apartment early in the afternoon and found Ria, Hilda, and one or two of the other girls who kept the quarters. They had finished their work and were sitting down, talking. I had learned to swear in German and started swearing, just kidding around.

Ria objected, possessively, I thought. That seemed funny. She made it plain she didn't think I should be swearing in front of them. The other girls laughed at Ria, and she got embarrassed.

Meanwhile, the battalion was enjoying the peace. Lt. Henry Russell, a former car salesman, decided he wanted to go on a thirty-day drunk. He had been known to put away a fifth a day before the war, he told me, and he said he often wanted to go on a thirty-day drunk but never had the opportunity. Russell was rooming with Lt. James Winningham, who felt the same way.

Henry went to Major Collins, battalion commander, and told him he wanted to go on a thirty-day drunk and would like to be excused from duties while he was on it.

"Okay," Major Collins said, "but stay out of trouble."

Russell and Winningham spent the next three days gathering supplies. They rounded up several cases of 10-in-1 rations and whatever booze they could find: schnapps, vodka, cognac, wines, scotch, and the like. On Sunday night, their buddies in the 356th Field Artillery threw them a little party to send them on their way.

It was a rousing send-off. Russell and Winningham got lit to beat hell and their buddies carried them down to their quarters and put them to bed. They lived in an old, smelly place with an archway leading into a courtyard, much like the one at our officers' mess. Henry's apartment was just above the archway. Their friends hoisted them into bed and went home.

On Monday, nobody saw them all day long. It was the same Tuesday. By Wednesday, two officers of the 356th thought they had better go down and check on them to see if they were dead. When they knocked on the door, nobody answered, so they started pitching pebbles at the windows.

Finally, Henry opened a window and looked out, bleary-eyed and half-dressed, with whiskers all over his face. One of his buddies yelled at him.

"You alive, Henry?"

Russell shook his head as if it hurt all over and came on down. He had on pants and an undershirt, the same clothes he had gone to bed in Sunday night. Everything was going fine, he said. They had plenty to eat and plenty to drink.

About that time, Winningham woke up and saw Henry talking to someone. He leaned out the window to say something, but he leaned too far and out he came through the window.

He hit the cobblestones in the courtyard head first, and lay there without moving. Henry thought he was dead and so did the others. They left him where he was and one of the other officers ran and called the duty sergeant of the 356th Field Artillery aid station and asked him to come down with an ambulance and the doctor. When they arrived, Winningham was still out cold and bleeding like a stuck pig.

The doctor looked him over and felt his pulse, which was weak. They stopped the bleeding and put some plasma into him and loaded him on the ambulance for the trip to Pilsen. None of us thought Winningham would make it. There was still a lot of his blood on the cobblestones.

That night Henry went up to battalion headquarters and found out they were having a party for a Hungarian dance troupe, mostly acrobats. I missed it because it was the 356th Battalion. Henry went to the party and woke up the next morning badly hung over. He pulled himself up out of bed and looked out the window at the cobblestones below and at Winningham's blood, and something must have happened to him. He quit drinking for a couple of days and went back to work. By Friday, the doctor said Winningham would live. He had a fractured skull and had lost a lot of blood, but he would make it. He wouldn't be back to the 356th, though. By the time he recovered, he would have enough points to go back home.

Despite Winningham's misadventure, there was a lot of drinking going on. A few days later, Capt. Bill Gausman found a German officer's uniform in the house where his shack woman lived in Winterberg. One night he put it on, steel helmet and all, and was sitting at a table in his quarters, next to mine, talking to three German women, when a lieutenant burst in. The lieutenant, half bombed himself, thought Gausman was a German officer and ran off to his room for his carbine. A minute later he came running back to where Gausman was sitting, ready to kill the German officer.

"Achtung!" he shouted in German.

Gausman, the women, and two other officers in the room didn't move a hair. That made the lieutenant even madder, and he pumped a round into the chamber. One of the officers standing nearby knocked the barrel upward, and two shots went off into the ceiling.

Bill Gausman came up from the table fighting mad in his Wehrmacht outfit and tried to slug the lieutenant. The row quieted down only when several of us came over to investigate the shooting.

The horseplay went on, well fueled by booze. Over toward the 356th's territory lived the widow of a German officer. She had two boys, six and eight, and she lived in an apartment over the brewery a long way from 301st. She was a nymphomaniac, I was told.

One night, Capt. Pete Moss woke up and couldn't go back to sleep. He had been drinking all evening and was pretty well smashed. When he woke up, he decided he would go down to the brewery and see this woman. He started at 1:00 A.M. on a chilly moonlit night.

Her apartment was above the entrance to the brewery and the whole front of the building was covered with English ivy that had been there for at least seventy years, the vines as thick as a man's wrist. They formed a perfect ladder, Moss thought. He started up the vines like a monkey and nearly made it to the window. What he didn't know was that Capt. Jack Daw, who had been with her all day and all evening, was still with her. When Moss got up the window ledge and tried to get in, Daw gave him a good hard push.

Clunk! Moss fell to the cobblestones twelve feet below and knocked himself colder than a block of ice. At dawn, one of the patrols found him and hauled him in, still unconscious, to the doctor, who patched him up. He came to at about 10:00 A.M.

It was September and getting cold. In the mornings, ice formed on the water and we had seen a little snow.

We got our liquor ration — scotch, champagne, and red wine — and a carton of cigarettes. Jim Russ and I split our rations; I took the champagne, he the scotch. We would have a few drinks together in my quarters, which were better than his, and write letters home.

There was a light snow falling when he showed up late in the afternoon and it kept on falling. By dark it must have been four or five inches deep. Jim, all bundled up, came in covered with snow, his ration under his arm. He was grinning from ear to ear.

We built a fire in the big tiled stove in the dining area and started working on the booze. I got out my writing portfolio to write Don and my mother. It was a portfolio I had liberated in Wolfenbuttel, leather and lined with linen and stamped with flowers on the front. Don's picture was taped inside. Steve came in later and had some drinks with us. By the end of the evening, Jim had drunk nearly a fifth of scotch and was lit up like a Christmas tree. He decided to go to his quarters because he wanted to stay in the sack until noon the next day.

He got up and took off out the front door of our quarters, with me following him. The way home for him was kind of tricky and I wasn't sure he could make it. If you left our quarters and went west, you crossed a road and soon came to a dropoff of about 110 feet on an incline of two to one. At the bottom of the incline was a valley about 200 yards wide with Ernstberger Creek running through it. Jim had to go west; there was no persuading him otherwise. I followed him, and when Steve saw what was going on, he came, too, but we weren't fast enough. The night was dark and it was snowing heavily.

Jim had forgotten about the slope. He took one step and fell, rolling all the way to the bottom about 200 feet below. As we stood at the top wondering what to do, he got up and shook himself. He wasn't hurt but wouldn't come back with us. He went on home to bed, and so did I.

The next morning, I was busy at headquarters until nearly noon. Then I thought I would go back to my quarters for a while before lunch, but when I got there my room was in disarray. The bed hadn't been made. Nothing had been picked up or touched in the kitchen-dining area. The table where Jim and I had been writing the night before had three empty bottles on it. My writing portfolio lay open, with the picture of my wife up.

Ria was sitting on the couch. She had her hands in her lap and she was quiet. Her eyes were red, as if she'd been crying.

"What's the matter?" I asked.

Her eyes swept the room. "Look at all this," she said.

"Yes, I see it." I folded the portfolio and put it away and threw the empty bottles into the trash box. "What's the matter?" I asked again.

"You drank last night?"

I told her yes, some friends came by and we drank some champagne and scotch. She looked up at me, eyes moist.

"You wrote your wife last night?"

I nodded yes.

"Do you love your wife?"

"Yes, Ria, I do."

I said it very quietly. A minute later, she started to cry. I didn't know what to do. She was hurt and there was nothing in it for either of us. I put my arm around her and tried to comfort her and she stopped crying.

She got up, wiped her eyes, and started to work. I went on back to headquarters, resolved to stay away for a while and not bother her. It would give her a chance to do some thinking without me around to confuse things. I thought time would help, as it usually does.

Saturday night I went to a party at the officers' mess. Just a few fellows were getting together for drinks. Nobody was bringing women, as far as I knew. It was cold with snow on the ground and I wore a semi-dress uniform with an Eisenhower jacket and a Luger in a shoulder holster. I wore it outside the jacket on the left. On top of that, I put on a short coat made out of khaki tank suit material. Capt. Bill Gausman had given it to me in Holland and nobody in the battalion had one like it. The party was loud when I arrived. Several girls were there but I didn't know any of them. It wasn't much of a party, so around 8:00 P.M., I decided to go home. I was putting on my coat and pistol when a young woman about twenty-five walked up. She was very attractive. A Czech, I thought.

"Captain Hardison," she said, "if you're leaving, would you please walk me home?" She was afraid to go by herself, she said.

I said, "Sure, I'll be glad to."

She lived on the same street as our quarters, not far away, she said. We took a path behind the water mill to a narrow bridge across the creek. She said that if we crossed the creek, went up the hill to the road, and turned right a hundred meters, we would come to where she lived. It was snowing lightly and the footing was treacherous. She slipped her arm through mine and held on until we came to the narrow bridge.

We were just about across when she slipped, or I did, and we fell, with a terrific splash, into the icy creek. It wasn't deep, but my Luger came out and I spent several shivering minutes groping around in the water until I found it. Then we climbed out shaking all over and headed for her house, 300 yards away.

She said, "Captain Hardison, why don't you come on in and dry off? It's warm inside. I live with my mother, but she's gone to be with my sister, who is having a baby."

She was soaked, but smiling. She was very pretty and I knew that it would be a lot warmer inside. But if I went in, I would just be making more problems for myself. And I had enough of those already. I told her I had to report back to battalion headquarters, then went on home to bed.

On Monday, I stayed home and talked to Ria for a while.

"My mother and father would like to meet you," she said.

I was surprised. I didn't say anything for a minute and she told me again, as if I hadn't understood.

"Ria, why do they want to meet me?"

"I told them about you," she said, "and they want to meet you."

That's all she would say, but I knew what was going on. We were not involved but we did like each other, and, as we both knew, more than one lovely young German girl had won the heart of an American officer whether he was married or not. This would not happen in my case and I wanted to make that clear without hurting her. On the other hand, I could take her invitation to meet her parents as it seemed to be on the surface. It was their right to meet her new friend, and so I asked her when.

"Can you meet them Wednesday after duty?"

I said all right and told her *auf wiedersehn* and left. On Tuesday, she said Wednesday night was okay. She would stay late and I could walk her home to meet her mother and father.

Next day, I got there about 3:00 P.M. We talked for a while and by 4:00 it was sleeting and quite dark. It was about a thirty-minute walk. The apartment where she lived with her parents was on the second floor of a very old complex of buildings. We went in and in the dim light were her mother and father and another woman, an aunt, all sitting around a big table.

"Guten abend," they said, adding some more German that got past me. Ria's father was a tall, dignified gray-haired man; her mother was gray, too, and smaller than Ria. The aunt was a tall, attractive woman who had lived in the West Indies.

I had told Ria that I studied Spanish in school and her aunt tried to speak to me in Spanish, but my Spanish was really Tex-Mex and we didn't get far at that.

Ria's father was a candle-maker and I gathered that the bulk of his work was for the Christmas trade. I realized that he was quite talented when he showed me some of the candles he made. They were beautiful, decorated with delicate flowers and vines.

Ria's parents seemed older than mine, in their late fifties — old to have a daughter Ria's age, nineteen. I was five or six years older than Ria.

I sat there rather stiffly, but Ria, who was interpreting for us, was quite charming and at ease. Her mother seemed as uncomfortable as I was, but her father was warm and courteous. I stayed about half an hour, trying to make conversation through Ria, then said, *"Gute Nacht,"* which I'd learned in Germany, and went back to my quarters, disturbed.

"You're invited to a hunting lodge for the weekend," the lieutenant said. He was from the 356th and had come to battalion headquarters and asked someone to point out "Captain Tex."

"Oh," I said. "What do you hunt? What kind of gun should I take?"

The lieutenant grinned and said, "Captain, you don't need to take any kind of gun. We're not after game. We have it."

"Well, what are you going to do? And who invited me anyhow?"

"A girl named Freda," the lieutenant said. "She would like to have Captain Tex as her guest for the weekend. You are Captain Tex, aren't you?"

I didn't know anybody named Freda.

"Hell," I said, "if you're not going to hunt, what are you going to do?"

He said there would be five girls and four officers. "You'll be the fifth," he said. "The girl who invited you has never been there, but she wants you to come and be her guest."

I told him I couldn't go. I had duty. "Tell her I'm sorry," I said, and forgot the whole thing.

During the week, I went by my quarters a couple of times during the afternoon for ten minutes or so to talk with Ria. She was getting more serious and I was a bit on edge. On Friday, the same lieutenant turned up.

"How would you like to go to the hunting lodge?" he asked.

It was twelve miles southwest of Winterberg, he said, near the village of Lipka. He described it and I knew I had seen it. It was unoccupied.

I said, "What did you do last weekend? Did you do any shooting at all?"

He grinned. "Nope, none at all."

"Well, what goes on up there? What do you eat?"

"You'd be surprised," he said. "We've got 10-in-1 rations and we've got some other things. Plenty to drink." He was grinning like a panther. "Since you didn't go with us last week, Freda was by herself, so that was five girls and four of us. We just played king and that sort of thing."

I said, "What in the hell is king?"

He told me about the weekend at the lodge.

"We built a big fire in the fireplace and visited around awhile, had several drinks, and then we decided we'd all play a game. The girls all took off their clothes and lay down on the floor on some blankets. Then they pulled some other blankets over their knees and put blankets over their heads down past their navels. Then we came out and we tried to identify them."

"The hell, you say . . ."

He nodded, still grinning. "Yeah. We didn't have much trouble there since one of them was a redhead and Freda was new."

I said, "I guess you were all fully clothed with field coats, boots, steel helmets, and a carbine in your hand."

"Nope, we were bare-ass, too. Then the girls put blankets over their heads and up past their navels to see if we could tell whose tits were whose."

Curiosity was getting the best of me. "What happened after that?"

"The girls all went in the next room and we lay down and put on blankets up above our knees and below our navels to see if the girls could tell us apart from looking at our cocks."

"Then what?"

"That's when the real fun started. It was too bad there were five of them and only four of us. Freda said for me not to come up this weekend if I didn't bring you."

I told him I couldn't make it and he went off looking for a fifth at whatever it was. I sat there wondering who in the hell Freda was. I didn't even know her.

On Tuesday, I got an urgent message from Colonel Morrow: "Report to battalion headquarters immediately." When I got there, he told me we had been ordered to move to Rokycany, Czechoslovakia, which was eighty miles north of Winterberg over winding roads and through numerous villages. He ordered me to leave immediately to mark the route for the battalion.

We used cardboard markers eight and one-half inches by eleven inches and our battalion symbol was an inverted "T." If there was no arrow on it, you went on straight ahead. Otherwise, an arrow would steer you to the left or right as you approached a crossroad. My job was to mark the route to Rokycany by way of Pilsen, which was the only way I knew to go. I got the maps and signs and detailed two men to help and went back to my quarters.

Ria was there. I told her that I had to leave and that this was goodbye. I wouldn't be back. I had a Val Pak with my uniform in it, a musette bag with some personal things, a duffle bag, a rifle and shotgun, and a foot locker. I took the Val Pak and the musette bag and asked her to put the rest of my things in the duffle bag and foot locker. I would have a lieutenant pick them up in a couple of hours.

She became very upset and began to cry. I tried to comfort her, but I had to tell her that was the way it was — no choice. I wished her the very best and that somewhere, someday, she would marry and be happy.

There was nothing for me to do but say goodbye and leave, so I did. I went out and got in the jeep. When I looked back, I saw her standing in the doorway, crying.

17 Rokycany

September 27, 1945–October 31, 1945

"The gale of war had blown itself out. Two recently isolated giants, the U.S. and the U.S.S.R., were suddenly everywhere. Russia was claiming colonies in Africa, making friends among the Arabs, gripping eastern Europe, regaining its economic position in Manchuria, actively concerning itself with the control of Japan. As rapidly as it could, the U.S. was stripping away its military strength. The War Department was turning out thousands of able, war-trained officers and noncoms who might have stayed to backbone the peacetime army if permanent rank and other inducements had been offered to them. The Army had already discharged more than 1,000,000 men and would soon be tearing itself down at the rate of 1,000,000 a month." —Time, *October 22, 1945*

We headed north, marking the route with signs as we went, passing through several villages, a large manufacturing town, and finally rolling into Pilsen. I routed the convoy straight through the center of the city, posting signs on utility poles, traffic signals, and whatever else I could find. From Pilsen, it was ten miles east to Rokycany. I had guides to direct the convoy there. In Rokycany, I arranged for a billet for the officers and took over the headquarters building and barracks of CCB, 8th Armored Division, my old division.

What I didn't know when I marked the route was that there was a Corps order that no military convoys would pass through Pilsen. My route took the convoy through town at the height of truck, bus, and streetcar traffic. The convoy, well disciplined, moved close together and fast, running rough-shod over the Czechs, stopping streetcars, trains, and buses.

The Czechs were madder than hell, but there wasn't anything they could do about it. Later, the mayor of Pilsen contacted Third Army, and Third Army called Corps command and raised hell with the division commander, who in turn raised hell with Colonel Morrow. The colonel called me in and read their letter to me. It said we had inconvenienced the Czechs and caused gigantic problems with the trains and streetcars.

"Colonel Morrow," I said, "I don't give a damn. They can all go to hell."

He couldn't help smiling. "I feel the same way," he said, "and it was the best marked route that I ever traveled."

We had come to Rokycany with the idea of trying to resolve some of the troubles between the Czech population, the Russians, the U.S. forces, and the few Sudeten-Germans who were in town. The Czechs were not as friendly as the Sudetens of Winterberg and I didn't like them as well. We settled into the officers' quarters, which were on the second story of a medical clinic. Captain Stevens, Lieutenant Myers, and Capt. Gardner Cook were my roommates. An old woman was there to take care of things.

The problems in Rokycany didn't seem all that bad. We were careful with the Russians, though I had already seen enough of them to hate their guts. They had a sentry post outside of town and a couple of guards could be seen standing around it with submachine guns, a weapon with a drum magazine that looked like it had been stamped out of tin.

We left them alone as much as possible, and kept them out of our area. We wouldn't let them go through Rokycany to Pilsen. They tried, though, and every time they tried, we stopped them.

Late one cold and snowy night, early in October, a train came in from the Russian zone of occupation. The train was put on a siding for a few minutes and one of our patrols saw it.

We had patrols out all the time, usually in jeeps with machine guns on them. The patrol that discovered the train came to my quarters, woke me up, and told me there was a train on the siding with eight or nine open gondola-type cars, all full of German civilians. They had no cover and it was continuing to snow.

A guard box was on each end of the cars with a Czech or Russian, holding machine guns on the people, who were crying. The sergeant leading the patrol wanted me to know about it. I got up and put on my clothes and armed myself.

The sergeant was right. The train had about eight cars, with about fifty people per car, most of them young women and children. They were being taken east. The only way I could stop this train was by putting something in front of it, which I had no authority to do. We had only wheeled vehicles, no tanks.

My first thought was to contact someone to see if I could get the train stopped. My second was to block the track with a truck. But before I could get a truck, the train pulled out, the people on it weeping and wailing. We watched it disappear into a curtain of snow.

We heard that the Czechs and Russians were moving the Germans out of Sudetenland as fast as they could, most likely carting them east to concentration camps, especially the young women. They probably didn't survive. The more I saw of the Russians, the more I hated them, and I had a lot of contact with them because I had become executive officer of the battalion.

Two or three days later, I hunted up the lieutenant I had sent to get my foot locker, duffle bag, and guns back in Winterberg. I had asked Ria to get together my rifle and a shotgun and give them to him. He said he had gone by the quarters, but Ria had told him I had taken everything. That meant Ria still had a lot of my stuff. I didn't know what to do about that, but I was so busy with other problems that I didn't have time to think about it. I had enough clothes for the time being, anyway.

The next evening, about 8:00 P.M., it was snowing and sleeting, as it always seemed to be, and I was out with a patrol. The guards had stopped a weapons carrier driven by a Russian major, a big man, about six-foot-two. Most of our Russian counterparts were smelly Mongolians, about five-foot-three and ugly as baboons.

This major was in an American weapons carrier demanding to pass through our checkpoint. Our people wouldn't let him through. They had sent for me, but I happened on the scene before the messenger found me.

The Russian officer was sitting inside the weapons carrier with a woman in a full-length fur coat. I asked him to step down from his vehicle. When he did, I noticed the back of the vehicle was covered with a tarpaulin and I told the guard to take the tarp off. We were in for a surprise. The weapons carrier was loaded with commodes, urinals, and sinks.

I beckoned the major over to a fire near the guard post, and in the firelight I noticed that he, too, had on a fur coat. We had a language barrier, but he understood my motion to take the coat off. He got out of it reluctantly. Underneath, he had a submachine gun. He also had three watches on each arm, and an alarm clock hung around his neck. He was a walking store.

I signaled for the woman to come over so we could have a look at her, too. She was really big, nearly six feet tall and weighing about 160 pounds, all tits and ass, and not too bad-looking, though I wouldn't have wanted to spend much time with her.

We had the authority to stop them, but I didn't want to fool with them, so I told them to go. I told the Russian major not to come back; if he did, he'd never get out again. He mouthed around in Russian and finally got back in his weapons carrier and drove off.

While we were in Winterberg, my friend Clair Stevens was ordered to write a history of the 301st Field Artillery Battalion. He finished it before we moved and made arrangements to have it published by one of the publishing houses there. We were ordered out of Winterberg before the publication of the history. Steve was going to Winterberg once or twice a week to edit the chapters. He had written it in English, of course, but it was being typeset by Czechs or Germans, so he had to proofread the chapters, too. I knew he was heading for Winterberg again so I asked him to go see Ria.

"Look, Steve," I said, "go talk to her and see how she feels. I hope I haven't hurt her and that she'll go ahead and forget me."

"Yeah," he said. "I know what you're talking about."

I asked him if he would get my guns and foot locker, too.

"Sure," he said. "I'll be back with them by tomorrow night."

Steve got back on schedule and we had dinner together that night. I asked him if he'd gotten the guns and the foot locker. He looked kind of sheepish and said he hadn't.

"What happened?"

"Ria wouldn't give them to me. She said she wouldn't give them to anybody but you. She says she wants to see you one more time. Take it from me, Tex. The only way you're going to get your stuff is to get in a jeep and go down there and get it."

I let three weeks go by before I decided I had to go down to Winterberg to get my stuff. Colonel Morrow gave me a day off and I got a command car and a driver and took off early down the road to Pilsen. We got into Winterberg around 11:00 A.M. and I went to the apartment where I had lived. No one was there.

Someone saw me, though, and soon I heard someone calling. It was Ria. She was next door.

We went back over to the old apartment. It was vacant and locked, but she had the key and there were all my things — the guns, foot locker, everything. She closed the door and locked it. From the door, she looked at me, and I could see her eyes begin to glisten.

"Are you leaving?"

"Yes, I have to, Ria. I have no choice. I'll be going home soon."

She began crying and I felt miserable. What had started as lighthearted fun in the afternoon had gone a lot deeper than that. When I got home, I was reasonably sure that I would have love and help from an understanding wife, but Ria wouldn't have the same sort of comfort. Because of the circumstances, Ria was more vulnerable.

I left depressed, flailing myself for letting it happen. After all, I was married. I was feeling glum when I got back to Rokycany. There I found that Colonel Morrow had been relieved. We had a new battalion commander, Maj. Hal Threadcraft, who had been with CCB of the 8th Armored Division. I had known him casually and I liked him.

The same kind of thing was still going on in Rokycany: drunk Russians trying to get into town, most of them mean drunk, and the Czechs trying to get at the few Sudeten-Germans. We were having constant problems with our men because of women, and it seemed like we needed a doctor for every battery.

A week after Major Threadcraft's arrival, we received orders to move to Klatovy for about three weeks. Capt. Henry Brooks, who was now battalion intelligence officer, was detailed to go to Klatovy to pick out quarters. I was ordered to stay and wind things down in Rokycany.

Klatovy, a manufacturing town of about 15,000 population, was stark, dirty, ugly, mean, and windy, much of it in bad repair. Garbage was everywhere, paper swirling through the streets, everything covered with dust and grime. It was a cold and depressing place.

Our quarters, nevertheless, were pleasant and our duties were not pressing. The first Sunday we were there I went out to a German army caserne to look around and found several propaganda posters the German army had distributed to the troops. One of them showed a soldier shot between the eyes and lying in a trench. Another soldier was cocking his rifle and looking at his dead comrade with contempt, the idea being that he shouldn't have stuck his head up, I guess.

About that time, we got some new second lieutenants, sharp lads from Norwich University, very "gung ho" but grass-green and ignorant about what life was like nowadays in the army. In Klatovy, two of them met some Czech girls who impressed them a lot. The mother of one of the girls was a countess. The lieutenants asked the girls and the countess to the officers' quarters for Sunday afternoon tea.

The officers' quarters were nice. They were on a street with a five-foot sidewalk. One entered the building off the street, across the walk, and through a double door. There were twenty-three rooms, including a kitchen, a parlor with a piano, and a fireplace.

On this cold, dreary, windy, dismal, overcast, red-ass Sunday afternoon, tea began splendidly. One of the lieutenants could play the piano and one of the girls was a singer. He was making a valiant effort to find something to play that she could sing. They had drunk some light wine and the old countess looked tickled to death. The wine and the fire in the fireplace had begun to work and they were feeling light-hearted. The lieutenants didn't know Capt. Elliott Thompson.

Thompson's room was down three windows from the parlor door, facing the street. He was drunk, as usual, and was looking out the window when a Czech prostitute passed by with everything in motion. Thompson quickly made a deal with her, the price being a pack of cigarettes, and hoisted her into his room through the window. In a few minutes, the girl left the same way she had come in and Thompson started to administer a GI prophylactic to himself, a crude process at best. He had on nothing but an undershirt, socks, and the prophylactic sack tied around his instrument when he got the urge to walk around.

He went down the hall and right through the parlor without noticing the piano-choral group at all. There were yelps of surprise, shock, and dismay. The countess let out an *eeeeeekkk!* that would have shattered crystal.

Thompson made no apologies. He just turned around and staggered out, his sacked instrument swinging to and fro a little as he went.

A couple of nights later, I was sitting in battalion headquarters minding my own business and thinking about home. I had the red-ass, a terrible case of it. The phone rang and it was the division special service officer. He wanted the name of one officer to go to Switzerland on ten days' leave beginning the next day.

"Capt. Richard Hardison," I said, without hesitation. He said he would cut the orders. "Fine," I said, and went off to wake up the battalion commander, who was sleeping nearby. I told him I was going on ten days' leave to Switzerland.

He said, "Okay, cut the orders," and went back to sleep. I was at division headquarters at 6:30 A.M. It was pitch dark and snowing with a wind chill factor of about thirty degrees below zero, but I was ready to go to Switzerland. I had whatever I needed packed in a musette bag and a duffle bag. Outside division headquarters, a long convoy of trucks was drawn up, with a sergeant in charge. He was MSgt. Albert O'Neill of the Division Special Service Office. He found my name on his list and told me the trip would be a long one; we wouldn't be in Basel, the Swiss border town, for fourteen hours.

"Better find a truck with a heater in it," he said. "I think there's one in the twelfth truck in line."

Counting twenty-three trucks in the convoy, I started down the line toward the twelfth and, sure enough, it had a heater. I spoke to the driver, a sergeant, and hoisted my gear into the front of the truck. It was warm and I quickly fell asleep.

Sometime later, I woke up to find we were bouncing along the road to Munich. Outside were picket fences strung up perpendicular and in some places parallel to the road. The driver said they were snow fences, designed to keep snow off the road. He knew because he was from Minnesota, where they had the same problem with snow. I had never seen anything like that. We stopped once to relieve ourselves and again for sack lunches. In the warm truck, I kept dozing off as we moved over the snowy roads toward Munich. I woke up again when we stopped somewhere near Munich. Conditions were bad. It was snowing hard and the road was covered with ice. I stayed in the truck until about twenty minutes later, when a lieutenant stuck his head in the door and woke me up.

"Captain, everybody has to get out. Colonel's orders."

It was very cold and I was the last one out. I put on my field coat and walked down the road a couple of hundred yards. All the traffic had been stopped on each end of the convoy. The enlisted men were lined up in two rows along the road: officers in front of the enlisted men, and lieutenants in one line, captains in another. I got in the right line and stood at attention.

The colonel walked straight over to me. He was a little man, about five-foot-two, in cavalry uniform, and he was madder than hell.

"Who the hell are you?" he demanded.

I said, "Capt. Richard Hardison of the 301st Field Artillery Battalion."

"What's your capacity in that organization?"

"Sir," I said, "I'm the executive officer."

He wasn't getting any less mad.

"Well, you're senior officer here and this convoy has been running at excessive speeds. They ran my sedan off into the ditch." He went into a tail-chewing tirade about the convoy being operated in a reckless and negligent manner. "I'll have your ass for this!" he yelled.

I looked at him with a poker face. I didn't really give a damn. I was not in charge of the convoy and I had no responsibility for it. All I wanted to do was to get back in the truck and get going. We'd already lost an hour.

The colonel stomped up and down in the snow. He was from the Third Army staff, he said, and he took down some information about me and threatened me one more time before getting back in his sedan. In a couple of minutes, the convoy started moving again.

The sergeant driving my truck, who was going to Switzerland for ten days' leave himself, thought the way I had been treated was chicken. After all, he said, the master sergeant at the head of the convoy was in charge. The driver said he would watch for the colonel's car in his rear view mirror and if he saw the sedan coming up, he would wipe it out. The road was covered with ice and it would be easy to make the truck slide into the car and crush it up against a tree or wall. I didn't say anything. I didn't give a damn. But the colonel's car didn't come.

We got into Basel that night at 10:00, settling down into some billets for the night. Next morning, we were divided into tours, officers together and enlisted men together. There were twelve tours to choose from, tours of various parts of Switzerland. I took one that went to Bern, Lausanne, Vevey, and finally to Lucerne for four days.

In our group were six officers, none of whom I knew, and two Red Cross women. One of the latter was a doughnut-type girl of about twenty-five, the other an administrative type in her mid-thirties. The eight of us were going to be together for the next ten days, and it turned out to be a congenial week and a half. We went out together every night and thoroughly enjoyed every minute of it.

Switzerland was warm, civilized, and untouched by the war. We especially enjoyed Lucerne. It was like another world. The air was cool, the sky was blue, and the white peak of the mountain near where William Tell is supposed to have shot an arrow off his son's head could be seen on the horizon. The Swiss were friendly and courteous, and you could walk into a restaurant and sit down and order dinner. We met two Swiss teenagers who wanted to talk "cowboy." It was fun hearing them say "podner" and "dogie" and all that.

Ten days went by in a blink. Back in Basel, we loaded onto trucks for the trip back to Czechoslovakia, this time heading through Strasbourg, which was full of wild French Sinhalese troops, back toward Czechoslovakia.

18 Klenci

November 1, 1945–November 18, 1945

"Last week a united House of Commons protested hotly against the continuation of Germany's misery. Charged Independent Sir Arthur Salter: 'If millions during this winter freeze and starve, this will not have been the inevitable consequences of war.' The implication was that Russia, Poland and Czechoslovakia were deliberately creating chaos in Germany." — Time, *November 5, 1945*

"The practical, patient Czechoslovaks have undergone occupation of one kind or another ever since the Middle Ages. Premier Zdenek Fierlinger announced that the last occupation was about to end as both Russia and the U.S. had agreed to withdraw their soldiers. In the State Department a spokesman said both armies would leave by December 1st." — Time, *November 19, 1945*

The 301st had moved. When I got back to division headquarters, they told me the battalion had gone from Klatovy to Klenci, a village not more than two miles from the Czech-German border and a place of some historical interest.

In recent times, it had been part of the fortress belt the Czechs had constructed on their German border after World War I. In medieval times, it had been a way station on the road from Munich to Prague. Now it was a collection of buildings on a road that passed through a small valley. Fog blanketed the valley now and it was a deadly quiet, depressing scene.

I saw Steve first thing and we went into the officers' mess for a cup of coffee. The building had been a small resort hotel and the mess had been combined with the staff officers' quarters, the headquarters battery officers, and the officers of Battery A.

We were sitting around drinking coffee and talking when I noticed a couple of women working around the kitchen, the roughest-looking pair of women I had ever seen. Steve said they were maids and they also worked in the mess. They had been there when the 301st relieved a British-trained Czech armored brigade, which had occupied the area.

They looked like old worn-out whores to me. I named the larger one Syphyllis and the smaller one Gonora. One of them obviously was, or had been, infected with venereal disease. I could see the blue scars of open sores on her legs. The doctor must have checked them out, though, and they must be clean because they were working in the kitchen. Steve said they were Slavic, probably Polish or Czech or Russian or a combination of all three. I went off to report to the battalion commander.

"Come on in, Tex," Major Threadcraft said. "I want to talk to you."

I told him the trip to Switzerland had been great, but I was glad to be back.

"Well," he said, "where did you have the trouble?"

I was puzzled. "I didn't have trouble anyplace."

He looked skeptical. "You're bound to have had some trouble someplace. Did you have a fight in Switzerland?"

I told him no, still baffled.

"Look at this," he said, handing me a thick sheaf of papers. The top one was a letter ordering me to report to the division artillery commander immediately upon my return to the unit. It was signed by Colonel Whiteley.

"Something must have happened," Major Threadcraft said, "because as you read down under this you will see that you're to be tried by a general court-martial."

I told him I didn't know a damned thing about it.

"Well," he said, "you'd better call Colonel Whiteley and talk to him."

I got on the phone. I knew Colonel Whiteley and he knew that I had planned to apply for a commission in the regular army.

He said, "Captain, come up to my office right away. I want to talk to you."

I was still puzzled when I drove up to division headquarters in the middle of a snow storm. In his office in Klatovy, Colonel Whiteley was distant and formal.

"You have got yourself in one hell of a jam," he said.

"Colonel," I said, "I don't know what you're talking about. I haven't done a damned thing."

"Well," he said, "I have this letter from Third Army directing me to try you by general court for negligence of duty, to wit, the reckless operation of a convoy."

Then I knew what he was talking about. It was that damned little colonel on the road. I told him the story, explaining that I was in no way responsible for that convoy. I had been just like every other officer in it. I had been on leave, not on duty, and on my way to Switzerland with no responsibilities whatsoever.

"But you were the senior officer."

"How in the hell was I to know that? There were twelve captains on the trip." I explained that the trip had been organized by the division special services officer and he had not put me in charge of the convoy. I was *not* in charge of it.

Colonel Whiteley was impassive. "You're going to be tried by court-martial and I want you up here in my office at 9:00 A.M. tomorrow. Have your number-one uniform on and we'll proceed from there."

This was the last straw, I thought. During the last few months, I had become increasingly disillusioned with the U.S. Army. I had planned to stay in, but now I was having some serious thoughts about getting out. I was concerned about civilian life, since I had never had a job. I had gone into the army the day I had graduated from college. The idea of getting out of a warm seat into a cold one didn't appeal to me, but in light of what was happening to me and around me, I knew I should go ahead and get out.

I was thinking about that as I drove back through the snow to Klenci in an open jeep, slipping and sliding all over the road. During the past five months, I had seen the finest army ever put together fall apart before my eyes. Divisions with fine combat records had been disbanded. The war was over, the job was finished, and with the finishing went the efficiency, the discipline, and the morale.

Most of the regular officers, from lieutenant colonel down, were moved out and given State-side commands or assigned as students in various army schools. As they departed, their jobs were given to the officers who were left. The company grade officers and non-commissioned officers with high points were sent home to be separated from the service. That meant the work of policing, vehicular maintenance, and training was left to those remaining, and, of course, the efficiency and snap were gone. Those of us left with the responsibility did the best we could with what we had to work with, but it was an exasperating period, and I saw that things were sliding downhill fast.

On the way back to the battalion, snow blowing into my face and falling down my neck, I made the decision. I was getting out. Regardless of how my immediate problem was resolved, I would not apply for a regular army commission. I would take my chances in civilian life, where I would be more in control of my destiny, whatever it might be. I had seen enough ass-kissing in the army to last me the rest of my life and I was aware of the success achieved by individuals practicing this art. I did not want to be in a situation ever again where this sort of low competition was a factor. I realized that whatever my future, it lay elsewhere. And, in a way, I felt relieved.

Back at battalion headquarters, I told Major Threadcraft I had got myself in a hell of a fix and repeated the story of the convoy on the road.

"We've got a lot to do in the meantime," he said. "We're getting out of Czechoslovakia."

I was glad about that. I was ready to go. We talked for an hour and then Steve came by and told me he had found us quarters in an architect's house, well away from the hotel, a comfortable upstairs room.

"I thought you'd like this better," Steve said. "It's pretty wild around the officers' quarters."

He was right. We turned in early. I lay there for a while, wondering what was going to happen to me in the morning, but finally drifted off to sleep.

I was up at 6:00 A.M. and got into my number-one uniform. I swallowed some coffee and a quick breakfast and went off in a jeep to Klatovy again to report to Colonel Whiteley.

When I got there, I threw a snappy salute at the adjutant and told him I was reporting to Colonel Whiteley. A minute later, the colonel told him to show me in.

The colonel was dressed just as I was and was sitting at a big desk with two flags behind it, one the flag of the United States, the other the standard of the 94th Division. He had a court recorder sitting at a table to his left and there were two guards, also in number-one uniforms, standing just inside the door of his office.

I went in and saluted, then formally reported to him. He returned my salute. "Captain, be seated," he said. He had found a wooden hammer and had a piece of wood on his desk. He slammed the hammer down on the wood.

"Court's in session." He chewed his lip in thought. "Captain Hardison," he said finally, "I'm not going to try you by general court-martial as directed by Third Army. Under the circumstances, I'm going to try you by summary court."

He asked me if I had any objections and I told him I didn't, realizing that a trial by general court-martial would be a time-consuming ordeal and would probably delay my departure for the United States.

"Then I want to read to you the charges prepared in Third Army Headquarters."

He read them in a dry voice. They said I was in charge of a convoy. I was negligent in my duties by allowing the trucks to run too fast, not keeping proper intervals. Then he read the specifications backing up the charges, which was just more bullshit.

"Do you understand the charges and specifications?"

I told him I did.

"How do you plead to the charges?"

"Not guilty," I said. "Same for the specifications."

About a minute later, he rapped the wooden block with his mallet, a crack that woke up the court recorder and made the guards jump.

"I find you guilty as charged," he said.

I just looked at him, dumbfounded. I had no responsibility for that convoy.

The colonel thought it necessary to repeat himself. "I find you guilty as charged and I sentence you to a reprimand. It will be written and you will have a copy delivered to you tomorrow. It will be in your 201 file as long as you are in the army."

The colonel got up from his desk, relieved, and the two guards, who had been standing at attention, stood at ease. The court recorder nodded that he had gotten everything. Colonel Whiteley walked up to me.

"Well, Tex, that wasn't so bad, was it?"

I didn't say anything. I couldn't believe it. I started toward the door and he walked up behind me and put his arm on my shoulder.

"I understand you plan on staying in the army. I want you to know that this isn't going to hurt you that much. It may make you wait a month or two for a promotion, but that's all. It isn't going to tear you up or hurt you."

I turned around, and said "Colonel Whiteley, sir, I understand your position under the circumstances. Your reprimand and court-martial are not going to hurt me. I'm getting out of this chickenshit army the first opportunity I have, and if I ever see that half-sized colonel, I'll give him a beating that he'll never forget as long as he lives!" I walked to the door, turned and saluted, and left. I never saw him again.

Colonel Whiteley had tried to help me, but he was in an awkward position. Though he knew I was not guilty, there was not much else he could have done with the tools he had. I understood all that. But what about me? I hadn't done a damn thing.

Pissed off to beat hell, I drove back to battalion headquarters. There I didn't have time to be pissed off. I had work to do. There was a message that we would be leaving on November 25. We would go to Neuberg Au Donau, moving into an assembly area there.

About noon, the battalion surgeon came in with a disgusted look on his face. "We've got a problem," he said.

Problems were just what I needed. I asked him what it was.

"We have fourteen cases of venereal disease among the officers of the battalion. There are thirty-two officers. That's nearly fifty percent."

I let out a low whistle. "What kind?"

"Most of it is gonorrhea," he said, "but three cases of syphilis."

"Any married officers infected?"

He held up four fingers.

"That does it! All right, let me have the names and I'll court-martial every son of a bitch!"

He said no, he couldn't give me the names. I told him it was my understanding that when an officer got a venereal disease it was a court-martial offense.

"That may be so," he said, "but we're way over here in Czechoslovakia and there's two feet of snow on the ground and I'm just not going to give you the names of those who've got the clap."

"Goddamnit, Doc," I said, "what did you come in here for anyway? To get warm? Why tell me this crap if you don't want something done about it?"

With that, he left.

I got up and went over to the officers' quarters. A lieutenant there I knew would tell me what was really going on. We went to a table in the dining room and sat down to drink a cup of coffee. Four of the new lieutenants were loafing around, talking to the two women working in the kitchen. The lieutenant, sipping his coffee, noticed me watching them.

Finally, I said, "What's going on over here at night?"

"Nothing much," he said. "Just disorderly to beat hell and everyone getting drunk and banging those two women around."

"What women?"

"The ones you call Syphyllis and Gonora. Somebody is always messing with one or the other. It goes on all night long."

I told him he had to be kidding, but he said he wasn't.

"There's only eight of us here who are not fooling with them. I don't see how they sleep any."

I groaned. That was about what I'd figured. I went off to the battalion commander's room. He had a bad cold and he had gone to bed the day before. He had hot water bottles on his head and he was feeling sick. I told him about the fourteen officers infected with VD and that I wanted to court-martial every last one of them. I didn't want any officers going home with venereal disease.

It was no surprise to Major Threadcraft, who had already heard the news.

"I agree with you," he said, "it's a hell of a note, but I can't court-martial them. When we get to Neuberg we won't be there long, a month or so, and we'll be broken up. It would be futile."

I was mad.

"It may be futile," I said, "but I'll tell you one thing, it will keep the married officers over here and in my opinion they ought not to be allowed to go home where they'll infect their wives and every other woman they can find."

"Well," he said, "that's my decision. I'm not going to allow you to press charges against them."

That pissed me off even further. A court-martial in the morning, and now this! I went back to my office and called the headquarters battery commander.

"Listen carefully," I said, "you've got thirty minutes to get those two whores out of the officers' quarters. I don't want to see them again. In thirty minutes, I'm going to come down to your battery and they had better be gone or it will be your happy ass!"

I told him they had infected fourteen officers and I wanted them out of there. A few minutes later, I looked out the window and saw the two women trudging down the road through the snow, each with a suitcase in her hand.

What a couple of days! I had come back from Switzerland, been court-martialed, threatened fourteen officers with court-martial, and run off two whores. And I had made a lot of officers mad at me for running off their recreation.

That it was getting colder and darker didn't make me feel any better. The next day was the same. Daylight didn't come until 9:00 A.M. and the clouds were about head high. There really wasn't much for us to do.

Late in the morning, the doctor came into my office. "If it isn't one damned thing, it's another," he said.

"What now?"

"Lieutenant Neighbors won't accept treatment for his infection."

I asked him what the lieutenant had. Gonorrhea for sure, he said, and probably syphilis. The lieutenant hadn't been too selective with the Czech women. I asked him why he wouldn't accept treatment.

"He heard from home that his wife's running around on him and he wants to give her a dose of clap."

"Forget it," I said. The silly bastard was sorry, his wife probably was too, and at any rate, they would be sharing, which was what marriage was all about.

He went out shaking his head.

The firing batteries were ready to leave and we were getting headquarters and service batteries ready when I got word from Ria. She needed to see me as soon as possible.

I knew it must be serious and I would go. Something was terribly wrong. The battalion commander was still in bed, but I called him and told him I was leaving and would be back late that night.

"Okay," he said. "Take care."

I got a command car and driver, put on all the clothes I had, and started off down the road to Winterberg. It was 3:00 P.M. by the time we got there, a dull gray afternoon with a chill that knifed through my double set of clothes and field coat.

Ria was in the old officers' quarters. She and a group of girls I recognized were waiting in an apartment next to the one where I had lived.

I stood for a minute without saying anything. Then she saw me and her face lit up as if someone had touched a match to a candle. In an instant, she was across the room and into my arms.

"I knew you would come," she said in a voice only I could hear. Finally she managed to say what was wrong. She was frightened, her voice halting. The Czech Communists would be taking over as soon as the Americans left, she said, and the local party secretary had told her father that she and all the girls who had worked for the Americans would be sent to a concentration camp in Slovakia, several hundred miles to the east.

The man had told her father, however, that if she would live in his house as his mistress, she would not have to go. The others, Hilda, Wally, and Maria, would have to go, but there was a way out for her. She despised the man, she said. He had been making advances toward her since she was thirteen years old. She hated him and she would never live in his house. But she didn't want to go to Slovakia either. She wanted me to know about the situation.

She looked at me with her eyes glistening, blinking back the tears.

I said, "Ria, how can I help you?"

"Do you think it would be possible for you to take me and the rest of us out of here?"

"Take you where?"

"To Germany," she said.

"Okay," I said, "I'll do it. I don't know how, but one way or another, I will."

I told her we would be leaving in a few days. I would go back to the battalion that night and I would pick her up Thursday afternoon. I told her to tell the girls who wanted to go to get what they wanted to take and be ready at the apartment. I would pick them up here and we would go to her house to get her things. She said she would.

"And tell them not to say anything to anyone," I said. "I have enough trouble already and don't need any more."

By then, it was dark, and I told her I had to go. We went back and told the other girls I would take them out.

"Please," I warned them again, "don't say a word to anybody."

When they heard that, they all brightened and started chattering among themselves, occasionally shooting glances in my direction. It was getting late.

We were back in Klenci by 9:30 P.M. I told Steve what had happened and went to bed, but I didn't get much sleep. Early the next morning, I went to see the battalion commander.

"Look," I said, "I've got a problem." He knew about Ria and the other girls from conversations among the staff. I told him what was about to happen to them. I said, "I want to get those girls out of Czechoslovakia and take them to Germany. I'll need a command car, a jeep, and a truck."

Major Threadcraft thought it over a minute, folding his hands into a steeple. "You know, Tex," he said, "you have the authority if you want a jeep or truck or whatever, but certainly I can't give you permission to do this." He paused a minute, tapping his fingertips together. "You can do it on your own."

We both relaxed a little. He asked me if I had given it serious thought. I told him I had. I'd been rolling and tossing and thinking about it all night long.

"You know it could cause some bad problems," he said.

"Yes, I'm aware of that."

"Do you think you can get through the Czech border guards?"

I told him I thought that would be the least of the problems. "We'll simply go in there and if there's a problem, we'll have the drop on them."

The biggest chance of a fight, I told him, was in Winterberg. The Czechs in Winterberg would probably think that Passau was a logical place to take the girls. If there was trouble, it would be in Winterberg or at the border between Winterberg and Passau. I didn't plan to take them to Passau. There wasn't time.

"I'm going to take them to Furth in Wald."

"What about the Czech who wants Ria? What if he gets four or five of his friends or the Czech police and tries to stop you?"

"I'll just have to play it by ear," I said. "I don't want to go in there and kill anybody. If I did, it would cause some real international problems."

"Yes," he agreed. "It would cause an international incident. You wouldn't get home for ten years and she wouldn't get out. Nobody would get out."

I went over to the window and looked out. Beautiful. The hills. The snow. I thought of Don and I wondered what the hell I was doing, getting involved like this. "This one man who wanted Ria so badly is the only one likely to cause trouble."

"You mean, one more won't make any difference?"

"No, I don't look at it that way. I don't want to shoot the bastard, but I won't be stopped. I don't want those girls sent to Slovakia."

In my mind, while we were talking, I could see the trainload of forlorn Germans moving out of Rokycany, disappearing into the snow storm. I wondered what had happened to them. I didn't want to see that happen to Ria.

"You're right," he said finally. "If there's a problem, it'll be in Winterberg. It'll be one man unless you've underestimated him and he has help from some others."

"I don't think they're that well organized."

The major shrugged. "Good luck," he said.

19 Home Again

November 19, 1945–January 6, 1946

Depicting the relief and the exultation that we all felt, Time *magazine reported on December 20, 1945: "The first year of the atomic age drew to a close amid a noisy bustle of Christmas shopping (most extravagant on record), unrationed auto traffic, of holiday travel and partying such as the U.S. had never seen before. The uniforms were disappearing; the face of the land and the face of the people took on a prewar complexion."*

About 10:30 the next morning, I got a thermos of coffee from the mess hall and found a command car with side curtains and moved out, followed by Lt. Bill Spitznas, two sergeants in a jeep, and a two-and-a-half-ton truck with a tarp and endcurtain. Spitznas had grown close to Hilda, one of Ria's friends who was coming out with her, and he had volunteered to help.

The weather was as frigid as ever and the wind and the snow chased each other past the windshield and the side curtains of the command car. The road was coated with ice; the adjacent forest was quiet as snow settled in layers on the honeysuckle and lichens. Ria's ancestors had been in Winterberg and the surrounding area for 500 years, but it looked as if that was all over now. It was strange, I thought. The feeling between the Czechs and the Sudeten-Germans might eventually subside, but if Ria went back to Winterberg to see her parents, she would still have trouble with the Czech official. It seemed to me that the best solution was to eliminate him, and I thought I might do it if I got the chance.

It was still snowing when we got into Winterberg about 2:30 in the afternoon, and a dull heavy gray fog hung over the village. It was mid-afternoon, but darkness was not more than a few minutes off. Ria and the other girls were waiting at the apartment and there was a crowd of their parents, relatives, and friends waiting with them. Word was out.

I noticed some other men standing together some distance away and I thought it was important to get in and get out quickly. Spitznas and the sergeants started loading up the truck with everything from an ironing board to a trunk sewing machine, and clothes — lots of clothes. I told him to keep an eye on the men standing together nearby while I took Ria and the command car to get her belongings. By the time we pulled up before the apartment house where her parents lived, it was dark. The darkness was made more impenetrable by the snow and fog. I waited while she went in to get her things and talk to her parents. Soon her father came down with some suitcases and boxes. Her mother was crying, and before long her father was, too. We loaded her things into the car and I stood a minute, talking to her mother and father. Then I saw the Czech man.

He was watching us from behind the corner of a building. I decided I would deal with him right then.

I took Ria's hand. "Is that the one?"

"Yes, that's him."

For a second, I felt like shooting him. I started toward him, but he moved away, fading into the curtain of snow.

We loaded Ria's things into the command car and drove back through the snow to the officers' former quarters. They were loaded and ready to roll, with Spitznas in the cab of the truck. It was still snowing when we left about 4:30 P.M., heading northwest toward Klenci.

We drove back to Klenci in silence, snow pelting the windshield. It was all right so far, but we weren't out of Czechoslovakia yet.

In Klenci, a vacant house was not far from where Steve and I lived. Though it had no furniture, it had fireplaces, and I had arranged for someone to come over and start fires and warm the place up. It was still snowing when we rolled into Klenci and pulled up into the frozen yard of the house. We unloaded sleeping bags and bedrolls and went inside. The girls took theirs upstairs. Bill and I and the rest of the men spread our bedrolls on the first floor and tried to get some sleep.

We were up at 6:00 A.M. It was dark. Outside, it was still snowing steadily, and cold. We planned to proceed to the Czech border station where I would tell the officer in charge that I had a jeep and a truck coming through and didn't want to slow them down. If they gave us any problem or wanted to search the truck or jeep, we would handle it at gunpoint.

We pulled off through the snow, tires crackling on the ice of the roads, heading directly toward the Czech border point. I got there first in the command car and had the driver pull it off by the side of the road. The post was a small guardhouse with a wooden barrier stretched across the road that could be raised or lowered to let vehicles pass. It was guarded by an NCO and two privates still in the uniform of the Czech army, Mauser rifles slung over their shoulders.

I went up to the three Czechs at the post and told them, as best I could in Czech, that I had a jeep and a truck coming through and to open the barrier and let them pass. They didn't seem to understand, and they didn't open the barrier. I motioned to the sergeant and he walked on past the guards and opened the barrier.

Meanwhile, I was holding a submachine gun and had it pointed in their direction, not threatening them, but pointing it toward them. They were aware of that and made no sudden moves.

When the sergeant opened the barrier, my driver turned the command car around and flashed the headlights. Then the jeep and the truck with the girls in it came up and passed through. We pulled in behind them and the Czech guards made no attempt to stop us.

Moving slowly over the icy road, we drove into Furth in Wald. I went to the burgomeister, told him what had happened, and asked if he could help. He said he would do his best, and I asked him where I could take the girls, and then gave him their names: Ria Allesch, Hilda Mueller, Anne Mueller, Wally Gerner, Gertil Schmidt, and Maria Hellmut.

"Well, there's a cafe downtown," he said. "Nobody's there. You can take them to the cafe where they'll be warm and can get something to eat. Then my wife and I will find a place for them until they can get settled." He nodded his head with assurance as he talked.

At the cafe, we said a quick goodbye to Ria and the girls, promising we would be back. Then, at 9:00 A.M., we turned our mini-convoy around and headed back to Klenci.

Ria and Hilda were in the cafe when Spitz and I returned that night. They had drawn a crowd, some GIs and a lot of Germans. I didn't get out of the command car, but Spitz went to the door and Hilda saw him. Then she and Ria came out and got into the command car with us.

It was cold, all of us in heavy coats, and we drove around some, then parked in front of the cafe. Ria and I were in the back seat, and she asked in a whisper, "What are you thinking of?"

It took me a minute to get it out. "I'm thinking that what you should do is forget about me. You should find a decent German man," I said, "and marry him."

She was silent. I couldn't see her eyes in the dark but I felt a tear on my hand.

Then, calmly, Ria said the other girls wanted to tell me goodbye. "Come on in," she said.

"No," I said, shaking my head. "I don't want to go in there. Please tell them goodbye for me."

She got out of the command car and walked back into the cafe. I wanted her to turn and look at me and maybe wave, but she didn't. I knew that I would never see her again. She would have to make it on her own. But she would. I was sure of that. She was strong. We turned the command car around and started back to Klenci, and I felt miserable.

"Tex, we're gone," the battalion commander told me the next morning. While I had been away, we received the march order. We were leaving at 11:00 A.M. in the morning for Neuburg Au Danau. Major Threadcraft had sent an advance party ahead under Captain Brooks. He said he didn't know exactly what was in store for us at Neuburg Au Danau, but he was sure most of us would be going home.

Steve left while I was in Winterberg, though it was no surprise. I knew he was leaving and asked him to call my wife when he got back to the States. I had given him a Browning Hi-Power 9mm pistol when I told him goodbye. He had been a close friend. I figured that I wouldn't be allowed to take home my cache of firearms, so I started giving them away. In the end, I brought home only a Luger (P-08, 9mm), a Mauser (7.65mm), a revolver, and a shotgun. In violation of orders, I also took my steel helmet with me. I thought I might need it.

We pulled out at 11:00 A.M., headquarters battery leading, rolling over the icy roads all day and throughout the night until finally, around noon, we got into Neuberg Au Danau, a day or so before Thanksgiving. We settled into decent quarters; we would be there at least a month. After that, the division would be broken up, high-point enlisted men going home first.

We were there four days when I got a phone call from an officer in the Division G-1 section, who said they had room for two officers to be redeployed, as the phrase went, to the continental United States the next day. The only requirement was that they have at least seventy-eight points.

"I must have these names as soon as possible," the officer said, "so I can cut the orders tonight."

I had both the howling red-ass and eighty-four points. Nothing mattered to me anymore as far as the army was concerned. I felt as though I had been thoroughly screwed around at least four times. And despite myself, I had become emotionally involved with a German girl in a hopeless situation. I wanted to go home.

When the assistant G-1 said he wanted the names of two officers, I said, "I'll give them to you right now, Capt. Richard M. Hardison and Capt. Henry E. Brooks." Brooks had eighty-four points, too. I gave him our serial numbers. Hank's was on file.

The officer said, "All right, I'm cutting orders now and you're to be at division headquarters in the morning at 9:00 sharp. You'll be heading back to the United States."

The battalion had eight officers with more than seventy-eight points and the decision as to who the two officers would be was the battalion commander's, not mine; but I was in the office and he was not. I was not hesitant about making this decision, however. I had been making a lot of battalion decisions and, besides, our eighty-four points were more than what the other six had. I called Hank and told him.

"God!" he said, "I don't give a damn about anything but going home."

I waited half an hour to give division headquarters time to cut the orders, then I called the battalion commander and told him I was leaving and so was Captain Brooks. The orders had been cut, I said.

He objected. I couldn't leave, he said, because there was still a lot to do, and he needed me. "I will be coming in to call Division and get the orders countermanded," he said. Twenty minutes later, he showed up at battalion headquarters, snow all over his coat. I confirmed that we were on orders to leave in the morning. He called Division, they told him the orders had already been cut, that we were qualified, and there was nothing he could do.

The major suddenly changed. He turned around. "Well, Tex," he said, trying to smile, "it looks like you're leaving."

I nodded.

"It's been a long trip, really, a long journey for those of us in the 8th Armored," he said. "I don't blame you. I wish I was going with you."

We had known each other a long time and he wished us the best, then turned away. When he turned to look at me again, his eyes were cloudy. "What in the hell am I going to do?"

I knew what he meant. "I don't know, sir," I said. "It's not going to be any fun the way things are."

He nodded. We shook hands and he left. I was damned well going home.

The next morning, Hank and I picked up our orders at division headquarters and caught a command car to a concentration center at Aschaffenburg. We were there for three days before boarding a train for France, heading for Camp Lucky Strike at Le Havre, which was a port of embarkation for the United States. We were leaving by the same door we had entered.

The train was not the Orient Express; it was a French "forty and eight," a small boxcar probably dating back to World War I. It got its name because it was designed to hold forty men or eight horses. There were eight officers aboard our boxcar, four on each end. The car had a wood stove with its stove pipe going out the door, and about a foot and a half of hay on the floor. We moved the hay away from the stove and laid our bedrolls down on the hay. All we had with us were K-rations, our duffle bags, and bedrolls. The foot lockers had been shipped ahead.

Some of the guys got a fire going in the stove, and late in the evening the train started rolling slowly toward France. We would enter France at Saarbrucken and go from there to Metz, west to Rheims, and on northwest to Le Havre, a four-day trip. About three days into the trip, our train rammed a train ahead of us and knocked down the stove.

At the same time, I fell backward onto Captain Roberts' duffle bag. It felt like it was full of iron.

"My God, man," I said, "what's in that duffle bag?"

He opened it up. There were two burp guns, a German MG-42 machine gun, and several rifles. I didn't know how he expected to get them through inspection, but there they were in his duffle bag.

Finally, we rolled into Camp Lucky Strike, a city of tents and boardwalks in the snow, tents with wooden walls about three feet up and wooden floors. Clerks checked our orders and told us a truck convoy would arrive in the evening to take us to a cross channel steamer to Southampton. Brooks and I settled into a tent to wait for the trucks.

When they came, they blew in like a "norther" and the drivers fanned out in all directions. I had been standing about eight feet in front of my tent when they drove in. A minute later, I went back into the tent where I had left my duffle bag and field coat, but my field coat was gone!

Meantime, everybody was loading up, heaving their duffle bags and bedrolls into the backs of the six-by-sixes, sixteen of them lined up. It was colder than a wedge and I was madder than hell! I looked around for the officer in charge of the trucks, but there wasn't any. A master sergeant was in charge. I found the sergeant and told him my field coat was gone, that one of his drivers had stolen it and the convoy wasn't moving until I found my coat.

The sergeant protested that the convoy had to leave, but I insisted. In fact, I stood in front of the first truck waiting. "Nobody leaves," I said, "till I get that coat."

I held them up about thirty minutes in the cold. Finally, the sergeant and two others started going through the trucks and found my coat in one of the side boxes of a truck. They brought me the coat and the driver, and I cussed him out in front of everybody. Stealing was bad enough, I told him, but it was even worse for some sorry rear-echelon yardbird like him to steal from a combat soldier. He hadn't seen a day of anything but rear-echelon duty, and I told him I was sorry I didn't have time to court-martial him.

Then I put on my coat and the convoy rolled off to the docks, pulling up next to an ancient channel steamer. There were no bunks; it was just a matter of finding a place to sit on deck, cold as it was. To make matters nearly unbearable, my stomach was hurting to beat hell and I hadn't the slightest idea why. I noticed a doctor aboard and told him my stomach was hurting.

"Let's get on down below," he said, "and see if I can feel anything."

We went down the narrow companionway and found a compartment where I could stretch out and open up my pants. He felt around and prodded and poked and finally, his examination finished, he looked me in the face.

"I think you've got stomach cancer. I feel a big lump here and I think that's what it is."

Suddenly, I felt even sicker, blood draining out of my head. I had been scared a few times in combat, but this time I was shaky and cold inside. Stomach cancer! I couldn't imagine anything worse than that. That's what I thought had killed my father.

I pulled on my clothes again and told myself that I would go to the hospital when I got to Southampton. If I did have something, I'd find out about it.

A few hours later, we landed at Southampton and were trucked to barracks nearby, where we were to stay until we could get passage home. It was December 20. We were supposed to board the *Queen Elizabeth* in the next day or two and land in New York before New Year's Day. But that didn't happen.

I was more worried about my stomach. As soon as we moved into the barracks, I reported sick at the station hospital. A few minutes later, the doctor, a captain, beckoned me to come in and asked me what the matter was.

I took a deep breath and told him about the doctor on the steamer who had told me I had cancer.

He asked who it was. I told him I didn't know, but I wanted a second opinion — quick. He told me to lie down on the table and he'd find out, so I shucked my shirt and trousers and stretched out on his examination table.

He felt my stomach in silence. Then he had several x-rays taken from the front and sides of my stomach. Half an hour later, he came back holding the x-ray pictures.

"You don't have a damned thing wrong with you," he said. "I can't imagine why that doctor would tell you what he did. You have no problem. I thought I felt a lump in your stomach, but it wasn't anything at all. Forget it."

It was like the war ending all over again and I felt like shooting artillery into the air.

Hank and I went to London, but it was a dreary place. Christmas passed in the barracks and we hardly noticed. We were told the *Queen Elizabeth* had already left and we would go home instead on the aircraft carrier USS *Wasp,* which was in the harbor. We would be in New York City by January 1, they said. That was good news. The *Wasp* was fast.

We were loaded on buses and taken down to the dock where the *Wasp* was moored, its superstructure looming like a mountain against the silver-gray sky. Hank and I shouldered our duffle bags and walked up the gangplank. A naval type was waiting with our room assignments. Hank and I would share a stateroom with two other officers: Capt. "Dog" Dawson of Crockett, Texas, whom I had known at A&M, and a lieutenant from Galveston.

The crossing was going to be like a vacation cruise, I thought, and I could spend my time reading. On the hangar deck were about 5,000 men in bunks, some of them seven tiers high. Anchored on the top and bottom, the bunks ran from the hangar deck to the bottom of the flight deck.

The seas got rough after we passed Lizard Head outbound, and south of Iceland the waves were so high that they crashed down on the flight deck. Instead of running at a normal twenty-five or thirty knots, the ship was moving at barely five knots. Then came messages on the speaker system that we would be slowing down to three knots and changing course.

The next thing I noticed was that the naval officers were wearing pistols. On the second day of the storm, I went down to the hangar deck. Waves were battering the ship and the propellers would jump out of the water and shake the ship like a dog shaking a rag. It was lurching, trembling, groaning, diving, rolling, and slipping, doing everything but going straight. The big ship was like a gigantic animal in pain.

The men were confined to their bunks. There wasn't room on the ship for everyone to be walking around. The one on the top bunk would be shaking the most and usually he would get sick and puke on those underneath and across from him. They, in turn, got sick and after a while the whole hangar deck was vomiting like Vesuvius. When I went to the hangar deck to see what was happening, vomit was cascading back and forth over the deck. Sailors were trying to hose it down and get it off the ship, but they were often themselves throwing up, three or four men to a hose and two or three of them vomiting on their buddies in front of the hose.

For four days, this went on. Finally, after twelve days at sea, we pulled into New York harbor. Boats came out to meet us and flash-bulbs popped. A picture of the ship, with its flight deck warped down over the bow on the port side, ran on the cover of a news magazine the next week.

That seemed less important than getting land under our feet again. We staggered down the gangplank and got on a train for Camp Kilmer, New Jersey, from which we had embarked sixteen months earlier. I was told I was going to Fort Sam Houston in San Antonio, Texas, and that I would be separated from the service there.

I called Don in Colorado City. "Don," I said, "I'm almost home."

"Richard! That's wonderful! I'll come and meet you! Where are you?"

"No, don't meet me here. I'll be back in Texas soon. And Don, I can hardly wait."

"Where will you be? I'll be there."

"San Antonio," I said. "And Don . . ."

"Yes?"

"I love you."

But I was jerked around again. They decided that I wasn't going to Fort Sam, I was going to Camp Fannin, Texas, near Tyler in East Texas. I called Don again, but she had already left. So now I was going to Camp Fannin, several hundred miles from San Antonio.

Hank Brooks and I shook hands goodbye. He wasn't far from home. We had gone overseas together, sharing the same stateroom, and we'd come back the same way. Dog Dawson and I boarded a train to Camp Fannin. Three days after I got there, I was promoted and out of the army, still in uniform.

I caught a taxi from the Separation Center and went to the bus station, which was in the lobby of a hotel in downtown Tyler. As I walked into the lobby, I heard a woman call, "Richard!"

I looked around, then I saw her. It was Jane Wilson, a school teacher I had dated years and years ago. A pretty brunette, she was wearing a Red Cross uniform, standing some distance away in front of the magazine rack.

"Richard! You're a major," she said. "I can't believe it!" From her tone of voice everyone in eye sight knew she meant it. I was not one of her favorites. By now, everyone in the lobby was looking at me. "Four years ago," she said, "you were a second lieutenant." She stood, looking at me, and then said, "I am glad for you . . . just surprised, that's all."

20 Getting On With It

January 7, 1946–April 17, 1946

Time *magazine, February 25, 1946: "At Nuremberg, the Russians were plugging a vengeful justice; everywhere else in Germany, they were plugging Communism. Combat-happy Red Army occupation troops who, until recently, had terrified Germans with their merry rounds of loot and rape, were being replaced by more disciplined units from Russia. The Western powers sought ways to strengthen their own occupation program to counter Russia's determined steps. Many a German looked on smugly; nine months after their victory, the victors were contending for the allegiance of the vanquished."*

The bus got into San Antonio at 9:15 that night. When I got off, somebody suddenly grabbed me from the side. It was Don, holding on and crying. We stood there in the bus station a long time, holding each other, not caring what anybody else in the world thought. The war was really over and I was home.

"Don," I said with a grin. "This is like a dream." And it *was* like a dream. Don was more beautiful than ever, and we were together again.

"It's a dream for me, too."

"Home," I said, taking Don in my arms. "Let me see if it's real or not." I kissed her, a long, warm, hungry kiss.

When it was over, she laughed. "Is it real?"

"It's real," I said. "And I love you." She laughed and we walked out of the bus station together.

Don had been in San Antonio for a week, staying with my sister and her husband, Lt. Ross T. Glover. He had been an infantry platoon leader in the 7th Division. The Japs had shot him up on Okinawa and he was an outpatient at Brooks Army Hospital. After a few days with them, we drove to Colorado City by way of Houston and College Station.

I didn't know what I was going to do. I went to see an uncle in Houston who was in business, hoping he might have a place for me, but he didn't. We drove on to College Station to see Prof. F. W. Hansel, head of the Landscape Architecture Department. He said he would have no problem getting me a job and asked me how I felt about it. I told him that after almost five years in the army, I didn't feel qualified to go into a professional office. My drafting was rusty, I said, and I didn't want to work for a nursery or a contractor. I told him I needed some time to think about it.

He leaned toward me, smiling. "I have a suggestion to make, Richard. Go home and come back on February 6. That's when graduate school starts."

I could take certain courses that would apply on a master's degree, he said. I should stay in school at least six months and get back into things and see what was going on. He would design some courses for me on the graduate level.

"Okay," I said, "I'll do it."

That settled, we left for Colorado City, getting in around 11:00 that night. Mother met us with hugs and kisses. It was good to be home.

Mother's house was comfortable, but small. We slept on a bed-type couch. The first day I stayed in and talked to Mother and Don. The next day was cold, with light snow falling, and I bundled up and went downtown about mid-morning to see who might be around. I ran across a fellow I knew who had been back from the war about three months. The town was dead, he said.

"A lot of the fellows are not back," he said, "and some of the others never will be back."

Many of them had come back shaken and jumpy. Those who had been discharged were for the most part farmers and ranchers and they had family businesses or interests to go into. Two or three had come back for a while and left to look for work in Houston or Fort Worth.

Finally I said, "Look, I've been gone a long time. I don't know what's happened. Who do you know of that was killed?"

"Quite a few," he said.

I pressed him for their names. Frank Blassingame had been killed at Anzio. Leon Callan died in an accident early in the war. J. W. Hodges was killed at Iwo Jima. Red Morrison had been killed when his Spitfire flew into a hill in England. Wilson Wyatt had been lost when the navy supply ship *Pecos* was sunk off the coast of Australia. James Bodine was killed on a destroyer in the Battle of the Coral Sea. Dick Jones had been killed when his P-51 blew up over the English Channel. Ted Hale died in Alsace. Archie Mohler was shot down over the Mediterranean Sea in 1943.

It was a terrible roll call. Some came back horribly shot up. Others returned to find that the families they left were no longer theirs. Some wives had gone off, others had grown apart. One or two soldiers received "Dear John" letters. I went to town once or twice a day, hoping to see someone I had known. I saw some new faces, soldiers who had married hometown girls and moved to Colorado City.

After five or six days, I began to relax a little and Don asked me what I planned to do.

"Plans?" I shook my head. "You know that we are going to College Station in February and I will enter graduate school and after that we will just have to wait and see."

"I understand," she said softly.

"For a long time, years now, I have not thought about things like this. I might have forgotten how. I thought that I was going to remain in the army. I thought that everything was settled. And then, well, it didn't work out."

"It's not all that bad, we will be happy as long as we are together," she said. Her hand was touching mine and she pressed it suddenly. "It'll work out, Richard. I know it will. But it will take some time."

"Of course it will work out," I said.

"And we've got plenty of time."

I told her I thought I would go down to the farm my father used to own, about twenty-five miles south of Colorado City. I had lived there by myself for a year after I finished high school, looking after my father's livestock and cooking all my own meals. It hadn't been too bad. I had liked it better than being at home. I wanted to see the house that I'd lived in, and there was a hill nearby that I wanted to climb again. I used to ride out there on my horse in the evening and just look over the landscape. You could see for twenty or twenty-five miles in any direction, mesquite-covered hills with a few houses in the distance. I had spent a lot of time on that hill. There was a road nearby and I thought I would drive out there, park on top, and think.

I let Don off at her parents' home, and as I started to pull away, she said, "Wait! I have something for you." She ran into the house and a minute later she was back with a small packet of letters.

"What's this?"

"You'll see," she said. "When you get out on top of the hill, take a look at it."

"Okay."

I drove the twenty-five miles over improved roads toward my personal hill. It was about noon and cold, the temperature down below freezing. From the crest of the hill, I could see the little frame house I'd lived in. Somebody lived there now, but it looked much as it had the year I'd lived there. My father sold the farm during my first year in college. I didn't know who lived there now and I didn't feel much like telling them I wanted to look around, so I just watched it for a while from the hill.

Then I opened the packet. The letters, unopened, were tied with a string. Some were postmarked 1944 and 1945, some in early 1946, about the time I got home. I began leafing through them. Four of the letters were from girls I had gone with while in college or at Ft. Sill. One said she had seen an article in the paper about me and wanted to know where I was and what I was doing. One letter was from the Red Cross girl in our tour group in Switzerland. Two were from Ria.

I put them all in a box and disposed of them. Then, about 3:00 P.M., I drove back to town to pick up Don. We didn't mention the letters, but she said, "We need to sit down and talk about some things."

"When?" I asked.

"After dinner?"

"Okay."

"I've got an idea," she said. "Why don't we go out to our old courting place?"

I nodded. It was a parking place on a hill. From it, you could look down on Colorado City and on a clear night see the lights of Sweetwater. We had dinner with my mother and grandmother, and after dinner we drove out to the hill. She leaned toward me as she always did and snuggled up against me. I leaned back against the door.

"Okay," I said, "what is it?"

"There were several things," she said. "First, you haven't asked me anything about money."

Money? I thought that I knew about how much we should have and was not worried about it. I had sent almost all of my army pay home by allotment and she was working.

"I know," she said, "but I just wanted to tell you what we have and how it looks." She hadn't spent a penny of my salary and she had saved three-fourths of her own. She had paid her parents a modest sum for room and board and had maintained the automobile and bought a few clothes. That was it.

We had a nice sum in our savings account. I was surprised and pleased, and I told her so.

"There's something else," she said.

"What is it?"

"You're different. I don't know what it is. I know you've been through a war and you've seen some terrible things. I've been talking to your mother about it and she agrees with me that you're different." She thought for a moment, then said, "I love you, Richard, but you're different."

I told her that I had changed and that she had changed, too. We had both matured. I had seen things and been to places that made me different. I had already told myself I wouldn't talk about the details of combat or about Ria until we got back to College Station, where I felt more comfortable. There was a park bench near the library where I went whenever I had free time from work or studies. It was under a big live oak and I liked the place for its peace and quiet. It was a good place to think. I used to sit there from time to time during my four years of college. When Don came up as my guest for the senior ring dance in May of 1941, we sat on that bench and talked about our future — our marriage, too. I would wait until we were back at A&M and it was spring and warm and the flowers were in bloom and the trees in full leaf.

A couple of days later, I was alone with my mother. She said, "You know, son, you're a lot different from when you left. I think there's something bothering you, something you need to talk about.

I'm not going to ask you what it is. You'll be ready to talk when the time comes."

I kept going to town, hoping to see friends. Julius Smith came home during this time. He was a close friend, and we spent some time riding around in the country shooting at crows with .22s and shotguns as we had when we were boys. By this time, too, Don's brother, R. C., had come home. We had often hunted together and we went out and shot at whatever we could find, crows or rabbits. I was beginning to relax. When February finally came, we packed up the car and headed for College Station.

Dormitory rooms were made available for returning servicemen and their wives. We lived in one room and ate in the mess hall. I was taking a full courseload of twenty hours and spent my time going to class and labs and writing reports. Don had nothing to do, though she was meeting some of the wives and getting acquainted.

I had been thinking a lot about the past years and decided that I had put it off long enough, that the time had come to talk to Don about things. I picked her up at the dorm and we went to lunch together, then I suggested a walk around the campus.

April was a lovely time of year, the flowers beginning to bloom and the leaves green against a pure blue sky. I took Don to my favorite bench where we had talked five years before. Nobody was there.

"Let's sit down," I said. "There's something I need to tell you."

She said, "I wondered when you were going to talk about it."

"Well, this is it," I said. Then I told her as objectively as I could about the battle at Rhineberg and some of the other actions we had been involved in. I told her about the death camp near Langenstein, and the slave laborers, and the displaced persons in Hann-Munden.

Finally, I told her about Ria. I told her what she was like and how she looked, though I didn't tell her then how strong my feelings for Ria had been. Maybe I still hadn't admitted it to myself.

"What I'm getting at, Don, is that nothing really happened, do you know what I mean? I mean that it was very different over there than it is here."

"I know that," she said, "and I understand."

Don said nothing for a long time and neither did I. Then suddenly she leaned over to me slowly and kissed me on the lips. "Richard," she said softly, "I'm sorry for the girl, but she knew that you were married. And so did you. I'm surprised, that's all. You knew better."

We sat for a long time without saying anything. I knew it was going to be all right between us. I had known that all along. And she was right, too, I guess, about knowing better. But things happen in a war that have nothing to do with knowing better.

At this time I was fully aware that what I had seen had broadened and changed me. There were many aspects of life that I did not look at as I did in 1941. For one thing I was more cynical, more impatient and critical.

I did not ever want to be involved in another war. But if I had to, there were many things that I would do differently.

I had recently learned that I was to become a father in November. Now was the time for us to think and plan for the future. With this in mind, we decided to remain in College Station, where I could complete the requirements for a master's degree, which we did.

Epilogue

Baldwin, Bun: Returned to Bridgman, Michigan, where he successfully operated a real estate brokerage company for many years. Died on February 2, 1989.

Brooks, Henry E.: Returned to Manchester, Connecticut, and his job in a plastics product manufacturing company. Was vice-president of sales when he retired in 1986.

Burba, Edwin: Remained in the army, was major general and killed in an aircraft accident on the last day of active duty.

Carroll, Edmund: Lived in New Albin, Iowa. Died there in 1987.

Collins, John J.: Was lieutenant colonel when discharged; graduated from Fordam University in 1949. Employed by Remington Rand in Australia and in England. Was senior vice-president of the Singer Corporation when he retired in 1983. Lives in Westport, Connecticut.

Cook, Gardner: Returned to his law practice in Lunenburg, Massachusetts. Now retired and lives in Lunenburg.

Davis, Gerald: no information.

Duckworth, Delmos: Returned to Sims, Indiana, and his automobile repair business. Retired; lives in Swaycze, Indiana.

Ezra, Harold: Returned to Crawfordsville, Indiana, and was employed in a manufacturing plant. Retired.

Gausman, Willis: Remained in the army; attained the rank of colonel. Lived in El Paso, Texas. Died in 1978.

Gillespie, Francis: Returned to New York City and his job with the police department. Retired from the PD and accepted employment with the IRS. Was colonel in the Reserves. Died in 1975.

Glover, Ross T.: Returned to Colorado City, Texas, then in 1952 accepted employment in Houston. Retired; lives in Houston, Texas.

Grant, Porter: Returned to his home in Dothan, Alabama. Remained active in the U.S. Army reserves; was brigadier general. Deceased.

Hale, Charles: Returned to his home in Scotland Neck, North Carolina. Retired from the lumber business several years ago. Lives in Scotland Neck.

Hardison, Richard M.: Returned to Texas A&M College for a master's degree in 1947. Lived in Houston, Texas, and operated a vegetative erosion control company for thirty-five years. Retired in 1985 and lives in Big Spring, Texas.

Hawley, William H.: Retired gentleman farmer and college professor. Lives in Oxford, Ohio.

Hughes, William F.: Discharged from the army and enlisted in the Air Force as master sergeant in 1946. Married in 1949 in Trieste. Died in 1966.

Lilly, Roger M.: Retired major general. Last duty was chief of staff of NORAD. Lives in Monument, Colorado.

Morris, William A.: Returned to his law practice in North Canton, Ohio. Elected municipal court judge in the early 1950s and served there until retirement in 1988. Lives in Canton, Ohio.

Oliver, Matthew A.: Employed by large forest products company for many years; later owned an office supply business. Retired and lives in Rancho Murieta, California.

Page, John U. D.: Remained in the army. Was colonel when killed in Korea in 1952.

Palmer, Thomas: Retired; lives in Bradenton, Florida.

Pieper, William: Retired from banking; owns automobile dealership in Burlington, Iowa. Lives in Dallas City, Illinois.

Polus, Peter: Retired tool and die maker. Lives in Galesburg, Illinois.

Pottish, Morris: Returned to New York City and the practice of law. No further information.

Quist, Lawrence: Returned to family masonry construction business. Is retired and lives in Chicago, Illinois.

Reed, Orr L.: Remained in the army and overseas for many years. Was field artillery group sergeant major when he retired. Lives in Spring Lake, North Carolina.

Rominger, James: Returned to his home in Breckenridge, Texas, and is president of a bank there.

Roth, John: Retired and lives in Pine Grove, Pennsylvania.

Russ, James E.: Returned to his home in Utica, New York, and was a cabinetmaker. Retired and lives in Clinton, New York.

Salisbury, George: Returned to the family ranch on the Colorado-Wyoming state line and soon became the manager of all operations. Served eight terms in the Wyoming legislature. Was featured in the documentary film *Cowboy* prepared on the ranch by the Alcoa Aluminum Company and was shown on the Alcoa Hour numerous times beginning in 1971. Lives in Slater, Colorado.

Sather, Marvin: Returned to River Falls, Wisconsin, entered college and earned a BA and an MA degree. Served many years as a county agricultural agent. Is retired and lives in Nelson, Nebraska.

Sears, Don: Received law degree after the war. Was dean of the University of Colorado Law School for several years. Is retired and lives in Boulder, Colorado.

Smith, Julius O.: Returned to Colorado City and his job in an oil refinery. Retired and lives in Colorado City, Texas.

Smith, Robert V.: Returned to Michigan State University to earn a master's and doctorate in chemistry. Was employed by Samuel Johnson and Sons for many years. Retired and lives in Fallbrook, California.

Snively, Robert Clark (R. C.): Returned to Colorado City, Texas, and entered Texas Tech University. Received a degree in Civil Engineering. Accepted employment with the Bureau of Reclamation and Survey in Denver, Colorado. Died there in 1962.

Starry, Dale: Returned to Shippensburg, Pennsylvania, and was employed for several years by GSA. Owns a bookstore and lives in Shippensburg.

Stephens, Lynn: Retired and lives in Wichita, Kansas.

Stevens, Clair: Returned to his job with American Bridge Company in Elmira, New York. Retired several years ago. Lives in Horseheads, New York.

Threadcraft, Hal: No information.

Verlinder, Raymond: Retired from Gulf Oil Co. and lives in Surfside, Texas.

Wakeman, Vincent: Returned to his home on Long Island and employed there until his retirement in 1987. Lives in Westbury, New York.

Weldon, Lloyd: Returned to Okemah, Oklahoma, and remained

in the Reserves. Was called to duty in the Korean Conflict and was a battery commander. Discharged and entered Oklahoma State University in 1956. Earned a degree in veterinary medicine. Received national publicity on several occasions for competence in his field. Died December 25, 1987.

Whiteley, Lt. Col. Hal: Deceased.

Zierler, Dr. Kenneth: Head, Department of Pathology, Johns Hopkins University. Lives in Baltimore, Maryland.

Appendix

I.

FIELD ARTILLERY SCHOOL
OFFICE OF THE COMMANDANT

FORT SILL, OKLAHOMA
April 16, 1942.

Brigadier General Waldo C. Potter,
Commanding General,
F.A. Replacement Training Center,
Fort Sill, Oklahoma.

My dear General Potter:

Upon relief of 2d Lt. Richard M. Hardison, Field Artillery Replacement Training Center, Fort Sill, as Post Improvement Officer, I wish to inform you of the splendid manner in which he has performed that duty.

Lieutenant Hardison was detailed as Post Improvement Officer on January 21, 1942, and relieved on April 9, 1942. He performed all duties pertaining to this assignment in a superior manner. He demonstrated marked qualities of leadership, initiative, and professional ability. He worked willingly, enthusiastically, and conscientiously, and cooperated fully in carrying out the directives of the Post Commander.

Very sincerely,

G. R. ALLIN,
Brigadier General, U.S.A.,
Commandant.

II.

HEADQUARTERS
399TH ARMORED FIELD ARTILLERY BATTALION
APO 258 US ARMY

S-2 AFTER ACTION REPORT-PERIOD 0001 4 APR–3 MAY 1945

1. *Enemy Situation at End of Period* — No contact with the enemy. Activities confined to patroling, maintaining martial law in assigned area.

2. *Enemy Operations During Period* — No contact with the enemy at beginning of period.

4 April 1945 — No contact with the enemy — Bn on the move.
5 April 1945 — No contact with the enemy — Bn on the move.
6 April 1945 — No contact with the enemy — Bn on the move.
7 April 1945 — Bn in position — intermittent artillery fire —Bn in close support to Task Force.
8 April 1945 — No artillery or SA Fire being received.
9 April 1945 — Resistance stiffens as Bn moves forward — intermittent fire by artillery.
10 April 1945 — Resistance continues — occasional small cal artillery and mortar fire on our positions — column fired on necessitating Bn going into position along road — several counter-attacks repulsed — Approx. 25 rounds landing in gun positions necessitating moving to alternate positions. Three casualties, 1 seriously wounded by mortar or small cal artillery shrapnel. It is quite evident that we are under observation at all times as we seem to be getting direct fire — close support of infantry and tanks.
11 April 1945 — Shelling of our position continues as the slightest movement draws medium cal artillery fire.
12 April 1945 — Resistance ceases — Bn released from present assignment.
13 April 1945 — No resistance — Bn moving.
14 April 1945 — No resistance — Bn moving.
15 April 1945 — Enemy activity consisting of ambushing trucks & small vehicles — med. cal. artillery fire coming from well selected positions that are difficult to locate due to unfavorable terrain & natural defenses.

16 April 1945 — Resistance continues — Approx. six rounds artillery landing in position — no casualties — activity increases.
17 April 1945 — Resistance continues — pocket diminishes. No
18 April 1945 shelling.
19 April 1945 — FOs with Infantry pinned down by mortar fire 1 officer and 1 sgt. wounded by SA and mortar fire while
20 April 1945 observing with Infantry.
21 April 1945 — Bn reld present mission.
22 April 1945 — Arrived Hann Munden.
23 April thru
3 May 1945 — Maintaining martial law in area.

3. *Section Operations* — The S-2 Section working in cooperation with the S-3 Section briefed observers & maintained communication with the observers while in contact with the enemy. The situation and operations maps were posted and pertinent friendly and enemy information kept up to the minute, by personal contact with front line troops. The Section was responsible for procurement and distribution of all maps used by the Bn. All information was sent to higher Hq. promptly and action reports hourly. All Burgomeisters were screened and it was found necessary to replace four of them. Several individuals whose activities before our occupation, made them dangerous to us, were arrested. All PW's located were cleared through the section. Displaced persons affairs, such as collection and census were taken care of by the S-2 Section.

4. *Weather & Terrain* — The weather throughout the period was generally fair, though some bad weather was experienced. Visibility was poor to fair. The terrain was favorable to armored action.

For The Battalion Commander:

R. M. Hardison,
Captain — F. A.,
S-2

Glossary

A-26: A light attack bomber, twin-engine Douglas airplane.

adjutant: A staff officer who is an administrative officer.

air control officer: An Air Force officer who was with the forward elements of the combat command and in communication with the squadron leader in the airplanes above.

anti-aircraft half-track: A half-track with an armor shield removed and with a flatbed mounted with quadruple .50-caliber machine guns or double 40mm Bouffer anti-aircraft guns. These guns were electrically operated and very effective against ground targets.

Air Force cadets: Those soldiers that were transferred to combat units toward the end of the war. They were considered surplus by the Air Force. They were pilot, navigator, and bombardier trainees.

air observer: An officer observer in a liaison plane with the mission of observing artillery file on the ground or any enemy activity he might be able to see.

airstrike: The bombing, strafing, and rocketing of certain areas when requested by combat troops; generally they were P-47s and occasionally the A-26s would participate.

anti-tank ditch: A ditch dug by the Germans with forced labor or machines that was generally fifteen to twenty feet wide at the top with sloping slides and a bottom of five to six feet. Usually, the ditches were eight to fifteen feet deep, depending upon the location.

anti-tank grenade: Generally, a rocket-propelled grenade with a shaped charge.

army: Consisted of two or more Corps and each Corps consisted of two or more divisions.

army group: A group of armies, two or more, such as the Twelfth Army Group — consisted of the army on the north; the army in the center; and the army on the south.

artillery concentration: The concentrated fire of an artillery battery, battalion, or several battalions.

ATS: An English organization, Army Transportation Service; truck companies whose drivers were female soldiers.

battalion executive officer: The second in command of a battalion, generally a major.

battalion intelligence officer S-2: The responsibilities included procurement and distribution of maps; briefing of forward observers; rendering shell reports to division artillery; occasional observation and direction of artillery fire; preparation of intelligence summaries; distribution to batteries; and miscellaneous other duties.

battalion packing and crating officer: This officer was designated by the battalion commander to oversee the packing, crating, labeling, and shipping of equipment, supplies, etc., in connection with overseas movement.

battalion surgeon: Each battalion had a medical doctor, who usually held the rank of captain.

battery clerk: A soldier clerk that took care of the typing and helped the first sergeant and the battery commander compile reports, fill out the morning reports, etc.

bazooka: A hollow tube through which an anti-tank rocket was propelled.

booby trap: An explosive placed around things that were considered valuable, such as stacks of rifles or other materiel. Sometimes they were hinged to doors, drawers of furniture, and that sort, and were triggered by moving or opening a drawer or door. This would in turn pull or release a wire that would set off the explosive.

Bosh: German soldiers.

Browning .50-caliber machine gun: A fine weapon that shot a slug about as big as a man's thumb, muzzle velocity higher than that of a .30-caliber rifle. Very accurate, very devastating.

burgomeister: The mayor of a German town.

buzz bomb: The V-1 rocket bomb of about 2,000 pounds, developed by the Germans.

carbine: A .30-caliber semi-automatic weapon; much lighter rifle than the .30-caliber M-1 rifle and much smaller shell cartridge.

CCA, CCB and **CCR:** A Combat Command unit comprised of one artillery, one infantry, and tank battalion, with one cavalry reconnaissance troop.

center battery: The geographic center of the three batteries.

chief, survey section: A sergeant in charge of the survey section; one who is capable of surveying and working out the locations of the batteries.

command post (CP): The location where the commanding officer of a given unit has established his headquarters and where communications are centered.

company grade officers: Second lieutenants, first lieutenants, and captains.

concussion hand grenade: A grenade for explosive purposes only, no fragmentation.

contact patrol: An infantry patrol dispatched at a given time to keep in contact with units, generally on the flanks.

converged sheath: The fire of a battery. Each gun is calculated and set for all shells to impact at the same point, not in relationship of the guns to each other on the ground.

CP tent: A command post tent when in the field.

counterbattery: When an artillery unit fires on enemy artillery.

D Series: Division maneuver series where one division participated alone and not with other divisions.

Department of Gunnery: A department in the field artillery school that taught all aspects of gunnery.

death camp: A German camp where displaced persons and others were systematically killed, by starving them to death or by gassing them.

DP: A displaced person foreign laborer that was in Germany as enslaved labor; included various Europeans, such as Poles, Russians, and Czechs.

division artillery commander: A colonel in overall command of the three artillery battalions when not in a combat situation. Usually, the command was broken up in combat, but he would supervise the training and the supply for the batteries, regardless of where they were.

field artillery officers' advanced course: A three-month course by which the field artillery school prepared an officer of given rank to become the operations officer of a battalion; a very technical course.

fire for effect: After adjustment, which is generally with one gun, all guns come in and shoot at the same target.

fire mission: A call to arms, so to speak. The observer decides to shoot at a target and his first words are "fire mission," which alerts the fire direction center.

firing chart: The fire direction center kept four firing charts (a ruled sheet of paper 24" x 24"). The master chart was kept by the operations officer or his assistant. A chart for each battery was maintained by the battery computer (a clerk, usually a corporal) and had the battery location pinpointed. Every target and gun position was plotted.

first sergeant: The ranking NCO of a given battery or company.

FOs: Forward artillery observers.

Folkwulf 190: A German high-performance fighter airplane which resembled the P-47.

foot locker: A small trunk, about twelve inches high, eighteen inches wide, and three feet long, to store excess winter or summer clothing and personal belongings.

G-1: Division personnel officer.

G-2: Division intelligence officer.

G-3: Division operation officer.

G-4: Division supply officer.

G-5: Division military government officer.

garbage sump: A hole in the ground where garbage is buried, much like a sanitary landfill today, but only on a very small scale. Garbage sumps generally were four to six feet long, three feet wide, and three feet deep. After the garbage was placed there, it was covered with dirt.

George W. Goethels: An army transport ship of about 10,000-ton displacement.

German 88: An 88mm dual-purpose high performance gun. The shell and the case itself is over three feet long and the muzzle velocity of this gun is 3,400 feet per second. The shell velocity was in excess of the speed of sound; one never could hear it coming.

good registration: A good clean hit with few rounds, on a given registration point.

grease gun: A term commonly given to the M-3, .45-caliber sub-machine gun. Made of stamped metal, generally not machined like the Thompson gun; a cheaply made but effective weapon in short range.

guidon staff: A staff to carry the guidon or flag of a given battery. Generally, the guidon staff is seven feet long.

half-track: A vehicle designed to transport personnel in an armored division. The vehicle itself was half-track, i.e., wheels in front and tracks in the rear. It was more mobile than a two-and-one-half-ton truck, much more powerful. It had a one-quarter-inch armor plate all around it, except on the top, and generally mounted a .50-caliber machine gun.

Headquarters Battery: A battery of about 130 men. Consisted of a communications section; the FO section; maintenance sections; and other supportive personnel. All of the staff of headquarters itself were in Headquarters Battery.

incendiary bomb: A bomb that, on impact, would set fire. It contained magnesium and started hot fires.

K Factor: A factor determined by putting map data corrected against observed data. A factor used in shooting off corrected maps.

K rations: Packaged rations in a box four inches wide, two inches thick, and ten inches long. Consisted of cheese, crackers, canned meat, and powdered drink.

L-4: An artillery observation aircraft, generally a Piper or Taylorcraft.

liaison pilot: An artillery officer trained to fly the light liaison artillery airplane.

Limey: An English national, either military or civilian.

line officer: An officer of one of the arms of the service — artillery, infantry, cavalry, or armor; not a quartermaster, finance, or ordnance officer.

litter jeep: A jeep equipped with two stretchers to carry wounded.

Lizard Head: A point of land off southern England, across the channel from Cherbourg.

LST: A landing ship tank.

maps: Generally small-scale maps 1/25,000 showing individual houses and often trees. Contour lines and elevations shown.

M-1: Model 1 army rifle. A Garand semi-automatic .30-caliber rifle.

map-located targets: Areas on a map in enemy territory that were thought to be significant.

ME-262: A German twin-engine, jet-propelled, plane fighter.

mess sergeant: The sergeant in charge of the kitchen, responsible for preparing and serving meals in the field and in garrison.

non-coms: Non-commissioned officers.

Panzerfaust: A bazooka anti-tank rocket of German origin.

parachute flare: A flare fired from a mortar. At the top of the trajectory a parachute would come out and a flare would ignite and light up an area for a given number of seconds, depending on how high it was.

rabbit ears: The lid on the top of the turret of a tank, made in two parts. Both parts raised when a man came out of the turret. The lid stuck up like jack rabbit ears.

red ass: A term used to express displeasure with the status quo; covers a broad spectrum of feeling, from mild dissatisfaction to paranoia.

howling (or screaming) red ass: A case of red ass that has progressed to the point that the person affected can no longer contain his indignation. Characterized by a vociferous outcry that tells all persons within a six-block radius more than they really want to know about the cause of his distress.

Bibliography

Bradley, Omar N. *A Soldier's Story.* Henry Holt and Company, New York.

Byrnes, Laurence G. *History of the 94th Infantry Division in WW2.* The Infantry Journal Press, Washington, D.C.

Krings, von Tony. *Eine Jugend Im Krieg.* Private printing, Heinsberg, West Germany.

Leach, Charles R. *In Tornado's Wake, A History of the 8th Armored Division.* Argus Press, Chicago.

MacDonald, Charles B. *The Last Offensive.* U.S. Government Printing Office, Washington, D.C.

Parker, Theodore W. *Conquer, The Story of the Ninth Army.* The Infantry Journal Press, Washington, D.C.

Ryan, Cornelius. *The Last Battle.* Simon and Schuster, New York.

Unpublished Sources

Brooks, Henry E. Numerous interviews, comments, and letters. Manchester, Connecticut.

Hawley, William. Letters describing events on maneuvers and actions in the Ruhr.

Sather, Marvin. Interviews, letters, and photographs. Nelson, Nebraska.

Starry, Dale. Letter describing events in the Ruhr. Shippensberg, Pennsylvania.

Steen, J. J. van der. Interview, letters, maps, and leaflets, describing events in and around St. Odilienberg and Malick, Holland.

Weldon, Dr. Lloyd. Numerous interviews, letters, and tapes describing events of the 399th Armored Field Artillery Battalion from 1943 until the breakup of the division in 1945.

Zierler, Dr. Kenneth. Interviews, letters, and comments regarding action in the Rhineland, the Ruhr. Baltimore, Maryland.

Other Sources

National Archives. Suitland, Maryland. After action report of the 8th Armored Division; after action report of CCB, 8th A.D.; after action report of the 399th AFA Bn.; letters and correspondence in 399th AFA

Bn. file. Audio Visual Section and Historical Section.

Hardison, Richard M. 8th Armored Division G-2 Periodic Report, daily from 1 February 1945 through 10 May 1945.

XIX Corps Artillery G-2 Intelligence Bulletin. Details the activities of the Divisions in the Corps as well as enemy activities.

8th Armored Division Artillery Intelligence Summary. Detailed information regarding mine fields, pill boxes, number of artillery rounds expended.

A howitzer being loaded for firing, January 25, 1945, near Sinz, Germany.

— *Courtesy U.S. Army Signal Corps*

An M-7 firing on strong points direct in February 1945.

— *Courtesy U.S. Army Signal Corps*

Three new tanks brought up by ordnance to replace some of those lost at Rhineberg, March 9, 1945.

— Courtesy U.S. Army Signal Corps

Tanks shelling the German village in the background. The 399th AFA Battalion was also shelling the town from another location.

— Courtesy U.S. Army Signal Corps

M7s in front of the château in Bazomesnil, France. The first overnight stop on the way to the front.

— Courtesy U.S. Army Signal Corps

The 49th AIB waiting in Rhineberg to make an attack on Ossenberg about one mile to the north, March 8, 1945.

— Courtesy U.S. Army Signal Corps

The business end of a 105mm howitzer, mounted on an M-4 medium tank chassis. It proved to be a fast and sturdy vehicle.

— *Courtesy U.S. Army Signal Corps*

Battery C in position in the Ruhr, April 1945.

— *Courtesy U.S. Army Signal Corps*

M7s crossing the Rhine on a one-way pontoon bridge, March 26, 1945.

— *Courtesy U.S. Army Signal Corps*

Field maintenance of an M-7 near Venlo, Holland, March 1945.

— *Courtesy U.S. Army Signal Corps*

A light pontoon bridge under construction across the Roer River at Hilfarth, Germany. We crossed it about two hours after this picture was taken on February 27, 1945.

— *Courtesy U.S. Army Signal Corps*

Men of the 49th AIB advancing on Rhineberg. The light tank pictured is disabled.

— *Courtesy U.S. Army Signal Corps*

"Dragons Teeth of the Siegfried Line" on the border between Holland and Germany near Heinsberg, Germany. This belt of concrete was designed to keep all vehicles on the roads where the gaps in the belt could be defended with anti-tank guns and other weapons.

— *Courtesy U.S. Army Signal Corps*

Infantry passing through Blankenberg, Germany, after two field artillery shellings and an air strike. This picture was taken about half an hour after 1st Lt. Weldon and I visited the police station there and relieved them of their guns.

— *Courtesy U.S. Army Signal Corps*

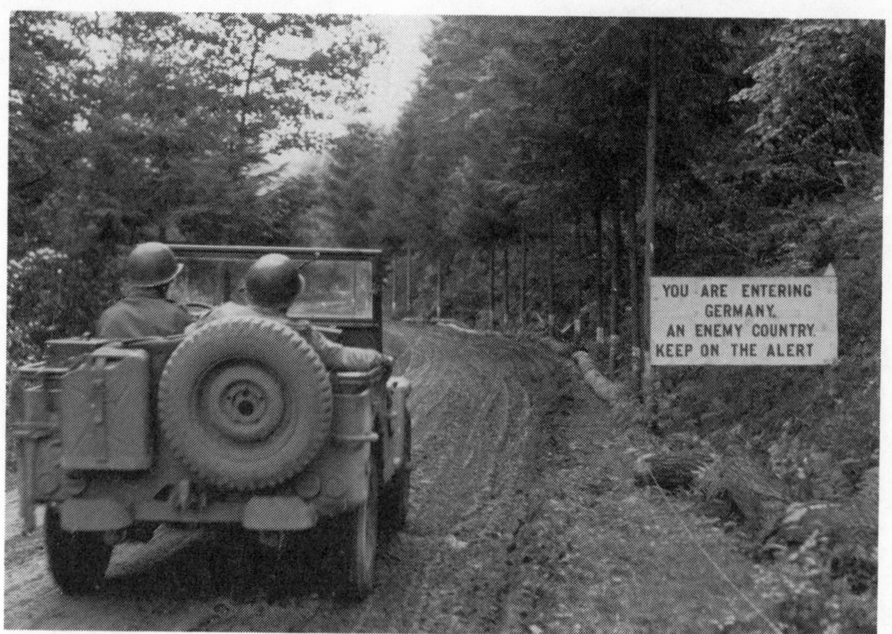

A sign on a logging road between Belgium and Germany in the Ardennes Forest.

— Courtesy U.S. Army Signal Corps

A carrying party moving mortar shells to two mortars near the last row of houses, January 29, 1945.

— Courtesy U.S. Army Signal Corps

An infantry squad has come under sniper fire in Heinsberg, January 1945.

— *Courtesy U.S. Army Signal Corps*

Sinz, Germany, was shelled for a week by several field artillery battalions both German and American. All of the destruction shown here was caused by that shelling.

— *Courtesy U.S. Army Signal Corps*

Men of the 49th Armored Infantry Battalion hurrying through Dorston. The structure in the center is a small hotel that housed the CP of the 36th Tank Battalion on the night of March 29, 1945. It was here that I talked to Lt. Col. Van Houten.

— *Courtesy U.S. Army Signal Corps*

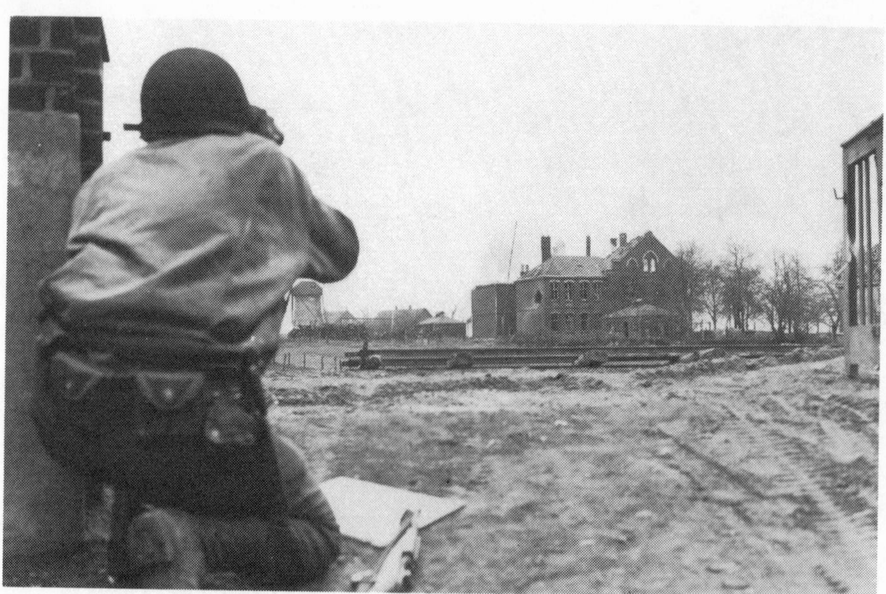

Artillery fire being adjusted on a German observation post in the large building. One round has hit the building and another one has struck on the other side of the house.

— *Courtesy U.S. Army Signal Corps*

Prisoners captured in the east end of Nening, Germany, January 1945.
— Courtesy U.S. Army Signal Corps

A few of the prisoners that were captured in the Ruhr pocket. Near Werl, Germany, in late April 1945.
— Courtesy U.S. Army Signal Corps

Prisoners in a large barbed wire temporary holding area. There are 89,000 in this cage. The area has been "carpet bombed" with anti-personnel bombs a few days before this picture was taken on April 28, 1945. Near Rhineberg, Germany.

— Courtesy U.S. Army Signal Corps

A horse-drawn German supply train, photographed near Halberstadt, Germany, in late April 1945. Note the fruit trees beginning to bloom in the background.

— Courtesy U.S. Army Signal Corps

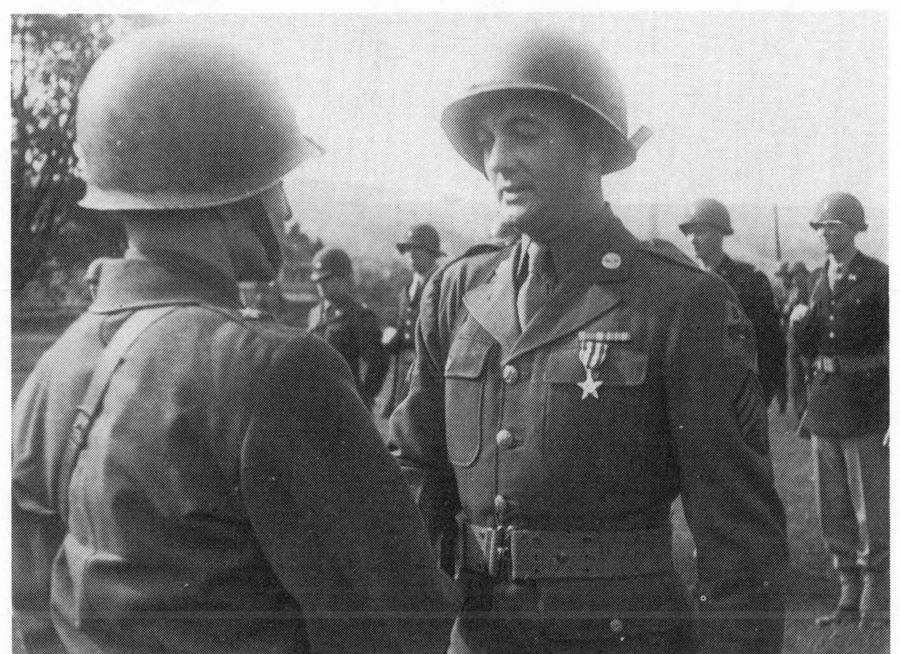

Sgt. Clayton Arnott receiving a Silver Star from Brig. Gen. John Devine, commanding general of the 8th Armored Division. Background (l. to r.) Capt. George R. Salisbury; unknown; 1st Lt. William H. Hawley; 1st Lt. Raymond Verlinder.

— *Courtesy U.S. Army Signal Corps*

1st Lt. James E. Russ signing "marriage certificates" for 250 couples that he has just married. They were French POWs and German or other women. Some had as many as four children.

— *Courtesy Author's Collection*

Officers of the 399th Armored Field Artillery Battalion, at Tidworth, England, December 1944.

— *Courtesy U.S. Army Signal Corps*

Ex-officers of the 399th Armored Field Artillery Battalion at a reunion, Colorado Springs, September 1970.

— *Courtesy Author's Collection*

. Col. Roger M. Lilly, battalion commander of the 399th, Hann-Munden, Germany. Photo taken by Capt. Ken Zierler on ay 25, 1945.

— *Courtesy Ken Zierler*

L. to r., Chief Warrant Officer John W. Mace, personnel officer of the 399th; 1st Lt. John Culhane, XO of Battery B; and Capt. Marvin Sather, CO of Battery B. Photo taken at Horsica, Czechoslovakia, June 1945.

— *Courtesy Author's Collection*

1st Sgt. William F. Hughes, Jr., of Headquarters Battery, 399th AFA Battalion, Hann-Munden, Germany, May 1945.

— *Courtesy Author's Collection*

1st Lt. Lloyd C. Weldon, communications officer of the 399th, April 1945.

— *Courtesy John Collins*

Capt. Henry E. Brooks, CO of Battery A, taken aboard the *Wasp* in New York harbor, January 1946.

— *Courtesy Author's Collection*

Don, photographed at Lawton, Oklahoma, February 1942.

— Courtesy Author's Collection

Richard Hardison at College Station, Texas, February 1946.

— Courtesy Author's Collection

Richard Hardison as a student at Texas A&M College, February 1941.

— Courtesy Author's Collection

Don Hardison at Camp Polk, Louisiana, in the summer of 1943.

— Courtesy Author's Collection

Photograph of a sketch of Hardison made by Cpl. Ralph E. Carlson on the night of our Rhine river crossing, 26 March 1945.

— *Courtesy Author's Collection*

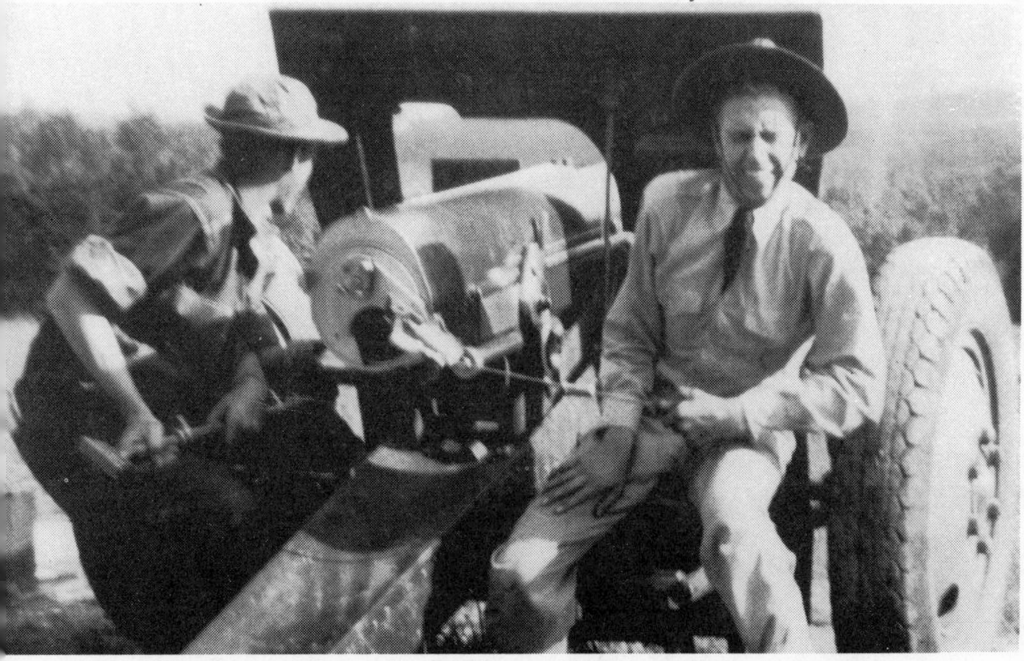

Richard Hardison serving as "gunner" on a WWI French 75. The man on the right is a member of the staff at the ROTC camp held at Camp Bullis, Texas. June 1940.

Index

T

U

V

W